UI Testing with Puppeteer

Implement end-to-end testing and browser automation using JavaScript and Node.js

Dario Kondratiuk

Packt>

BIRMINGHAM—MUMBAI

UI Testing with Puppeteer

Copyright © 2021 Packt Publishing

All rights reserved. No part of this book may be reproduced, stored in a retrieval system, or transmitted in any form or by any means, without the prior written permission of the publisher, except in the case of brief quotations embedded in critical articles or reviews.

Every effort has been made in the preparation of this book to ensure the accuracy of the information presented. However, the information contained in this book is sold without warranty, either express or implied. Neither the author, nor Packt Publishing or its dealers and distributors, will be held liable for any damages caused or alleged to have been caused directly or indirectly by this book.

Packt Publishing has endeavored to provide trademark information about all of the companies and products mentioned in this book by the appropriate use of capitals. However, Packt Publishing cannot guarantee the accuracy of this information.

Associate Group Product Manager: Pavan Ramchandani

Publishing Product Manager: Kaustubh Manglurkar

Senior Editor: Sofi Rogers

Content Development Editor: Aamir Ahmed

Technical Editor: Shubham Sharma

Copy Editor: Safis Editing

Project Coordinator: Manthan Patel

Proofreader: Safis Editing

Indexer: Tejal Daruwale Soni

Production Designer: Shankar Kalbhor

First published: March 2021

Production reference: 1100321

Published by Packt Publishing Ltd.
Livery Place
35 Livery Street
Birmingham
B3 2PB, UK.

ISBN 978-1-80020-678-6

www.packt.com

To God, who makes all things possible.

To my wife, Abigail, for all her unconditional support all these years. I am who I am thanks to you.

To my dad, Carlos. You always knew that I was going to write a book.

-Dario Kondratiuk

Contributors

About the author

Dario Kondratiuk has been a web developer since 2001. He won the Microsoft **MVP** (**Most Valuable Professional**) award in 2020 for his contributions to the developer community. Dario has been working with Puppeteer since the beta versions, back in 2017. He is the author of *Puppeteer-Sharp*, a Puppeteer port to .NET, and *Playwright-Sharp*, a Playwright port to .NET. He writes about web automation on his blog, `https://www.hardkoded.com`, and he's active on Stack Overflow.

> *I want to thank my family, Abigail, Carlos, Graciela, Yanel, Eduardo, and Nacho, for all their support during this project. I would also like to thank Mauro, Ezequiel, Facundo, Lucas, Javier, Fede, and Fercho, for helping me be a better professional. Lastly, I would like to thank Pablo, Roge, Fran, Faa, Marcos, Martin, Jere, and Christian for helping me be a better person.*

About the reviewers

David Rubio Vidal is a senior software test engineer, AWS solutions architect, and professional Scrum Master with international and multi-disciplinary experience in software engineering. He has worked in the subsea/oil and gas, aerospace, and multimedia industries as well as in the public sector. Regarding software testing, he has proven experience at all levels and disciplines: from UI to API, accessibility, layout, mobile, and more. David is also capable of deploying and managing infrastructure in the cloud, with cutting-edge technologies and methodologies. Finally, as well as working as a software engineer, he has developed his career as a Scrum Master to ensure Agile methodologies are applied properly in the teams he has worked with.

Jim Munro has two decades of professional experience as a test automation engineer. He is passionate about the quality and usability of software and generally enjoys breaking things.

He has spent most of his career writing code in Python and JavaScript and testing with tools such as Puppeteer, Cypress, and Selenium. He lives near Boulder, Colorado with his wife, his daughter, Stella, and their dog, Kipper. He can be reached via email at jim@jimmunro.net or on Twitter as @jimfmunro.

I would like to thank Manthan Patel, Nitin Nainani, and the team at Packt Publishing. For my parents, Bill and Patricia, who have kindly never asked me to be their tech support.

Table of Contents

Preface

1
Getting started with Puppeteer

What is browser automation?	2	Setting up the environment	12
Selenium and Puppeteer	3	Node.js	12
		Visual Studio Code	13
Introducing Headless browsers	4		
Available headless browsers	5	Our first Puppeteer code	14
The Chromium DevTools Protocol	6	Installing Puppeteer	15
Introducing Puppeteer	8	Hello world in Puppeteer	18
The Puppeteer object model	9	Asynchronous programming in JavaScript	19
Puppeteer use cases	10		
Task Automation	11	Promise.all	21
Web Scraping	11	Promise.race	21
Content generation	11	Fulfilling our own promises	22
End-to-end testing	11	Summary	22

2
Automated Testing and Test runners

Technical requirements	24	Test runner features	32
Introduction to Automated Testing	24	Available test runners	35
		Creating our first test project	37
Unit tests	26	Organizing our code	44
Service tests	28	Introducing the Page Object Model	45
End-to-end tests	31	Summary	50

3
Navigating through a website

Technical requirements	52	Options in practice	63
Introducing the tests sites for this chapter	52	Navigating through a site	65
Creating a Puppeteer browser	55	Timeouts	65
		waitUntil	66
Using the Puppeteer.launch function	56	Referrer	68
Headless	57	Using the response object	69
The user data directory	58	Getting the response URL	69
Executable Path	59	Getting the response status code	70
Default Viewport	60		
Product	62	Introduction to continuous integration	73
Browser Arguments	62		
Mobile options	63	Summary	81

4
Interacting with a page

Technical requirements	84	Interacting with Elements	104
Introduction to HTML, the DOM, and CSS	84	Typing on input elements	104
		Clicking on elements	104
HTML	85	Selecting options in drop-down lists	105
The DOM	91	Keyboard and Mouse emulation	108
CSS Selectors	94	Debugging tests with Visual Studio Code	115
Finding elements	95		
Finding elements using XPath	100	Summary	118

5
Waiting for elements and network calls

Technical requirements	121	Waiting for network calls	130
Waiting for the page to load	121	Arrange, Act, Await	131
Waiting for elements	127	Fire and forget	133
Await a wait function	128	Promise.all	134

Waiting for page events	135	The console event	139
The close event	138	The dialog event	140
The popup event	138	The headless recorder	141
Target created event	139	Summary	144

6
Executing and Injecting JavaScript

Technical requirements	146	Enforcing server rules	155
Executing JavaScript code	146	Finding elements using JavaScript	156
Variable scopes in JavaScript	146	Waiting for functions	157
Manipulating handles with JavaScript code	150	Exposing local functions	163
		Running our checks with Checkly	166
Getting information from the elements	152	Summary	170
Acting on elements	154		

7
Generating Content with Puppeteer

Technical requirements	172	Generate PDF files	182
Taking screenshots	172	Creating HTML content	190
Using screenshots for regression tests	178	Summary	192

8
Environments emulation

Technical requirements	194	Pixel ratio	202
Understanding the browser's market share	194	The touchscreen	204
		The user agent	205
The browser's popularity over the years	195	Emulating mobile devices with Puppeteer	207
Operative Systems market share	197		
Screen resolution distribution	198	Emulating network conditions	212
Emulating mobile devices	199	Emulating localization	216
The Viewport	200	Emulating geolocation	218

Emulating time zones	221	Other emulations	224
Emulating languages	222	Summary	227

9
Scraping tools

Technical requirements	230	How to avoid being detected as a bot	250
Introduction to web scraping	230		
Does the site allow scrapers?	231	Dealing with authorization	254
Creating scrapers	238	Summary	259
Running scrapers in parallel	246		

10
Evaluating and Improving the Performance of a Website

Technical requirements	262	Using the node module	268
The Issue of Performance	262	The performance category	270
Getting started with Google Lighthouse	265	Using Lighthouse for testing	275
As part of Chrome DevTools	266	Tracing Pages	279
Using PageSpeed Insights	267	Analyzing code coverage	285
Using the command line	267	Summary	287
		Why subscribe?	289

Other Books You May Enjoy
Index

Preface

Puppeteer is a multi-purpose browser automation tool created by Google. You will see Puppeteer being used in many different ways. It's used for web scraping, task automation, content generation, web monitoring, and UI testing.

This book focuses on UI testing, but we won't stop there. For instance, we have a chapter focused on content generation and another chapter that focuses on web scraping. If you read this book from cover to cover, you will be able to use Puppeteer in all fields.

When I found that there was no book about Puppeteer available on the market, that really motivated me: I wanted this book to cover the entire Puppeteer API. By the end of this book, you'll have learned about the whole Puppeteer API.

Who this book is for

If you are a quality assurance professional looking for a better and more modern tool to do your job, this is the book for you.

These days, UI testing is not only for the QA team. There is a new wave of frontend developers looking for tools to test their UI components. If you are a web developer using JavaScript and Node.js in your daily job and you want to test your UI components, this book is also for you.

Web developers will also learn from this book how to use browser automation tools to automate tasks such as taking screenshots, generating PDF files, or doing web scraping.

What this book covers

Chapter 1, Getting started with Puppeteer, lays the foundation for the book. It will help you get started with Puppeteer by introducing you to the tool and getting you acquainted with the essentials. You will also learn how to write async code in JavaScript.

Chapter 2, Automated Testing and Test runners, covers end-to-end testing fundamentals and the difference between different types of tests. In the latter part of the chapter, we will cover creating and organizing a test project and getting started with test runners.

Chapter 3, *Navigating through a website*, sees you start coding your tests. You will learn how to launch a browser, navigate to a page, and make some assertions. Then, you will see how to publish your tests to the cloud to be tested.

Chapter 4, *Interacting with a page*, is all about interaction. Once you get to a page, how do you test it? How do you simulate user interaction? This chapter takes you through the most common ways of interacting with a page. This chapter also covers some basic HTML concepts, so you can take advantage of all the tools Puppeteer provides.

Chapter 5, *Waiting for elements and network calls*, teaches you how to wait for the different scenarios on the page you are testing—waiting for the page to load and be ready, waiting for a button to be enabled, waiting for an Ajax call to be completed, and so on. This chapter covers all the tools that Puppeteer offers to handle these scenarios.

Chapter 6, *Executing and Injecting JavaScript*, shows you one of the best features of Puppeteer: injecting JavaScript code easily. In this chapter, we will leave the end-to-end testing world for a moment and dive into web automation using a general-purpose tool.

Chapter 7, *Generating Content with Puppeteer*, expands on the usage of Puppeteer and shows you how we can create content using Puppeteer. We'll start by learning how screenshots are created and how they can be used for regression tests. Then, we will cover PDF generation, and finally, we will learn how to create pages on the fly.

Chapter 8, *Environments emulation*, explains all the tools Puppeteer provides to emulate different scenarios. It will show you how to emulate mobile devices, different screen resolutions, various network speeds, geolocation, and even things such as vision deficiency.

Chapter 9, *Scraping tools*, demystifies web scraping, showing you how it can be used to your advantage. You will learn how to create scrapers and run tasks in parallel using Puppeteer Cluster.

Chapter 10, *Evaluating and Improving the Performance of a Website*, shows you how Puppeteer can help developers to evaluate and improve the performance of their sites. We will learn how to extract and analyze all the performance metrics you can see on the Developer Tools. This chapter also has a great introduction to Google Lighthouse and how to automate its reports and integrate them into your tests.

I also want this book to fill your toolbox with more tools besides Puppeteer. During the course of this book, you will learn about other tools, such as GitHub Actions, Visual Studio Code, Checkly and its Puppeteer recorder, and many others.

To get the most out of this book

This book assumes that you have some knowledge of JavaScript, but you don't need to be an expert. All the examples will run on Node.js. If you have experience with this framework, you will find it easier to get started. If you don't, don't worry; we won't go deep into Node.js.

All the tools we will use are cross-platform. You will be able to follow the code of this book using any popular operating system, such as Windows, macOS, or Linux. In *Chapter 1, Getting started with Puppeteer*, we will see how to install Node.js and Visual Studio Code. If you already have these tools installed, notice that Puppeteer relies on Node 10.18.1+.

If you are using the digital version of this book, we advise you to type the code yourself or access the code via the GitHub repository (link available in the next section). Doing so will help you avoid any potential errors related to the copying and pasting of code.

Download the example code files

You can download the example code files for this book from GitHub at `https://github.com/PacktPublishing/UI-Testing-with-Puppeteer`. In case there's an update to the code, it will be updated on the existing GitHub repository.

We also have other code bundles from our rich catalog of books and videos available at `https://github.com/PacktPublishing/`. Check them out!

Disclaimer

Many of the examples of this book will be based on real websites that most of us use every day. We are going to test websites like `GitHub.com`, `StackOverlow.com`, The Weather Channel, and PacktPub. That means that you will learn how to automate real websites using the latest technologies. However, this also means that some of the code examples might eventually fail. This could be due to network conditions, problems with the server, or a website redesign. However, our main aim is that you can learn the concepts and apply them to your own solutions besides these changes.

Download the color images

We also provide a PDF file that has color images of the screenshots/diagrams used in this book. You can download it here: `https://static.packt-cdn.com/downloads/9781800206786_ColorImages.pdf`.

Alternatively, you can also find the color images for the book at: `https://github.com/PacktPublishing/UI-Testing-with-Puppeteer/blob/master/ColorImages.pdf`

Conventions used

There are a number of text conventions used throughout this book.

`Code in text`: Indicates code words in text, functions, variables, folder names, filenames, file extensions, pathnames, dummy URLs and user input. Here is an example: "Every HTML document will be contained inside an `<html>` element."

A block of code is set as follows:

```
const productId = config.productToTestId;
const productDiv = await this.page.$(`[data-test-product-id="${productId}"]`);
const stockElement = await productDiv.$('[data-test-stock]');
const priceElement = await productDiv.$('[data-test-price]');
```

Any command-line input or output is written as follows:

```
~ % /Applications/Google\ Chrome.app/Contents/MacOS/Google\ Chrome --headless --remote-debugging-port=9222 --crash-dumps-dir=/tmp
```

Bold: Indicates a new term, an important word, or words that you see onscreen. For example, words in menus or dialog boxes appear in the text like this. Here is an example: "When you call `page.click`, that function will return a **Promise**."

> Tips or important notes
> Appear like this.

Get in touch

Feedback from our readers is always welcome.

General feedback: If you have questions about any aspect of this book, mention the book title in the subject of your message and email us at `customercare@packtpub.com`.

Errata: Although we have taken every care to ensure the accuracy of our content, mistakes do happen. If you have found a mistake in this book, we would be grateful if you would report this to us. Please visit `www.packtpub.com/support/errata`, selecting your book, clicking on the Errata Submission Form link, and entering the details.

Piracy: If you come across any illegal copies of our works in any form on the Internet, we would be grateful if you would provide us with the location address or website name. Please contact us at `copyright@packt.com` with a link to the material.

If you are interested in becoming an author: If there is a topic that you have expertise in and you are interested in either writing or contributing to a book, please visit `authors.packtpub.com`.

Reviews

Please leave a review. Once you have read and used this book, why not leave a review on the site that you purchased it from? Potential readers can then see and use your unbiased opinion to make purchase decisions, we at Packt can understand what you think about our products, and our authors can see your feedback on their book. Thank you!

For more information about Packt, please visit `packt.com`.

1
Getting started with Puppeteer

I remember the first time I heard about browser automation. A friend told me that their QA team was testing using "automation." That sounded magical to me. People testing websites using "automation." After a few years, I learned that automation wasn't a magic potion, but instead a powerful tool not only for QA but also for developers, because we developers love to automate stuff, right?

That's why in the first part of this chapter, I want to show you how browser automation works and what makes Puppeteer unique. In the latter part of this chapter, we are going to review some asynchronous techniques that are going to be useful throughout the rest of the book, and throughout your automation journey.

This chapter will cover the following topics:

- What is browser automation?
- Introducing headless browsers
- Puppeteer use cases
- Setting up the environment
- Our first Puppeteer code
- Asynchronous programming in JavaScript

What is browser automation?

If you go and look for the word "automation" in Wikipedia, it will tell you that it is *"a process or procedure performed with minimal human assistance."* If you are a developer, or just a geek, I bet you love to create scripts to automate tasks. You might also create environment variables, so you don't have to type long paths, or even create cool Git commands, so you don't need to remember all the steps required to create a new branch upstream.

When I got my first Mac, I discovered an app called Automator. I fell in love with it. You can automate tasks and connect applications just using drag and drop. If you use macOS and you've never played with Automator, please give it a try! But Automator isn't the only app. There are many workflow apps in the market, such as Hazel or Alfred.

Automation is even in the cloud and is available to the general public. Apps such as IFTTT and Zapier allow users to automate everyday tasks. You can create automations such as "When I post on Instagram, share the same image on Twitter," all from your phone. Regular people doing automation, that's great!

We also have mail rules. Most mail clients, even web clients, let you create rules, so you can mark emails as read, label them, or even remove them based on conditions. That's also automation.

Maybe you've taken it to the next level and coded an application for some of your daily tasks. You have that report that you need to send to your boss every month. That report is the result of many CSV files. You just wrote a tiny app, using your favorite language to make that report for you.

In a few words, automation means using an app to do a repetitive task for us. And as we have seen, it doesn't necessarily involve coding that app. So now, we can say that **browser automation is telling an app to do a repetitive task in the browser for us**.

Ok, that's a simple statement. But how's that possible? When you automate an app, you accomplish this using some kind of **application program interface (API)**. For example, when you write a bat/bash file, you use the command-line arguments as an interface. If you use IFTTT, it employs Twitter's and Instagram's HTTP APIs to fetch images and create tweets. You need some kind of API, some way to interact with the app you are trying to automate. How are we supposed to interact with the browser? Good question.

To make things a little bit more complicated, we also need to consider that we have two apps to automate: the browser itself and the website. We don't want just to open a browser, create a new tab, and navigate to a page. We also want to go to that page and perform some actions. We want to click on a button, or enter some text in an input element.

Automating a browser sounds challenging. But, luckily for us, we have some brilliant people who did an excellent job for us and created tools such as Selenium and Puppeteer.

Selenium and Puppeteer

A quick search on Google will show that Selenium is one of the top, if not *the* top, UI testing tool on the market. I think a question many people would ask is: **Why should I choose Puppeteer over Selenium? Which one is better?**

The first thing you need to know is that Puppeteer was not created to compete with Selenium. Selenium is a cross-language, cross-browser testing tool, whereas Puppeteer was created as a multi-purpose automation tool to exploit all the power of Chromium. I think both are great automation tools, but they tackle browser automation in two different ways. They are different in two important aspects that define the target audience of a browser automation library:

- The interface between the tool and the browser
- The interface between the tool and the user

Let's first unpack how Selenium works.

Selenium's approach

In order to automate most browsers in the market, Selenium wrote a spec (an API) called **WebDriver**, which the W3C then accepted as a standard (`https://www.hardkoded.com/ui-testing-with-puppeteer/webdriver`), and asked the browsers to implement that interface. Selenium will use this WebDriver API to interact with the browser. If you take a look at the paper at the preceding URL, you will find two words showing up over and over: **testing** and **simplicity**. In other words, they defined an API with a clear focus on testing and simplicity and asked the browsers to implement that interface. Cross-browser testing is, in my opinion, the main feature of Selenium.

> **What is an API?**
> An API is the set of classes, functions, properties, and events that a library allows us to use. An API is critical for a library's success because it will determine how much you can do with it and how easy (or not) the interaction will be with the library.

The API that Selenium exposes to users is also considered a part of the WebDriver spec, and it follows the same philosophy: it's focused on testing and simplicity. This API provides a layer of abstraction between the user and all the different browsers and provides an interface that will easily help the developer write tests.

Puppeteer's approach

Puppeteer doesn't need to think in terms of cross-browser support. Although there are some efforts to run Puppeteer on Firefox, the focus is on grabbing all the developer tools that Chromium has and making them available to the user. With this goal in mind, Puppeteer can access way more tools than those exposed by the WebDriver API that Selenium uses.

The difference in how they communicate with the browser is also reflected in the APIs. Puppeteer provides an API that will help us take advantage of all the power of Chromium. I think it's important to highlight that Puppeteer was created in JavaScript, so the API will feel more natural than Selenium's, which comes from a cross-language philosophy.

Puppeteer doesn't need to ask anybody to implement the API because it takes advantage of the headless capability of Chromium. Let's now see what headless browsers are.

Introducing Headless browsers

What is a headless browser? No, it's not something from a horror movie. **A headless browser is a browser that you can launch and interact with using a particular protocol over a particular communication transport, with no UI involved**. This means that you will have one active process (or many processes, as we know how browsers are these days), but there will be no "window" for you to interact with the browser. I think that "windowless browser" would have been a more accurate name.

Available headless browsers

Both Chromium and Firefox support headless browser mode. It's important to mention that, at the time of writing this book, Firefox's headless mode was still experimental. That might sound bad, compared with the six browsers Selenium offers (`https://www.hardkoded.com/ui-testing-with-puppeteer/selenium-browsers`), but, as you might have noticed, I didn't say Chrome, I said Chromium. Chromium is the engine Chrome uses under the hood. But Chrome is not the only browser using Chromium; in the past few years, many browsers have started to use the chromium engine. These are a few examples of chromium-based browsers:

- Google Chrome
- Microsoft Edge, a.k.a. Edgium, to avoid confusion with the previous version of Microsoft Edge based on Trident
- Opera
- Brave

That's much better. We can automate at least five browsers. But there are two major browsers with no headless support: Microsoft Internet Explorer and Safari. The case of Safari is interesting. In the same way that Chromium is the engine behind Chrome, Webkit is the engine of Safari and, although Safari doesn't support headless mode, there are a few Webkit builds created for testing purposes with headless support. Microsoft Playwright has its own Webkit build to support cross-browser automation.

Do you want to see a headless browser for the very first time?

Let's try this out:

If you have Chrome installed, grab the full path of the executable and pass these command arguments: `--headless --remote-debugging-port=9222 --crash-dumps-dir=/tmp`:

```
~ % /Applications/Google\ Chrome.app/Contents/MacOS/Google\ Chrome --headless --remote-debugging-port=9222 --crash-dumps-dir=/tmp
```

> **Tip**
> If you are a macOS user, the Chrome executable will be inside the "Google Chrome.app" pseudo-file. As you can see, it's: "Google Chrome.app/Contents/MacOS/Google Chrome".

After executing that command, you should get something like this in the console:

```
DevTools listening on ws://127.0.0.1:9222/devtools/browser/
e7e52f93-8f1e-491c-b718-94ae7a8e81b7
```

Now we have a headless chrome browser waiting for commands through a WebSocket on ws://127.0.0.1:9222.

Firefox also provides a headless mode:

```
~ % /Applications/Firefox.app/Contents/MacOS/firefox --headless
*** You are running in headless mode.
```

It doesn't say much, but trust me, now we have a Firefox browser running in headless mode.

As I mentioned before, a headless browser doesn't have a UI. The only way to interact with the browser is to use the transport the browser created, in this case, a WebSocket, and to send messages using some kind of protocol. In the case of Chromium and Firefox, it's the Chromium DevTools Protocol.

The Chromium DevTools Protocol

If you are a web developer, I'm 100% sure you have used Chrome DevTools. If you don't know what I'm talking about, you can open DevTools by clicking on the three dots button in the top-right corner, and then go to `More Tools > Developer Tools`. You will get something like this:

Chrome DevTools

It's impressive all the things you can accomplish using this fantastic tool:

- Inspect the DOM.
- Evaluate CSS styles.
- Run JavaScript code.
- Debug JavaScript code.
- See network calls.
- Measure performance.

And the good news is that it's the **Chromium Developer Protocol** (which we'll call **CDP** from now on) that drives most of the DevTools' features. And that same CDP is the protocol that headless browsers use to interact with the outside world.

CDP sounds perfect. We can interact with the browser and do all the things I have mentioned. You can create a Node.JS app to launch a browser and start sending CDP messages through a WebSocket, but that would be quite complex and hard to maintain. That's where Puppeteer comes to the rescue and offers a human-friendly interface to interact with the browser.

Introducing Puppeteer

Puppeteer is nothing more, and nothing less, than a Node.js package that knows how to open a browser, send commands, and react to messages coming from that browser. At the time of writing this book, Puppeteer supports Chromium and Firefox, but Firefox support is still considered experimental. I think it's a good time for you to go to the Puppeteer repository (`https://www.hardkoded.com/ui-testing-with-puppeteer/puppeteer-repo`) and check whether things have changed since then.

There are also some community projects that implement Puppeteer in other languages. You will find Puppeteer-Sharp (`https://www.hardkoded.com/ui-testing-with-puppeteer/puppeteer-sharp`) for .NET or Pyppeteer (`https://www.hardkoded.com/ui-testing-with-puppeteer/pypeteer`) for Python.

When you use Puppeteer, you are, in fact, using more than just a JavaScript library. Many people call this the "Puppeteer pyramid":

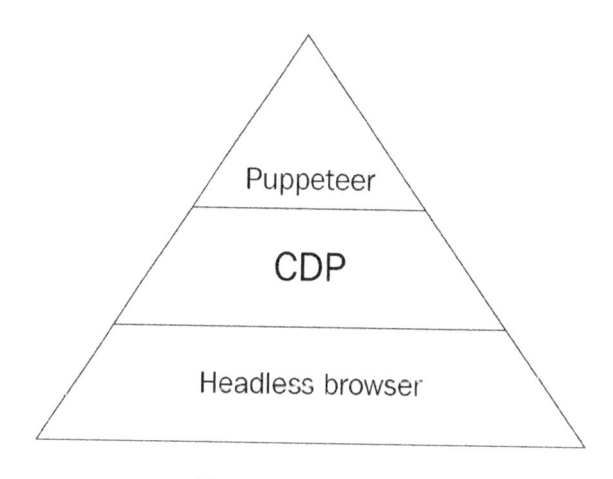

The Puppeteer pyramid

The Puppeteer pyramid consists of three components:

- The headless browser is the engine that will run the pages we want to automate.
- The Chromium DevTools Protocol allows any external user to interact with the browser.
- Puppeteer provides a JavaScript API to interact with the browser using the CDP.

What I find valuable about Puppeteer is that its model clearly represents the browser structure:

The Puppeteer object model

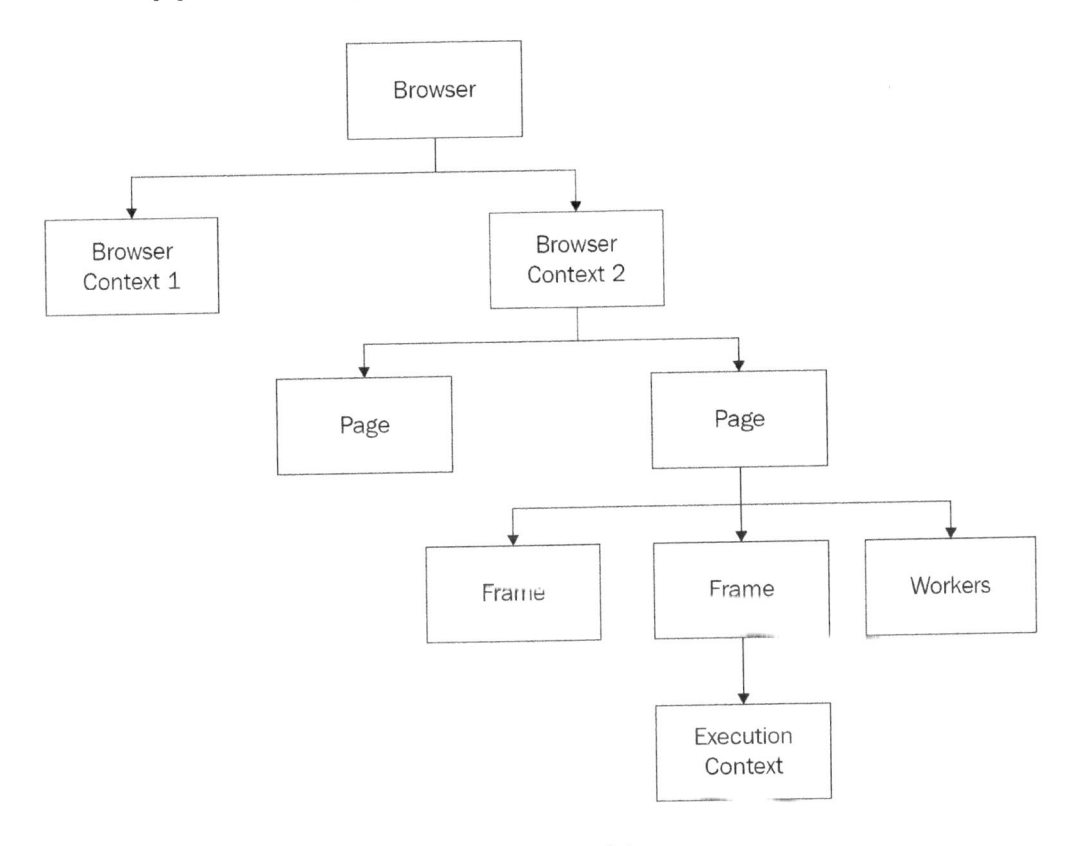

Puppeteer Model

Let's see what these objects represent inside the browser.

Browser

The browser is the main class. It's the object created when Puppeteer connects to a browser. The keyword here is **connect**. The browser that Puppeteer will use can be launched by Puppeteer itself. But it could also be a browser that is already running on your local machine, or it could even be a browser running in the cloud, like Browserless. io (https://www.hardkoded.com/ui-testing-with-puppeteer/browserless).

Browser context

A browser can contain more than one context. A context is a browser session (not to be confused with a browser window). The best example is the Incognito Mode or private mode, depending on the browser, which creates an isolated session inside the same browser process.

Page

A page is a tab in a browser or even a pop-up page.

Frame

The frame object is more important than it looks. Every page has at least one frame, which is called the main frame. Most of the page actions we will learn across this book are, in fact, a call to the main frame; for example, `page.click` calls `mainframe.click`.

The frame is a tree. One page has only one main frame, but a frame can contain many child frames.

Worker

A worker is a model that interacts with Web Workers. This is not a feature we will talk about in this book.

Execution context

The execution context is a mechanism Chromium uses to isolate the page from the browser extensions. Each frame will have its own execution context. Internally, all the frame functions that involve executing JavaScript code will use an execution context to run the code inside the browser.

There are other objects involved, such as `ElementHandles` and `JSHandles`, but we are going to talk about them later in the book.

Now that we know some of the differences between Selenium and Puppeteer, it's a perfect moment to review many possible use cases for Puppeteer.

Puppeteer use cases

Remember, the main difference between Puppeteer and Selenium is that Selenium is designed for end-to-end testing. In contrast, Puppeteer is designed as an API to exploit all the power of the DevTools, which means that besides end-to-end tests, there are also other use cases where you can use Puppeteer, as we will see now.

Task Automation

There are many things we do on the web that you can automate. For example, you can download a report, fill in a form, or check flight prices. You might also want to check your website's health, monitor its performance, or check whether your website is working correctly. In *Chapter 6, Executing and Injecting JavaScript*, we will see how to use Checkly to monitor your website in production.

Web Scraping

Most library authors won't like to say that you can use their library to do web scraping. Web Scraping has a reputation for being illegal. But in *Chapter 9, Scraping tools*, we will see how to do web scraping in the right way, without getting banned or sued.

Content generation

Generating content is not a use case that would come to your mind if you had to think about possible use cases. But Puppeteer is a great tool for generating two kinds of content:

- **Screenshots**: Why would you need to take screenshots using an app? Think about thumbnails or previews. Imagine you want to create a paywall, showing part of your website content but as a blurred image. You could use Puppeteer to take a screenshot of your site, blur it, and use that image.

- **PDF files**: Invoices are a great example of PDF generation. Imagine you have an e-commerce site. When the user makes a purchase, you show them a nice, well-designed invoice, but you need to send them that exact invoice by email. You could use Puppeteer to navigate to that invoice page and print it to PDF. You could also use your landing page to generate a PDF and use it as a brochure.

In *Chapter 7, Generating Content with Puppeteer*, we will talk about this use case and how to use screenshots to write UI regression tests.

End-to-end testing

I think Puppeteer is great for testing modern web apps because it's close to the browser. The API feels great, modern, and is designed for the JavaScript developer. It lets you execute JavaScript code easily and gives you access to all the power of Chromium. But I also have to say that Selenium's tolling for end-to-end testing is impressive. Puppeteer is not even close to what Selenium offers with its Selenium Grid. It's up to you to decide which is the right tool for you.

Enough with the theory. It's time to get started and set up our environment.

Setting up the environment

What's good about Node.js and Puppeteer is that they are cross-platform. My local environment is macOS Catalina 10.15.6. But you won't see much difference if you use a Windows or a Linux environment.

Time is a tech book's worst enemy. At the time of writing this book, I was using Node.JS 12.18.3 and Puppeteer 7. I'm pretty sure that by the time you read this book, new versions will have come to light. But don't feel discouraged about that; we expect that to happen. That's why I encourage you to go now and take a look at the GitHub repository of this book (`https://github.com/PacktPublishing/ui-testing-with-Puppeteer`). If you see that something is not working or has changed, please create an issue on that repository. We will try to keep it updated.

We only need two things to run our first Puppeteer code: Node.JS and Puppeteer. Let's begin with Node.JS.

Node.js

For the purposes of this book, the only thing you need to know about Node.js is that it's a runtime that allows us to run JavaScript code outside the browser.

It's important to highlight that the website we want to automate doesn't necessarily need to run on Node.js. You wouldn't need to know the language used to write the website, nor the platform that the website is running, but if you get to know those details, that could give you some ideas to write better automation code. For instance, if you know that the site is an ASP.NET Webforms project, you will know that it uses some hidden inputs to perform postbacks. That becomes more evident if you know the client-side frameworks, such as Vue or React.

As I mentioned before, we will install Node.JS v12.18.3 (or higher). The process is quite simple:

1. Go to the official site: `https://nodejs.org/`.
2. Download the LTS version. **LTS** stands for **Long-Term Support**.

3. Run the installer as you would typically do on your platform:

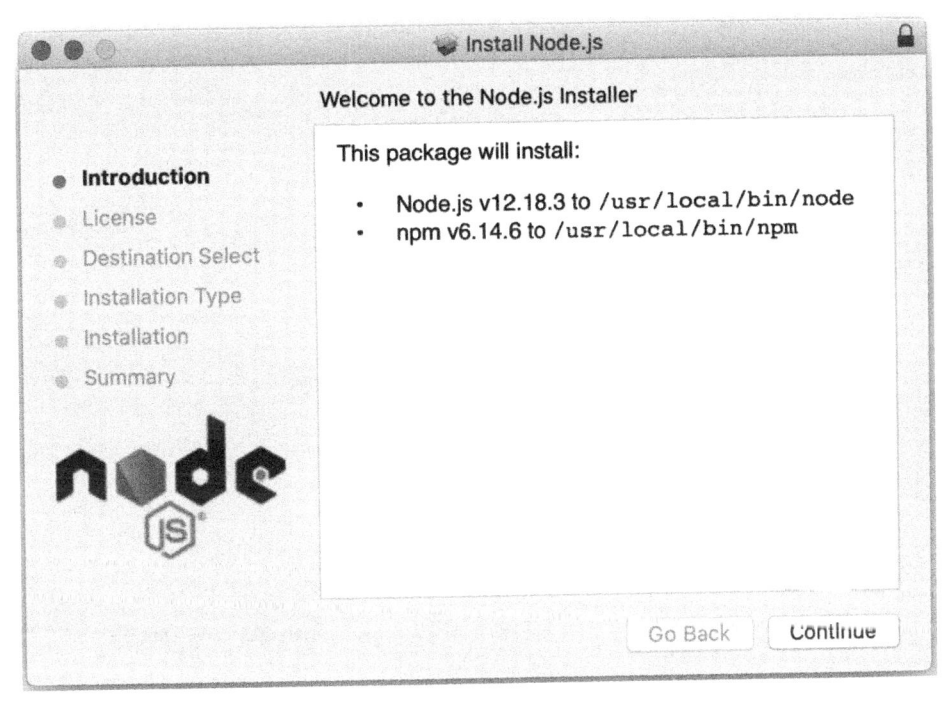

Node.js setup

If you want to see whether the installation was successful, you can open a terminal and execute `node --version`:

```
~ % node --version
v12.18.3
```

Visual Studio Code

You don't need any special code editor to write a Node.js app. But Visual Studio Code is a great editor. It's free, cross-platform, and you can use it not only to code JavaScript, but also to code in many other languages as well.

14   Getting started with Puppeteer

You can download it at `https://code.visualstudio.com/`. It doesn't even require running a setup on macOS. It's just an app you copy to your `Applications` folder:

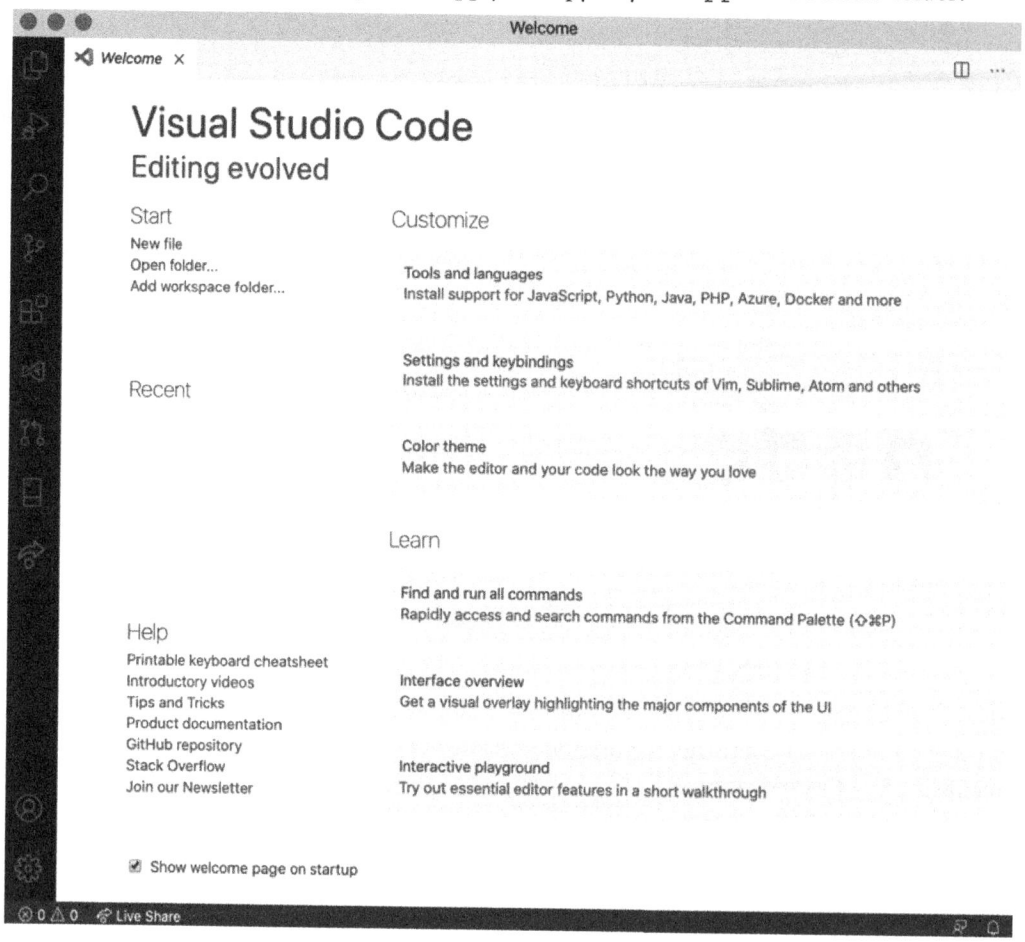

Visual Studio Code

Now that we have Node.js installed along with a code editor, we can create our first app.

Our first Puppeteer code

We first need to create a folder where our `hello-puppeteer` project will be located. I'm going to use a terminal, but you can use whatever you feel more comfortable with. Our project will be called `hello-puppeteer`:

```
> mkdir hello-puppeteer
> cd hello-puppeteer
```

We now need to initialize this brand-new node.js application. We create new applications in node.js using the `npm init` command. In this case, we will pass the `-y` argument, so it creates our app using default values:

```
> npm init -y
Wrote to /Users/neo/Documents/Coding/hello-puppeteer/package.json:
{
  "name": "hello-puppeteer",
  "version": "1.0.0",
  "description": "",
  "main": "index.js",
  "scripts": {
    "test": "echo \"Error: no test specified\" && exit 1"
  },
  "keywords": [],
  "author": "",
  "license": "ISC"
}
```

This output doesn't say much. It shows us that it has created a `package.json` file with some default values. Now, I will create an `index.js` file using the `touch` command. Again, you can perform this action in the way you feel most comfortable:

```
> touch index.js
```

Touch should have created the entry point of our app. But before coding our app, we need to install Puppeteer.

Installing Puppeteer

Most frameworks, if not all of them, have a way to publish and reuse components from different authors. The most popular package manager in Node.js is **NPM** (https://www.npmjs.com/). Does that sound familiar? We used `npm init` to create our app. As Puppeteer is a package published in NPM, we can download and install it using the `npm install` command.

If you don't want to jump between apps, you can open a terminal inside Visual Studio Code. If you are still in the terminal, you can open Visual Studio Code using the following command:

```
> code .
```

That will open Visual Studio Code. Once there, you will be able to launch a new terminal from the **Terminal** menu, as shown in the following screenshot:

Terminal inside Visual Studio Code

After opening a terminal, we can install Puppeteer using `npm install`:

```
> npm install puppeteer@">=7.0.0 <8.0.0"
Downloading Chromium r848005 - 128 Mb [=========        ]
44% 5.3s
```

I would like to highlight two things here. As this book is based on **Puppeteer 7**, we are specifying the version as `@">=7.0.0 <8.0.0"`, which means that we want the latest Puppeteer version greater than or equal to `7.0.0` and less than version `8.0.0`. By forcing this version to be used, you will be able to follow the examples in this chapter using the same version I used.

> **Puppeteer versioning**
>
> Puppeteer follows the **Semantic Versioning Specification (SemVer)** to version their releases, which means that those three numbers in the version follow a rule. A change in the major number (the first number) means that there was a breaking change in the API. When a package changes the major number, it tells you that the new version might break your code. A change in the minor number (the second number) means that they added new functionality, maintaining backward compatibility. Lastly, a change in the patch number means that they fixed a bug, maintaining backward compatibility.
>
> If you see that Puppeteer is in version 8, 9, or 10, it doesn't mean that this book is now obsolete. It means that they changed something that broke someone else's code. For instance, the change from version 6 to version 7 was just some change they made in the way they take screenshots.

In real life, you can use the latest version available. And second, you might have noticed that the package downloaded a specific version of Chromium, in this case, `r848005`. That doesn't mean that your code won't work with any version of Chromium you download from the internet. But, remember, Puppeteer interacts with the browser using the Chrome DevTools Protocol, so it needs a version of Chromium that reacts in the way Puppeteer expects. In the case of Puppeteer v7.0.1, it needs Chromium 90.0.4403.0, and there is no guarantee that any other version of Chromium (newer or older) would work with your current Puppeteer version. It doesn't mean that it won't work. It means that it's not guaranteed. You need to experiment and see. You can check which chromium version you should use for every version of Puppeteer on the API page (`https://www.hardkoded.com/ui-testing-with-puppeteer/puppeteer-api`).

Hello world in Puppeteer

Every language has its own hello world program. Puppeteer's hello world program would be navigating to `https://en.wikipedia.org/wiki/%22Hello,_World!%22_program` and taking a screenshot of the page. Let's see what it would look like:

```
const puppeteer = require('puppeteer');

(async function() {
    const browser = await puppeteer.launch();
    const page = await browser.newPage();
    await page.goto('https://en.wikipedia.org/wiki/%22Hello,_World!%22_program');
    await page.screenshot({ path: './screenshot.png'});
    browser.close();
})();
```

This is what we are doing in this small script:

1. We import the Puppeteer library using `require`.
2. Launch a new browser.
3. Open a new page (tab) inside that browser.
4. Navigate to the Wikipedia page.
5. Take a screenshot.
6. Close the browser.

I love how simple and easy it is to get started with Puppeteer. It's now time to run it. Using the same terminal you used to run `npm install`, now run `node index.js`:

```
> node index.js
```

A Chromium browser opened, navigated to Wikipedia, and closed by itself. You didn't see it because it was a headless browser, but it happened. Now, if you check your working directory, you should have a new file called `screenshot.png`:

Screenshot

Our code worked as expected. We got our screenshot from Wikipedia.

I bet you noticed that we used four **awaits** in our small hello puppeteer example. Asynchronous programming plays a big role in Puppeteer. Let's now talk about asynchronous programming in JavaScript.

Asynchronous programming in JavaScript

Normally, a program runs synchronously, which means that each line of code is executed one after the other. Let's take, for instance, these two lines of code:

```
const x = 3 + 4;
console.log(x);
```

Those two lines will run in order. The result of 3 + 4 will be assigned to the x constant, and then the variable x will be printed on the screen using `console.log`. The `console.log` function can't start until x is assigned.

But there are tasks, such as network requests, disk access, or any other I/O operation, that are time-consuming, and we don't necessarily want to wait for those tasks to finish to keep executing our code. For instance, we could start downloading a file, perform other tasks while that file is loading, and then check that file when the download is completed. Asynchronous programming will allow us to execute those long-running tasks without blocking our code.

An asynchronous function returns a **Promise** immediately to avoid blocking your code while waiting for a task. This Promise is an object that can be in one of the following three states:

- **Pending**: This means that the asynchronous task is still in progress.
- **Fulfilled**: This means that the asynchronous task was completed successfully.
- **Rejected**: This means that the asynchronous task has failed.

Let's say that we have a function called `downloadAFileFromTheInternet`. The most common way to wait for a task to finish is to use the `await` keyword:

```
await downloadAFileFromTheInternet();
```

It's important to highlight that the `await` keyword here is not waiting for the function itself; it is waiting for the `Promise` returned by that function. That means that you can also assign that `Promise` to a variable and `await` it later in the code:

```
const promise = downloadAFileFromTheInternet();
// some code
await promise;
```

Or you can just not wait for the promise at all:

```
downloadAFileFromTheInternet();
```

If you want to learn more about asynchronous JavaScript, check out the *Asynchronous JavaScript Deep Dive* videos by Steven Hancock (https://www.packtpub.com/product/asynchronous-javascript-deep-dive-video/9781800202665).

Puppeteer relies on asynchronous programming techniques because the communication between Puppeteer and Chrome DevTools is asynchronous. After all, the communication between Chrome DevTools and the browser is asynchronous. Think about what would happen under the hood when you click a link:

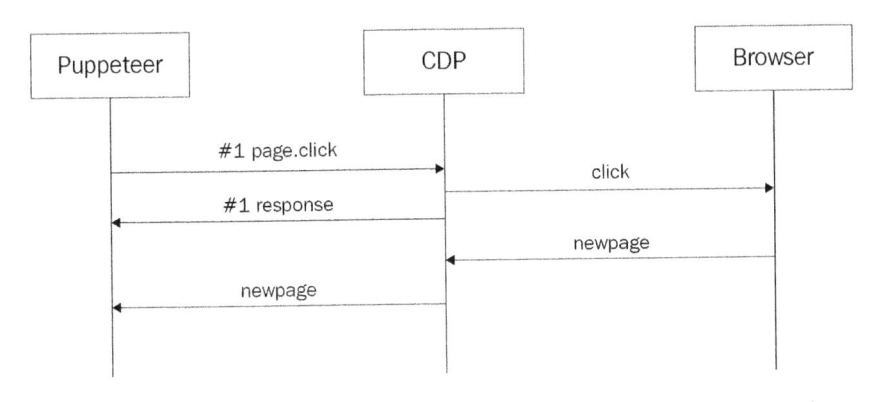

Click timeline

When you call page.click, the result of that action is not immediate. As we saw, there are many things going on under the hood. When you call page.click, you will need to do one of the things mentioned previously: await it; keep the promise in a variable and await it later; or don't await it at all.

Now that we know more about asynchronous programming, I would like to review five utilities that we will use across the book.

Promise.all

Promise.all is a function that expects an array of promises and returns a promise that will be **resolved** when **all** the promises are **fulfilled or rejected**. Yes, a promise could be fulfilled, completed successfully, or rejected, which means it failed.

A common scenario is clicking on a link, and waiting for the page to navigate to the next page:

```
await Promise.all([
    page.click('a'),
    page.waitForNavigation()
]);
```

This promise will wait for the link to click and the waitForNavigation promises to be either fulfilled or rejected.

Promise.race

Like Promise.all, Promise.race expects an array of promises, but in this case, it will resolve when **any** of the promises are resolved.

A typical usage is for timeouts. We want to take a screenshot, but only if it takes less than 2 seconds:

```
await Promise.race([
  page.screenshot(),
  new Promise((resolve,reject)=>{
    setTimeout(()=>{
      reject(new Error('Too long!!!'));},2000);
  })]);
```

In this case, if the `screenshot` promise takes more than 2,000 milliseconds, the promise created as the second element in the array will be **rejected**, rejecting the Promise.

Fulfilling our own promises

You saw in our previous example how you can create a promise, return that Promise or assign it to a variable, and then fulfill it.

This is great when you want to wait for an event to happen. We can create a promise that will be resolved when the page closes:

```
const promise = new Promise((x) => page.on('close', x));
// ...
await promise;
```

This kind of `await` is quite risky. If the Promise is never fulfilled, your code will hang. I recommend using these promises with `Promise.race` and timeouts.

We will see lots of promises throughout this book. Maybe some recipes such as "fulfill our own promises" look odd now, but we will use them a lot.

Summary

We covered a lot in this first chapter. We learned about browser automation and the difference between Selenium and Puppeteer. Then we saw that Puppeteer isn't limited only to end-to-end testing and reviewed some use case scenarios. Then we got our hands dirty and coded our first Puppeteer script. In the last section of the chapter, we covered many asynchronous techniques that we will use in this book.

In the next chapter, we are going to focus on end-to-end testing. We will review some tools available on the market and will consider how to organize our code to create reliable end-to-end tests.

2
Automated Testing and Test runners

In *Chapter 1*, *Getting started with Puppeteer*, we covered the first fundamental pillar of this book: browser automation and headless browsers. In this chapter, we are going to cover the second pillar: UI testing. We learned that Puppeteer is not just about testing, but that doesn't mean that it's not an excellent tool for the job.

In this chapter, we are going to learn the fundamentals of Testing Automation. We are going to see the differences between UI Testing and End-to-End testing. If you have tried to write tests in Node.js before, you might have come across some weird names: Mocha, Jest, Jasmine, AVA, or Chai. That feels quite overwhelming if you are not used to these tools. We are going to see which are the right tools for us.

We will cover the following topics in this chapter:

- Introduction to Automated Testing
- Test runner main features
- Available Test runners
- Creating our first test project
- Organizing our code

Once we understand these foundational concepts and we learn how test runners work, we will be able to dive deep into the Puppeteer API.

Technical requirements

You will find all the code of this chapter on the GitHub repository (`https://github.com/PacktPublishing/UI-Testing-with-Puppeteer`) under the `Chapter2` directory.

Introduction to Automated Testing

Testing is a fundamental task in software development. Even if you consider yourself a bad tester, or even a bad developer, you do some testing when you code your app. At the very least, you open the app to see whether it works as expected.

Maybe you are a little bit more methodical and you have a test plan, at least in your mind. You know that when you code a form, you have to validate some common scenarios:

- Try to save a form with empty fields.
- Try to save with good data.
- Try to enter bad data. You might enter text in numeric fields, invalid dates, and so on.

More experienced developers will cover all the possible scenarios. They will write code based on those scenarios and then test accordingly.

Then we get to the word that's driving this book: we **automate** stuff. We want to automate our tests. We don't want to forget any scenarios or have to test the same thing over and over.

As you will notice, I haven't mentioned **Quality Assurance** (**QA**) analysts yet, because I want to highlight that testing is not something relegated to the QA team. Those who are involved in the testing process include the following:

- Backend developers
- Frontend developers
- QA analysts
- Managers (product or project managers)

We need to know that there are different types of tests. Some types of tests will be performed by developers and QA analysts. Other tests will be specific to either developers or QA analysts.

Mike Cohn, in his book *Succeeding with Agile* (Addison-Wesley Professional), introduced his very popular Testing Pyramid:

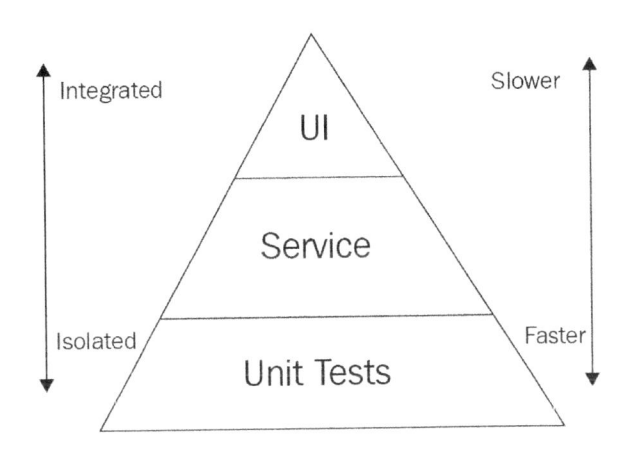

Mike Cohn's Testing Pyramid

Although Mike's book is more than 10 years old, this pyramid is still valid.

This pyramid is based on three characteristics:

- Number of tests
- Isolation
- Speed

I have only one thing against this pyramid: the word **UI**. Modern apps rely more and more on client code, "UI" code. Frameworks such as React, Angular, and Vue.js allow developers to write reusable components. Many apps now have most of their business rules running on the client.

Frontend developers should not be limited to the top of this pyramid. They should be able to write unit tests and service tests for their UI code. This might look like a small change, but I think it's important. With this change in the paradigm, we get a pyramid that looks like this:

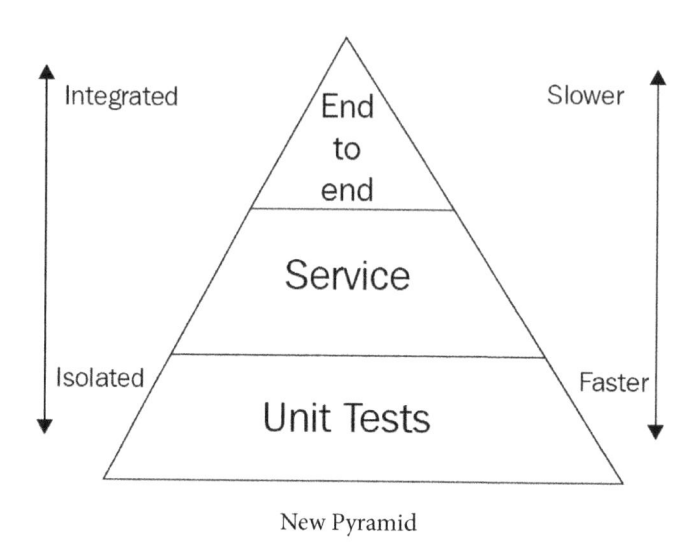

New Pyramid

Now that we have a better understanding, let's talk about the different levels of this pyramid.

Unit tests

Unit tests are the base of the pyramid. The more business logic you cover in unit tests, the less ground you will need to cover in service or UI tests.

As we can see in the pyramid, unit tests need to be **fast and isolated**. That means that a good unit test shouldn't depend on the environment or any other function. Sometimes this is easier said than done. For instance, if you want to test that the total amount of an invoice is equal to the sum of its items, you should be able to test that specific functionality in the code, without launching a web server or getting data from a database.

What roles use Unit tests?

Backend developers: For sure, Unit tests are for them. They follow the **Test-Driven Development** (**TDD**) process if possible. TDD is a technique in software development where tests are written even before any source code has been written. Once the tests have been written, the developer will program the source code to make them pass.

Frontend developers: Writing unit tests was almost impossible in the past. If you didn't have the right tools, you couldn't do your job correctly. But now, many modern libraries support unit testing. If you use React and Redux, you will find that Redux has a way to write unit tests for your components (`https://www.hardkoded.com/ui-testing-with-puppeteer/redux-unit-tests`).

That's not all. In the same way that backend developers need to think about how to make their code testable, if frontend developers, using modern frameworks, start creating small and testable components, **they should be able to use Puppeteer to write UI unit tests**. And here is where the "UI" at the top of the testing pyramid stops making any sense. Now we can write **UI unit tests**.

We can run a small test, rendering a component and testing, for instance, that it "*renders a textbox and when I enter a value, the label below changes,*" or "*if I pass a list of 10 items, 10 elements are rendered.*"

We moved UI testing to the bottom of the testing pyramid.

QA Analysts are not involved yet. Unit tests are about testing the internal code.

How about **Managers**? If you are a developer, I believe you are going to show this paragraph to your boss. Managers won't write unit tests, but they need to know the importance of writing unit tests and investing time in them.

These are the four benefits you (or your boss) need to know about.

Unit tests show how the code works

Unit tests explain how the code works. When I review code, I start by reviewing unit tests. If I find unit tests saying, for instance, "*Create order should send email*". I could read that test first, and then, check how that rule was implemented.

Business Analysts or project managers could read these tests and see whether there are any scenarios that haven't been covered or some missing validation.

Unit tests make refactoring possible

I took a risk using the word possible. But I believe that's true. You can't refactor your code if you don't have unit tests backing your changes. Remember, refactoring is changing the implementation of your code without changing the result given specific inputs. Unit tests guarantee that premise.

Unit tests prevent regressions

Regression is an involuntary change in the expected behavior of an app. If we have a good set of tests, they will prevent us from breaking any behavior of the app while we implement new features or while fixing bugs.

How can I make sure that some other developers won't come and break the precious function I just wrote? By writing unit tests. A unit test is a version of you in the future enforcing how a piece of code should work. "*Create an order should send an email*" – no one will be able to break that rule.

When I review code, changes in unit tests are a red flag to me. I'm not saying that unit tests shouldn't change. But if a test changes, there must be an explanation. Now, the "*Create and order should send an email*" shows that the sent email count is 2. Is that right? Are we sending another email? Or do we have a regression? Pay attention to changes in unit tests.

Time to go up in the test pyramid.

Service tests

Service tests are also known as **Integration Tests**. These tests will check how your code interacts with other components. When we talk about components, we are talking about the following:

- Databases
- Other components in the app
- External services

Frontend developers would also need to integrate their code with the following:

- Other UI components
- CSS files
- REST APIs

As we mentioned before, when we go up in the testing pyramid, tests become **slower and less stable**. And it's supposed to be like that. You will be connecting to a real database or interacting with a real REST API that would use real network calls. That would also mean that your tests would expect the environment to respond in a certain way. For instance, you would expect the database to have some set of data ready to be used, or a REST API to be available.

That's why the more tests you have in the unit test layer, the fewer integration tests you will need to code.

Let's take, for instance, the class that sends an email, could you code an integration test for that? Sure. You set up a local email server that would write emails in a temp folder, so after creating an order, you could check that folder and see whether the email server processed the email your app should have sent. But, as you can see, these kinds of orchestrations are harder to code than small unit tests.

Why do we need integration tests? Why don't we code unit tests only?

Well, you need to tests your integrations. Your code won't run in isolation. If you are testing the backend, you need to see how the database reacts to the data you are inserting, or whether a SQL query returns the data you expect.

If you are a frontend developer, this is where you would invest most of your time, checking how your component interacts on a page or how the HTML being generated affects other elements in the DOM. You would need to test how your component is being rendered with a real REST endpoint, instead of using a dummy JSON file.

What roles use Integration tests?

Backend developers: I've heard people say that these are the only tests that matter. Although I disagree with that strong opinion, I do believe these tests are essential. Say I created a unit test where, for instance, when I call `CreateOrder`, I get a new `Order` object. But now, I need to test that when I make a `POST` request to `/orders`, an order is created in the database.

Frontend developers will create tests to check how all the different components interact with each other on a page. Again, it's UI testing down in the testing pyramid.

QA Analysts will create tests similar to the tests backend and frontend developers create but with a different perspective.

Developers and QA Analysts create the same kinds of tests but with a different perspective.

Developers will create tests to back their job, so they can check whether they broke anything. And, as we mentioned before, they need tests to be able to refactor their code in the future.

QA Analysts will create tests to guarantee the application quality to the stakeholders.

There is one interesting type of test that QA Analysts can implement in this layer: the **Visual Regression Test**. These tests are used when we want to check whether there was any visual change regarding the style of the app. We don't want to check whether there is a button, or whether that button works. We want to check whether the button looks like how it was before. How can we achieve that? By comparing images. This technique is based on four steps:

1. We take a screenshot as a baseline:

Baseline image

2. We make a change in the code.

3. We take another screenshot:

Image after making a change

4. We compare both images:

Differences

This type of test can be quite unstable. I bet you have seen that pages sometimes "move" when they are loading, so you have to be very sure when the page is ready for a screenshot. But it is doable. Another downside is that for every error you get, you have to analyze whether the change was a regression (a change made by mistake) or we are in the presence of a **new baseline**.

The role of **managers** is still important. They need to provide the tools and the time for developers to implement the required integration tests. They will also help QA Analysts to determine what the integrations to test are.

And so we come to the top of the pyramid, the **end-to-end** tests.

End-to-end tests

You might also find these tests referred to as **E2E** tests. The goal of E2E tests is to guarantee that an application works as expected through the entire workflow. Most applications will have more than one workflow. That would mean that it will require a number of E2E tests to cover all the possible workflows or scenarios.

Let's take a cart app as an example. These could be our tests:

- Unit tests:

    a) Passing a cart object, the `AddToCart` component renders an **Add to cart** link if the product is not in the array.

    b) Passing a cart object, the `AddToCart` component renders a "View cart" link if the product is in the array.

- Integration tests:

    a) Go to a product page and click "Add to cart." The link changes to "View cart."

    b) Go to the checkout page. After clicking on the **Checkout** button, it gets disabled.

- One E2E test testing the cart flow:

    a) Go to a product page, click **Add to cart**, then click on **View cart**.

    b) You should have got to the checkout page. Click **Checkout**.

    c) You should have been redirected to the receipt page.

    d) The receipt should show the product added to the cart.

    e) The price should be the product price.

We are at the top of the pyramid. That means that these will be the **slowest and least stable** tests.

Why least stable? Check the workflow. Many bad things can happen there. The add to cart endpoint might take a little bit more than expected. The scroll to the **Checkout** button could have failed for just a few pixels. Your database might be in an unexpected state. Maybe your user already purchased that product, so the **Add to cart** button is not enabled.

How about roles?

This is the **QA Analyst's** land. This is where they need to take advantage of all the features Puppeteer provides to make reliable tests. But **Developers** play an important role, helping the QA team to do their job efficiently. As we are going to see in the next chapters, a developer can leave hints so that the QA team can find the components they need.

I hope the picture of the pyramid makes more sense now. We need lots of small and isolated unit tests, many integration tests testing our pages, and finally, a good set of E2E tests, checking the workflow's health.

This is the famous testing pyramid, but how do we write a test? Where do we write them? How do we run a test?

First, we need to know what we need from a test runner.

Test runner features

What would the world be like without a test runner? Let's say you don't know what a test runner is, and you want to code a unit test. Would that be possible? I think it would. For instance, say we have this small `Cart` class:

```
class Cart {
    constructor() {
        this._cart = [];
    }
    total() {
        return this._cart.reduce((acc, v) => acc + v.price, 0);
    };
    addToCart(item) {
        this._cart.push(item);
    };
}
module.exports = Cart;
```

If we want to test it, we could run some code like this:

```
const Cart = require('./cart.js');
const c = new Cart();
c.addToCart({ productId: 10, price: 5.5});
c.addToCart({ productId: 15, price: 6.5});

if(c.total() !== 12)
    console.error('Nooo!!!');
else
    console.log('Yes!!!!!');
```

A test is basically a piece of code testing our code. Will this work? Yes. Is this a unit test? Yes. Will this scale? Definitely not. This file will become massive and hard to maintain. Keeping track of what has failed would be an impossible task. We need a tool to help us scale and to help us keep our tests maintainable. We need a test runner.

Before exploring possible test runners, I would like to review what we would expect from a test runner. What are the features we would need in a test runner?

Easy to learn and run

We have a lot of things to learn. We need to learn Node and React; we even have to buy a book about Puppeteer. We want a test runner that is simple and easy to use.

Group tests by functionality

We want to have our tests separated by functionality, component, or workflow. Most test runners have a `describe` function that helps us to group tests.

Ignore tests if needed

We want to skip a test if it becomes noisy, but we don't want to remove it.

Run only one test

Being able to run only one test is extremely important while debugging. Imagine you have over 1,000 tests (yes, you are going to have over 1,000 tests). If you want to fix only one test, you wouldn't want to run all of them. You would like to run only the one you are working on.

Assertions

Assertions are essential. An assertion is an expression to check whether the program we are testing worked as expected. Do you remember my `console.log` and `console.error` to check whether the cart worked as expected? Well, Assertions are way better than that. What do we want to check with Assertions? This is a possible list:

- Whether a value is equal to a test value.
- Whether a value is null or not null.
- Whether a string or a list contains a value. We might have a huge block of text, and we only want to check whether it has some string in it, or an item in an array.
- Whether we expected something to fail, because sometimes, we would expect some piece of code to fail.

Tools to set up and clean up the environment

Before starting the tests, we need our application to be in a certain state. For instance, in the cart test, we would like to make sure that the customer has not already purchased the product before starting the test.

There are also technical setups that might need to be performed. In our case, we would need to have Puppeteer and a browser ready to be used before each test.

Another important concept is that tests should be independent and detached from each other. This means that the result of one test must not affect other tests. This is why, very often, it is required to clean up after each or all tests.

Reports

We want to see which tests passed and which tests failed. We would expect a test runner to at least show a good report in the terminal. It could be even better if we can get results in other formats, such as JSON, XML, or HTML.

There are many other features we could mention, but these are the most important features we need to know about before getting started.

Let's now see what the test runners available on the market that can cover the features we are requesting.

Available test runners

There are many types of tennis racquets. Some racquets give you more control. Others give you more power. If you have just started learning how to play tennis, you won't feel any difference. You would if you compared a cheap racquet with a professional one. But you wouldn't be able to say why one is better than the other. You would say that it just *feels better*.

It's the same with test runners. There are test runners that offer some features. Other runners offer other features. But what's important for us now is to get a test runner that provides us with all the required features to write our automated tests.

Another important thing to mention is that this book is not about "using Puppeteer with X." We are going to pick a test runner after this chapter, but it doesn't need to be the test runner for you. The idea is that you can choose what's best for you, or what your team is using right now. It is also probable that by the time you read this book, a better test runner will have become popular. You should be able to apply the concepts you learned from this book to that test runner.

These are the most common test runners in the market today.

Jest

According to the Jest site (https://jestjs.io/), "*Jest is a delightful JavaScript Testing Framework with a focus on simplicity.*" Pretty nice introduction. Facebook maintains this project, and it currently has over 32,000 stars on GitHub. I'm not saying this is what makes a project a good project, but knowing who is behind a project and its level of community support are some of the things to take into consideration.

Jest has all the features we mentioned before, such as group tests with `describe`, and each test is an `it` or `test` function. You can skip tests with `describe.skip`, `it.skip`, or `test.skip`. You can run only one test with `describe.only`, `it.only`, or `test.only`. You also have `beforeEach`, `afterEach`, `beforeAll`, and `afterAll`, to run setup and cleanup code.

It also has some features that differentiate it from other runners. It has a **Snapshot** tool. The snapshot tool would process a React component and return some kind of DOM representation as JSON, which will allow us to test whether the DOM created by the component has changed. Is this a kind of UI test? Sure it is!

Another thing to consider when evaluating a test runner is available plugins. For instance, there is a package called **jest-puppeteer**, which helps us integrate our tests with Puppeteer. You don't need to use **jest-puppeteer**. It's just a helper.

There is also a package called **jest-image-snapshot**, maintained by American Express, which provides a set of tools to perform visual regression tests. In this case, if you want to code visual regression tests, I recommend you to use one of these packages. Managing all the screenshot baselines can be quite tedious.

Mocha

Mocha is another popular framework. It is a community project with over 19,000 stars. Something worth mentioning is that the Puppeteer team uses Mocha.

Mocha also has functions like Jest. It has a `describe` function to group tests. Tests are `it` functions. You can skip functions using `describe.skip` or `it.skip`, and use `describe.only` or `it.only` to run only one test. You also have `beforeEach`, `afterEach`, `beforeAll`, and `afterAll`, to run setup and cleanup code.

You will also find many plugins for Mocha. You will find **mocha-puppeteer** and **mocha-snapshots**.

A recipe you are going to see a lot on the web is Mocha + Chai. **Chai** is an assertion library that extends the assertions a test runner provides. It lets you express assertions in a pretty specific way:

```
foo.should.be.a('string');
foo.should.equal('bar');
foo.should.have.lengthOf(3);
tea.should.have.property('flavors').with.lengthOf(3);
```

There are many other test runners, such as Jasmine by Pivotal Labs with over 15,000 stars, Karma by the AngularJS team with over 11,000 stars, AVA, a community project with over 18,000 stars, and the list goes on.

As I mentioned at the beginning of this section, we just need a good tennis racquet, that is, a good test runner. When you become an expert, you will be able to move from one test runner to another that fits your needs. For the purpose of this book, we are going to use **Mocha + Chai**.

Creating our first test project

We will create a Node application in the same way we created our first app in *Chapter 1*, *Getting started with Puppeteer*. We are going to create a folder called `OurFirstTestProject` (you will find this directory inside the `Chapter2` directory mentioned in the *Technical requirements* section) and then execute `npm init -y` inside that folder:

```
> npm init -y
```

The response should be something like this:

```
{
  "name": "OurFirstTestProject",
  "version": "1.0.0",
  "description": "",
  "main": "index.js",
  "scripts": {
    "test": "echo \"Error: no test specified\" && exit 1"
  },
  "keywords": [],
  "author": "",
  "license": "ISC"
}
```

Now it's time to install the packages we are going to use:

- Puppeteer 7
- Mocha (any version)
- Chai (any version)

Let's run the following commands:

```
> npm install puppeteer@">=7.0.0 <8.0.0"
> npm install mocha
> npm install chai
```

For this first demo, we are going to use the site `https://www.packtpub.com/` as a test case. Let's keep our test simple. We want to test that the page title says *Packt | Programming Books, eBooks & Videos for Developers.*

> **Important Note**
> The site we are using for this test might have changed over time. Before testing this code, go to `https://www.packtpub.com/` and check whether the title is still the same. That's why, in the following chapters, we will be downloading sites locally, so we avoid these possible issues.

We mentioned that we would use `describe` to group our tests. But separating tests into different files will also help us to get our code organized. You can choose between having one or many `describe` functions per file. Let's create a file called `home.tests.js`. We are going to put all tests related to the home page there.

Although you can create the files anywhere you want, Mocha grabs all the tests in the `test` folder by default, so we will to create the `test` folder and then create the `home.test.js` file inside that folder.

We are going to have the following:

- `home.tests.js` with the home tests
- A `describe` function with the header tests
- An `it` function testing *"Title should have Packt name"*
- Another `it` function testing *"Title mention the word Books"*

The structure should look like this:

```
const puppeteer = require('puppeteer');
const expect = require('chai').expect;
const should = require('chai').should();

describe('Home page header', () => {
    it('Title should have Packt name', async () => {

    });

        it('Title should mention Books', async () => {
```

```
    });
});
```

Let's unpack this code:

1. We are importing Puppeteer in line 1.
2. Lines 2 are 3 are about importing the different types of assertion styles **Chai** provides. As you can see, `expect` is not being called with parentheses whereas `should` is. We don't need to know why now. But, just to be clear, that's not a mistake.
3. How about Mocha? Are we missing Mocha? Well, Mocha is the test runner. It will be the executable we will call later in `package.json`. We don't need it in our code.
4. It's interesting to see that both `describe` and `it` are just simple functions that take two arguments: a string and a function. Can you pass a function as an argument? Yes, you can!
5. The functions we are passing to the `it` functions are `async`. We can't use the `await` keyword in functions that are not marked as `async`. Remember that Puppeteer relies a lot on async programming.

Now we need to launch a browser and set up everything these tests need to work. We could do something like this:

```
it('Title should have Packt name', async() => {
    const browser = await puppeteer.launch();
    const page = await browser.newPage();
    await page.goto('https://www.packtpub.com/');
    // Our test code
    await browser.close();
});
```

> **Tip**
> Don't try to learn the Puppeteer API now. We are going to explain how all of these commands work in *Chapter 3, Navigating through a website*.

This code will run perfectly. However, there are two things that could do with optimization:

- We would be repeating the same code over and over.
- If something fails in the middle of the test, the browser won't get closed, leaving lots of open browsers.

To avoid these problems, we can use `before`, `after`, `beforeEach`, and `afterEach`. If we add these functions to our tests, this would be the execution order:

- `before`
- `beforeEach`
- `it('Title should have Packt name')`
- `afterEach`
- `beforeEach`
- `it('Title should mention Books')`
- `afterEach`
- `after`

It's not a rule of thumb, but we can do something like this in our case:

1. `before`: Launch the browser.
2. `beforeEach`: Open a page and navigate to the URL.
3. Run the test.
4. `afterEach`: Close the page.
5. `after`: Close the browser.

These **hooks**, which is what Mocha calls these functions, would look like this:

```
let browser;
let page;

before(async () => {
    browser = await puppeteer.launch();
});

beforeEach(async () => {
```

```
    page = await browser.newPage();
    await page.goto('https://www.packtpub.com/');
});

afterEach(async () => {
    await page.close();
});

after(async () => {
    await browser.close();
});
```

One thing to mention here is that we could do what's called **Fire and Forget** when closing the page or the browser. Fire and forget means that we don't want to `await` the result of `page.close()` or `browser.close()`. So, we could do this:

```
afterEach(() => page.close());
after(() => browser.close());
```

That's not something I love doing because if something fails, you would like to know where and why. But as this is just cleanup code for a test, it's not production code, we can afford that risk.

Now our test has a browser opened, a page with the URL we want to test read. We just need to test the title:

```
it('Title should have Packt name', async() => {
    const title = await page.title();
    title.should.contain('Packt');
});

it('Title should should mention Books', async() => {
    expect((await page.title())).to.contain('Books');
});
```

I used two different styles here.

In the first case, I'm assigning the result of the `title` async function to a variable, and then using `should.contain` to check whether the title contains the word *"Packt"*. In the second case, I just evaluated `((await page.title())`. I added some extra parentheses there for clarification. You won't see them in the final example.

The second difference is that in the first case, I'm using the **should** style, whereas in the second case, I'm using the **expect** style. The result will be the same. It's just about which style you feel more comfortable with or feels more natural to you. There is even a third style: **assert**.

We have everything we need to run our tests. Remember how `npm init` created a `package.json` file for us? It's time to use it. Let's set the `test` command. You should have something like this:

```
"scripts": {
  "test": "echo \"Error: no test specified\" && exit 1"
},
```

We need to tell npm to run **Mocha** when we execute `npm test`:

```
"scripts": {
  "test": "mocha"
},
```

Time to run our tests! Let's run `npm test` in the terminal:

```
npm test
```

And we should have our first error:

```
1) Home page header
       "before each" hook for "Title should have Packt name":
     Error: Timeout of 2000ms exceeded. For async tests and
hooks, ensure "done()" is called; if returning a Promise,
ensure it resolves.
```

That's bad, but not that bad. Mocha validates by default that our tests should take less than 2,000 ms. That sounds OK for an isolated unit test. But UI tests might take longer than 2 seconds. That doesn't mean that UI tests shouldn't have a timeout. **Speed is a feature**, so we should be able to enforce some expected timeout. We can change that by adding the `--timeout` command-line argument to the launch setting we set up in the `package.config` file. I think 30 seconds could be a reasonable timeout. As it expects the value in milliseconds, it should be `30000`. Let's make that change in our `package.config` file:

```
"scripts": {
  "test": "mocha --timeout 30000"
},
```

> **Tip**
> The command-line argument is not the only way to set up the timeout. You can call `this.Timeout (30000)` inside the `describe` function or configure the timeout using a config file (https://mochajs.org/#configuring-mocha-nodejs).

Once we set up the timeout, we can try our tests again by running npm `test`:

```
/Code/OurFirstTestProject > npm test

> OurFirstTestProject@1.0.0 test /Users/neo/Library/Mobile Documents/com~apple~CloudDocs/Docs/Books/Up and running with Puppeteer/CH2/Code/OurFirstTestProject
> mocha --timeout 30000


  Home page header
    ✓ Title should have Packt name
    ✓ Title should should mention Books


  2 passing (5s)
```

Test Result

Mocha not only ran our tests but also printed a pretty decent report. We have there all the tests Mocha ran, the final result, and the elapsed time. Here is where many test runners offer different options. For instance, Mocha has a `--reporter` flag. If you go to `https://mochajs.org/`, you will see all the available reporters. We could use the `list` reporter, which shows the elapsed time of each test. We can add it to our `package.config` file:

```
"scripts": {
  "test": "mocha --timeout 30000 --reporter=list"
},
```

With this change, we can get a better report:

```
/Code/OurFirstTestProject> npm test

> OurFirstTestProject@1.0.0 test /Users/neo/Library/Mobile Documents/com~apple~CloudDocs/Docs/Books/Up and ru
nning with Puppeteer/CH2/Code/OurFirstTestProject
> mocha --timeout 30000 --reporter=list


  ✓ Home page header Title should have Packt name: 6ms
  ✓ Home page header Title should should mention Books: 3ms

  2 passing (5s)
```

Test Result using the list reporter

This project looks fine. If you had only a few tests, this would be enough. But if we are going to have lots of tests using many pages, this code won't scale. We need to organize our code so that we can be more productive and reuse more code.

Organizing our code

Our first test was quite simple: we were just checking the page title. But let's take a look at the home page:

Packtpub home page

There are many actions we would like to test there:

- Search for an existing book.
- Search for a non-existing book.
- Check the cart when it is empty.
- Check the cart when we add a product.

Let's take, for example, *Search tests*. We would be doing the same steps every time:

1. Click on the search box.
2. Enter the text.
3. Click on the search button.

We would be doing the same thing over and over in all our search tests. Sometimes there is a misconception that, as the test code is not production code, the code can be a mess. So, people go and copy/paste their tests over and over, duplicating code and hardcoding values. That ends up with hard-to-maintain tests. When tests are hard to maintain, they tend to be pushed down the priority list. Developers lose, QA analysts lose, and in the end, clients lose.

We are going to see two techniques to improve our test code: the **Page Object Model** (**POM**) and the test data config.

Introducing the Page Object Model

The POM is a design pattern that will help us separate our test code from the implementation of the interaction our tests will perform.

Let's build our `HomePageModel` together. What are the possible interactions on that page?

- **Go** (to the page)
- **Get page title**
- **Search**
- **Sign In**
- **View Cart**
- **Go to Checkout**
- **Subscribe**

Well done! We just created our first Page Model. This is how it will look:

```
module.exports = class HomePageModel {
    go() {}
    title() {}
    search(searchValue) {}
    signIn() {}
    viewCart() {}
    gotoCheckout() {}
    subscribe() {}
}
```

Let's focus on the two first functions: the `go` function, which will navigate to the home page, and the `title` function, which will return the page title.

We will reuse a lot of code here. If we want to start using this model, we would need to do two things: implement the title fetching here and pass a Puppeteer page to this model:

```
export default class HomePageModel {
    constructor(page) {
        this.page = page;
    }
    // Unused functions...
    async go() {
        await this.page.goto('https://www.packtpub.com/');
    }
    async title() {
        return await this.page.title();
    }
}
```

Now it's a matter of importing this class into our tests using `require`. I will put this class into a **POM** (**Page Object Model**) folder inside the test folder. Once we create the file, we import it:

```
const HomePageModel = require('./pom/HomePageModel.js');
```

We declare a variable inside the describe:

```
let homePageModel;
```

We create an instance of this class in the `beforeEach` hook:

```
beforeEach(async () => {
    page = await browser.newPage();
    homePageModel = new HomePageModel(page);
    await homePageModel.go();
});
```

And now, we simply replace the `page.title` we are using with `homePageModel.title`:

```
(await homePageModel.title()).should.contain('Packt');
```

As I mentioned earlier in the chapter, UI tests help us see whether our refactoring broke our code. Let's run `npm test` again to confirm that we didn't break anything:

```
ning with Puppeteer/CH2/Code/OurFirstTestProject
> mocha --timeout 30000 --reporter=list

  ✓ Home page header Title should have Packt name: 13ms
  ✓ Home page header Title should should mention Books: 2ms

  2 passing (5s)
```

Test result after the first refactor

There's only one thing left to do so that we can be proud of our first project. We need to get rid of our hardcoded values. We only wrote two tests, and we have three hardcoded values: the site URL and the `Packt` and the `Books` words.

For these tests, we can leave these hardcoded values. But what if you have different environments? You would need to make the URL dynamic. What if your site were a generic e-commerce site? The brand name would depend on the test you are navigating.

There are many other use cases:

- Test users and passwords
- Product to test
- Keywords to use

We can create a `config.js` file with all the environment settings and return only the one we get on an environment variable. If not set, we return the local version:

```
module.exports = ({
    local: {
        baseURL: 'https://www.packtpub.com/',
        brandName: 'Packt',
        mainProductName: 'Books'
    },
    test: {},
    prod: {},
})[process.env.TESTENV || 'local']
```

If this looks a little bit scary, don't worry, it's not that complex:

- It returns an object with three properties: `local`, `test`, and `prod`.
- In JavaScript, you can access a property by using `object.property` or by treating the object as a dictionary: `object['local']`.
- `process.env` allows us to read environment variables. We won't be using environment variables in this book, but I wanted to show you the final solution.
- Finally, we are going to return only the `local`, `test`, or `prod` property based on the `TESTENV` variable or `'local'` if the environment variable was not set.

I bet that by now, you will know that we will be able to access this object using a `require` call:

```
const config = require('./config');
```

And from there, start using the `config` variable instead of hardcoded values. We would also need to pass this config to the page model because we have a hardcoded URL there.

After making all these changes, this is what our tests should look like:

```
const puppeteer = require('puppeteer');
const expect = require('chai').expect;
const should = require('chai').should();
const HomePageModel = require('./pom/HomePageModel.js');
const config = require('./config');

describe('Home page header', () => {
```

```
    let browser;
    let page;
    let homePageModel;

    before(async () => browser = await puppeteer.launch());
    beforeEach(async () => {
        page = await browser.newPage();
        homePageModel = new HomePageModel(page, config);
        await homePageModel.go();
    });
    afterEach(() => page.close());
    after(() => browser.close());
    it('Title should have Packt name', async () => {
        (await homePageModel.title()).should.contain(config.brandName);
    });
    it('Title should mention Books', async () => {
        expect(await homePageModel.title()).to.contain(config.mainProductName);
    });
});
```

If we remove all the unused functions, our final page model would look like this:

```
module.exports = class HomePageModel {
    constructor(page, config) {
        this.page = page;
        this.config = config;
    }
    async go() {
        await this.page.goto(this.config.baseURL);
    }
    async title() {
        return await this.page.title();
    }
}
```

As you can see, we didn't need to implement complex design patterns to make our tests reusable and easy to maintain. I think it's time to get started with our tests, which we will do in *Chapter 3, Navigating through a website*.

Summary

In this chapter, we started with the foundations of automated testing. Mike Cohn's pyramid helped us to understand the different types of tests. We also gave this pyramid a new look, showing how it should be used from a Frontend developer perspective. We also made it clear that both developers and QA analysts are part of this pyramid, but with different perspectives.

In the second part of the chapter, we got more practical, and we looked into test runners. A learning point here is that we used Mocha as a test runner, but everything you learned in this chapter should be possible with any test runner; that is, we used Mocha, but we could have used any other test runner.

We use many Puppeteer APIs in our tests. In the next chapter, we are going to dive deep into these APIs and see how we can use Puppeteer in different scenarios.

3
Navigating through a website

We have already laid the foundations for the rest of the book. In *Chapter 1, Getting started with Puppeteer*, we learned about browser automation and headless browsers. *Chapter 2, Automated Testing and Test runners*, was about automated testing and test runners. Now it's time to get more practical. In this chapter, we will learn about UI testing, but in the real world.

In the following chapters, we will pick an open-source website made with Vue.js to test, but we are also going to navigate through many other public websites. I want you to learn techniques that help you test websites no matter the framework they use.

I also want to share some tools with you, so you can finish this book with a complete toolbox. In this chapter, we will learn how to ship our code to GitHub and run our tests using GitHub Actions.

In the previous chapter, we created a test project, and we ran a few tests without paying too much attention to the Puppeteer APIs we were using. In this chapter, we will create a test project again, but this time we will go deeper and see what Puppeteer has to offer on each API.

We will cover the following topics in this chapter:

- Introducing the test site for this chapter
- Creating a Puppeteer browser
- Navigating through a site
- Using the Response object
- Introduction to Continuous Integration

By the end of this chapter, we will have tested a real website, pushed it to GitHub, and run our tests automatically, learning many new APIs. Let's see what test sites we can use in this chapter.

Technical requirements

You will find all the code of this chapter in the GitHub repository (`https://github.com/PacktPublishing/ui-testing-with-puppeteer`) under the `Chapter3` directory. We will consider `Chapter3` as the base path for all the demos. Inside the `Chapter3` directory, you will find three directories:

- `vuejs-firebase-shopping-cart` contains the test site.
- `init` is the directory you can use to follow this chapter.
- `demo` contains the final code from this chapter.

Introducing the tests sites for this chapter

In this chapter, we will test a site made with Vue.js. Thang Minh Vu (`https://me.coddeine.com/`) wrote a great Vue.js example: **vuejs-firebase-shopping-cart** (`https://github.com/ittus/vuejs-firebase-shopping-cart`).

> **Tip**
> When you look for projects on GitHub or any other site like GitHub, you need to pay attention to the license the project uses. The fact that the code is open source doesn't mean that you can use it as you wish. This project uses the **MIT License**, which is one of the most permissive licenses. This license basically states that you can use the code *without restriction, including without limitation the rights to use, copy, modify, merge, publish, distribute, sublicense, and/or sell copies of the Software, and to permit persons to whom the Software is furnished to do so.*

As we don't want you to deal with firebase setup, I forked this project (made a copy on GitHub), removing all the firebase code. You can find the base structure of the code used in this chapter inside the `init` directory. You just need to run `npm install` in the base folder and then run the following commands on the `vuejs-firebase-shopping-cart` folder.

```
> cd init
> npm install
> cd vuejs-firebase-shopping-cart/
> npm install
> npm run build
> npm run serve
```

In the terminal, you should have got a success message and the URL the site is now running:

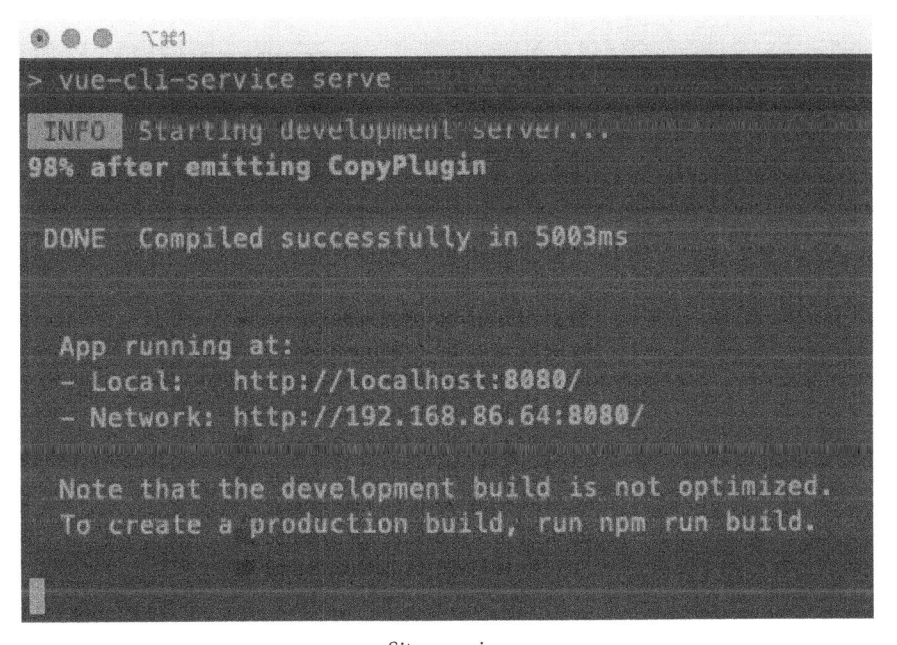

```
> vue-cli-service serve

 INFO  Starting development server...
98% after emitting CopyPlugin

 DONE  Compiled successfully in 5003ms


  App running at:
  - Local:   http://localhost:8080/
  - Network: http://192.168.86.64:8080/

  Note that the development build is not optimized.
  To create a production build, run npm run build.
```

Site running

Now we should have a nice site running on port 8080.

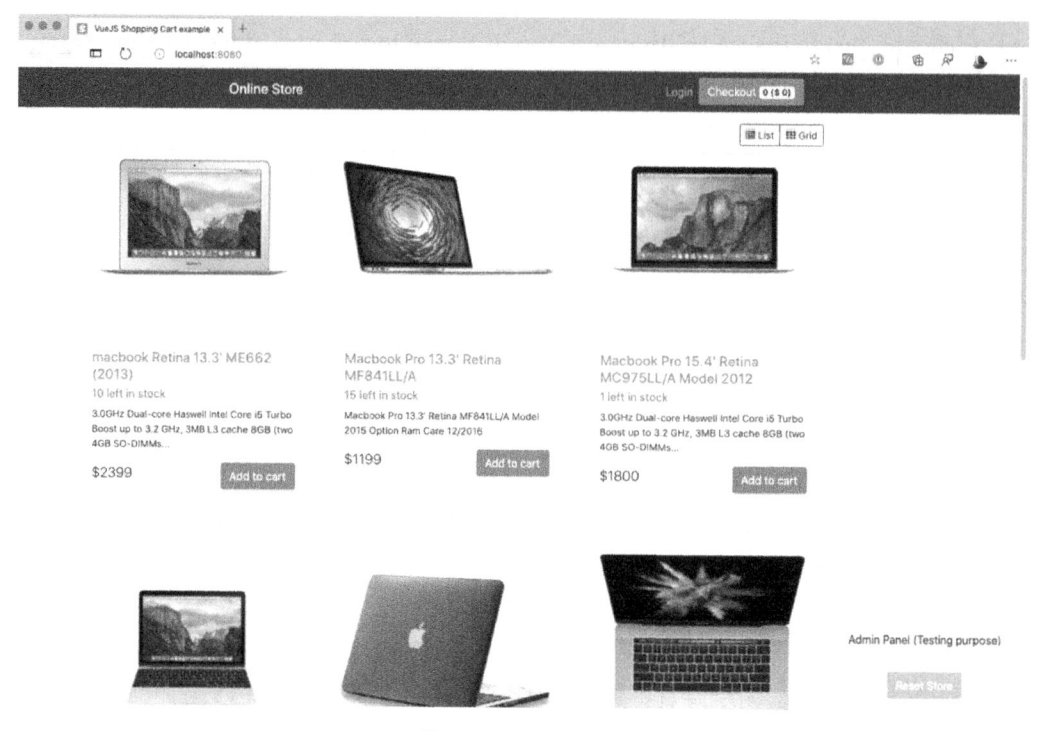

Demo site running

We'll need two terminals to work on this project. In one terminal, we are going to run the website. In the second, we are going to launch our tests.

If you are using VS Code, notice that the **TERMINAL** tab has a plus button. If you click on that button, a new terminal will be created. You can switch between terminals using the selection list to the left of that button.

New terminal option

Let's run the site in one terminal using the same commands we used before:

```
> cd vuejs-firebase-shopping-cart
> npm run build
> npm run serve
```

You should get something like this:

```
DONE  Compiled successfully in 5523ms
1:42:33 PM

  App running at:
  - Local:   http://localhost:8080/
  - Network: http://192.168.86.64:8080/

  Note that the development build is not optimized.
  To create a production build, run npm run build.
```

Now let's run the tests in another terminal:

```
npm test
```

And here, you should be getting something like this:

```
> mocha --timeout 30000 --reporter=list
  ✓ Login Page Should have the right title: 3ms

  1 passing (875ms)
```

In the previous chapter, we didn't pay much attention to how we were using Puppeteer. We just knew that if we did `browser = await puppeteer.launch();` we would get a new browser. How? No idea. Well, it's time to understand a little bit more about how Puppeteer works.

Creating a Puppeteer browser

The signature of the `launch` function is not `launch()`, but `launch(options)`. Thanks to the freedom we have in JavaScript, we can just avoid passing that argument, and the `launch` function will get `options` as `undefined`.

Using the Puppeteer.launch function

These are all the options `Puppeteer.launch` supports in Puppeteer 7 according to the official docs (https://github.com/puppeteer/puppeteer/blob/v7.0.0/docs/api.md#puppeteerlaunchoptions):

- `product`: Which browser to launch. At this time, this is either `chrome` or `firefox`.
- `ignoreHTTPSErrors`: Whether to ignore HTTPS errors during navigation. This option will become handy when you want to automate websites with invalid or missing SSL certificates. This will prevent Chromium from returning an invalid certificate page in those cases.
- `headless`: Whether to run the browser in headless mode. Defaults to `true` unless the `devtools` option is `true`.
- `executablePath`: Path to a browser executable to run instead of the bundled Chromium.
- `slowMo`: Slows down Puppeteer operations by the specified number of milliseconds. Useful so that you can see what is going on.
- `defaultViewport`: Sets a consistent viewport for each page. Defaults to an 800x600 viewport. `null` disables the default viewport. A viewport is an object with the following properties:

  a) `width`: page width in pixels.

  b) `height`: page height in pixels.

  c) `deviceScaleFactor`: Specify device scale factor.

  d) `isMobile`: Whether the `meta viewport` tag is taken into account.

  e) `hasTouch`: Specifies whether the viewport supports touch events.

  f) `isLandscape`: Specifies whether the viewport is in landscape mode.

- `args`: Additional arguments to pass to the browser instance.
- `ignoreDefaultArgs`: If `true`, then do not use `puppeteer.defaultArgs()`. If an array is given, then filter out the given default arguments.

- `handleSIGINT`: Close the browser process on *Ctrl +C*.
- `handleSIGTERM`: Close the browser process on `SIGTERM`.
- `handleSIGHUP`: Close the browser process on `SIGHUP`.
- `timeout`: Maximum time in milliseconds to wait for the browser instance to start. Defaults to `30000` (30 seconds). Passing `0` disables the timeout.
- `dumpio`: Whether to pipe the browser process `stdout` and `stderr` into `process.stdout` and `process.stderr`.
- `userDataDir`: Path to a user data directory.
- `env`: Specify environment variables that will be visible to the browser.
- `devtools`: Whether to auto-open a DevTools panel for each tab. If this option is `true`, the `headless` option will be set to `false`.
- `pipe`: Connects to the browser over a pipe instead of a WebSocket. Defaults to `false`.
- `extraPrefsFirefox`: Additional preferences that can be passed to Firefox.

That's a long list, I know. But I didn't want to just write about the features I think are interesting. I want you to have the full picture of the `launch` option. Now, let's talk about about the options you do need to know.

Headless

I think the `headless` option is the most used. Remember I told you we were going to use headless browsers? I won't say that I lied, but I lied. Headless mode is the default mode, but in fact, you could launch a browser with `headless` in `false`, also known as *"headful mode."* Headful mode is useful while debugging automation code because you will see what is going on in the browser. I bet that will be the default local setting. This is how you can launch the browser in headful mode:

```
const browser = await puppeteer.launch({ headless: false });
```

This line of code will launch a browser that will almost look like a normal browser.

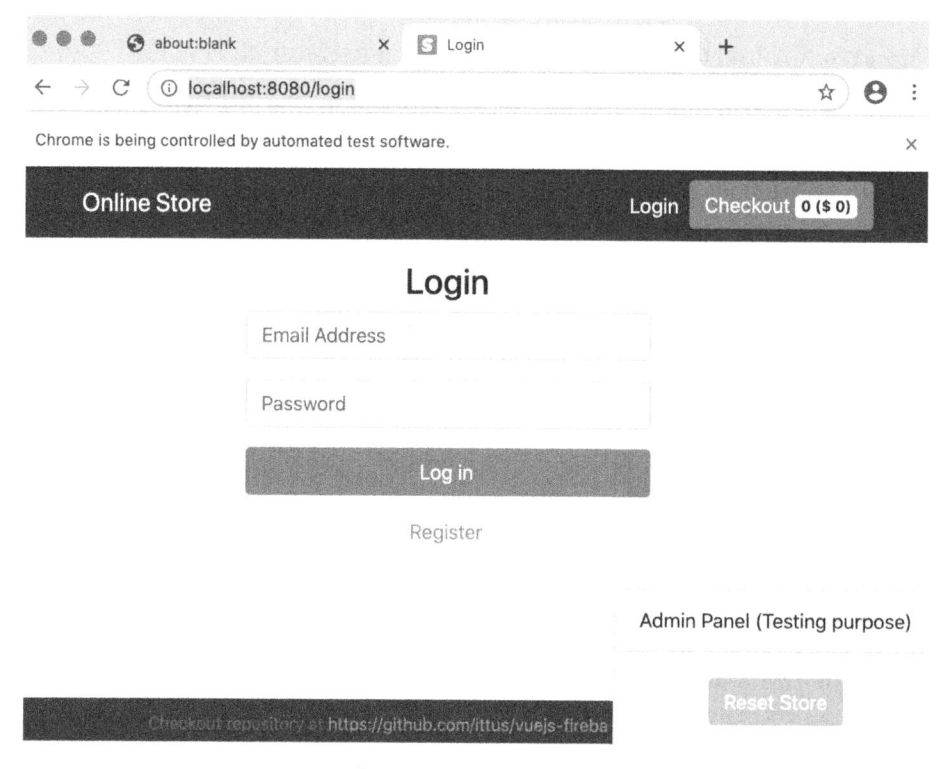

A browser in headful mode

As you can see, that's a full working browser. The only difference is that you will get that banner saying that *"Chrome is being controlled by automated test software."* If someone asks you, no, you can't remove that banner. I believe that with so much phishing and hacking around the internet, it's important to tell a potential user of the browser that there is an app behind it controlling and monitoring the browser activity.

The user data directory

The **user data directory** is where the browser stores user data, such as history, bookmarks, and cookies. If we don't pass a `userDataDir`, Puppeteer will create a new directory before launching the browser. Then it will delete it when the browser is closed. That would mean that sessions or anything we store in cookies won't be preserved across test runs.

In UI testing, we might want to use this option to check whether the site uses the local storage (for example, cookies) as expected. Does the site remember the logged-in user? Is the cart being preserved?

Executable Path

The `executablePath` option is not common on UI testing. Most tests will run using the browser downloaded by Puppeteer. Still, this option is used a lot in task automation or scraping, when you want to use the browser you would normally use, or in some continuous integration environments, where you want to run an already downloaded browser.

As we saw in *Chapter 1, Getting started with Puppeteer*, Puppeteer is guaranteed to work with a specific version of Chromium. In the case of Puppeteer 7.0.0, the Chromium version is 90.0.4403.0. That doesn't mean that it will not work with any other version, but it's not guaranteed.

> **Tip**
> If you are a macOS user, the Chrome executable will be inside the application bundle `Google Chrome.app`. For example, `/Applications/Google Chrome.app/Contents/MacOS/Google Chrome`.

Using the `executablePath` option won't be enough if we want to use the exact same browser we would normally use. Remember that Puppeteer will create a new user data directory if we don't pass one. We need to pass the user data directory our browser uses. It should be `%LOCALAPPDATA%\Google\Chrome\User Data` in Windows, `~/Library/Application Support/Google/Chrome` in Mac, or `~/.config/google-chrome` in Linux. If you want to double-check that value, you can navigate to `chrome://version/` using your browser. There you will see the current **Profile Path**. You need to remove the Default directory in macOS.

> **Tip**
> If you are going to use your own browser, you can install puppeteer-core instead of Puppeteer. puppeteer-core won't download a browser, speeding up your install time and saving disk space.

60   Navigating through a website

Default Viewport

If you tried the headful mode, you might have seen something like this:

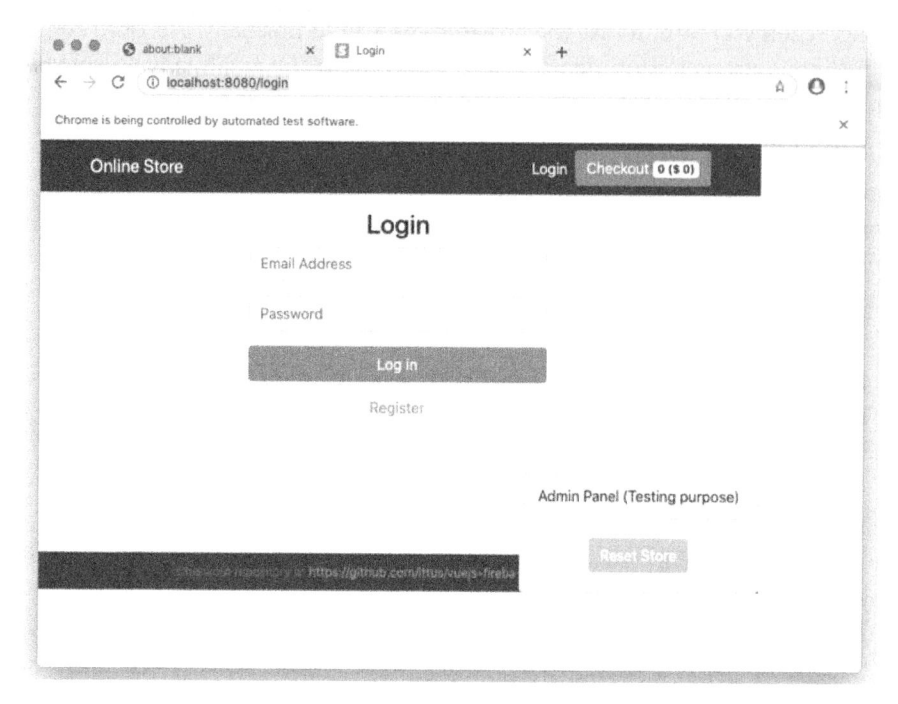

Headful mode with no default viewport

No, the site is not broken. If we don't pass a `defaultViewport`, Puppeteer will default to a viewport of 800x600. If you were wondering what a viewport is, according to Wikipedia, *a viewport is the visible portion of the entire document*.

The viewport is an important piece of UI testing. UX experts and designers make a significant effort trying to give the user the best experience for the device they are using. Frontend developers use CSS breakpoints to determine which layout to show based on the viewport size. Rico Sta. Cruz, on his blog post *What media query breakpoints should I use?* (`https://ricostacruz.com/til/css-media-query-breakpoints`), posted this excellent list of breakpoints:

- Mobile devices in portrait: From 320px to 414px.
- Mobile devices in landscape: From 568px to 812px.
- Table in portrait: From 768px to 834px.
- Table in landscape: From 1024px to 1112px.

- Laptops: From 1366px to 1440px.
- Desktop displays: 1680px to 1920px.

You don't need to have many devices to test this. Just open a browser and change the size of the window.

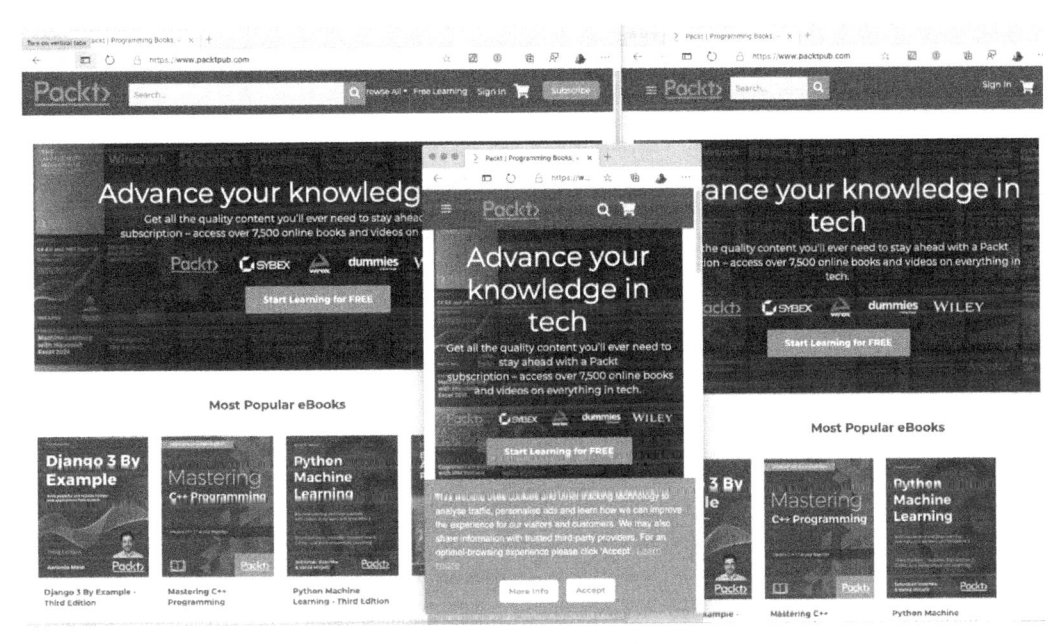

Different breakpoints Packtpub.com uses

If you look at that screenshot, you will see that the site shows or hides different elements based on the viewport. It would show a big search bar in a big viewport, assuming a desktop experience. When it detects a small viewport, assuming a mobile device, it will hide the search bar and show a hamburger button.

We need to consider all these changes when writing our tests.

> **Tip**
> Instead of trying to guess viewports, ask your frontend team what breakpoints they are using. But keep in mind that many bugs emerge on those precise breakpoints, test the breakpoints, and check whether they are appropriate.

We will go deeper into this topic in *Chapter 8, Environments emulation*, when we talk about mobile emulation. One last trick here. If we pass `null`, the viewport will adapt to the window size, as you would expect in a normal browser.

Product

Are you saying that we can automate Firefox with Puppeteer? Yes, we can. Although it is still experimental. This is the official definition of "experimental": *Official Firefox support is currently experimental. The ongoing collaboration with Mozilla aims to support common end to end testing use cases, for which developers expect cross-browser coverage. The Puppeteer team needs input from users to stabilize Firefox support and to bring missing APIs to our attention.* My unofficial definition would be: *It uses a nightly build of Firefox, and the long-term support doesn't seem guaranteed.*

Disclaimers aside, if you want to launch a Firefox browser, you need first to install Puppeteer setting the `PUPPETEER_PRODUCT` variable:

```
PUPPETEER_PRODUCT=firefox npm install puppeteer@7.0.0
```

And then you can set Firefox as a product:

```
browser = await puppeteer.launch({ product: 'firefox' });
```

Browser Arguments

The `args` option is an array of arguments or **flags** you can pass to the browser. There are over 1,400 flags (https://www.hardkoded.com/ui-testing-with-puppeteer/chrome-flags). It would be impossible to cover all 1,400 flags.

`--no-sandbox` is the most common flag. From the official documentation: *In order to protect the host environment from untrusted web content, Chrome uses multiple layers of sandboxing. For this to work properly, the host should be configured first.*

The key phrase here is *"the host should be configured first."* You might need to create a user with the right permissions to use Puppeteer in a more restricted context, such as **Docker** images. A (risky) shortcut would be the `--no-sandbox` flag, which would bypass the sandboxing system.

Other common flags are the following:

- `--window-size` to set the window size.
- `--proxy-server` and `--proxy-bypass-list` to set up proxy settings.

There is another option called `extraPrefsFirefox`. You can use this property to set Firefox flags. Hopefully, you won't need to deal with these flags much.

Mobile options

`deviceScaleFactor`, `isMobile`, `hasTouch`, and `isLandscape` will help us set up mobile emulation. We will cover these options more deeply in *Chapter 8, Environments emulation*.

As you can see, `puppeteer.launch()` is way more than that, and there are many others for you to keep digging.

Options in practice

Now let's see how we can apply these new features in the real world. The first thing we can do now, and you should do from now on, is to load the options object from the config file. Remember that the config class we have is JavaScript code. We can add a property there called `launchOptions` and pass that to the `launch` function. You don't even need to populate it if you don't want to, but it will be there, ready to be used.

Your config file will look like this:

```
module.exports = ({
    local: {
        baseURL: 'http://localhost:8080/',
        launchOptions: { headless: false }
    },
}) [process.env.TESTENV || 'local'];
```

Now, when we run these tests using the `local` config, it will launch the browser in headful mode. The next step is passing this option to the `launch` function:

```
before(async () => {
    browser = await puppeteer.launch(config.launchOptions);
});
```

Now let's try to code a real-life test. We want to test that the login action is being persisted after closing a browser.

These are the steps:

1. Open a browser using a user data directory.
2. Check that we are logged out (checking that the login button says **Login**).
3. Log in.
4. Check that we are logged in (checking that the logout button says **Logout**).

5. Close the browser.
6. Open the browser.
7. We should be logged in.

We won't be able to reuse the browser we are using in other tests because we will need to create our own user data directory:

```
it('It should persist the user', async() => {
    const userDataDir = fs.mkdtempSync('profile');
    const options = config.launchOptions;
    options.userDataDir = userDataDir;
    let persistentBrowser = await puppeteer.launch(options);
    let persistentPage = await persistentBrowser.newPage();
    let loginModel = new LoginPageModel(persistentPage, config);

    await loginModel.go();
    (await loginModel.logState()).should.equal('Login');
    await loginModel.login(config.username, config.password);
    (await loginModel.logState()).should.equal('Logout');

    await persistentBrowser.close();

    persistentBrowser = await puppeteer.launch(options);
    persistentPage = await persistentBrowser.newPage();
    loginModel = new LoginPageModel(persistentPage, config);
    await loginModel.go();

    (await loginModel.logState()).should.equal('Logout');

    await persistentBrowser.close();
    deleteFolderRecursive(userDataDir);
});
```

This test is longer than the others because we need to create a browser, a page, and a model twice. Ignore how the `logState` and `login` functions work. We will cover those functions in the following chapters.

It's impressive, all the functionality that can be hidden inside a single line. Now let's see how we can improve our navigation skills.

Navigating through a site

If you look at how you navigate through different pages on a browser, there are basically four ways:

- You type a URL in the address bar or using a bookmark.
- You use the browser functions to go back, forward, or reload a page.
- You click on elements on a page.
- The site you are browsing redirects to another page.

The `goto` function emulates the first option, navigating to a site. We use that to navigate to the page we want to test:

```
await this.page.goto(this.config.baseURL + 'login');
```

Now, guess what? The `goto` signature isn't `goto(url)` but `goto(url, options)`. You will see this pattern being repeated over and over – a function with one or more required arguments (or none), and then a set of extra options.

Luckily for us, the options `goto` expects is not as big as the one we saw in the `launch` options. It only has three options:

- `timeout`: Maximum navigation time in milliseconds.
- `waitUntil`: When to consider navigation succeeded.
- `referrer`: Referrer header value.

Let's unpack these options.

Timeouts

You will see the `timeout` argument in many functions. Puppeteer groups timeouts in two groups: **navigation timeouts** and **generic timeouts** (this is not the official name; I named them in this way just to make these concepts easier to understand).

If we wanted to set a default timeout in all our navigation calls, we could create a property in our config file and use it in every place. That sounds like a great idea, but there is an even better solution. We can use a property in our config file, but instead of passing that to every function we use, we can call `page.setDefaultTimeout(timeout)` or `page.setDefaultNavigationTimeout(timeout)`.

The `page` object will store the timeout you pass to these functions and use them as a default value.

> **Important note**
> If you don't pass a timeout to a function, nor set a default timeout, Puppeteer will set the timeout to 30 seconds (30,000 milliseconds).

If we are testing a site locally, waiting 30 seconds for a page to load sounds like a lot. Let's reduce that time to 5 seconds. We can add a new property in our config file:

```
local: {
    baseURL: 'http://localhost:8080/',
    timeout: 5000,
},
```

And then, we can set that value using the default timeout:

```
page.setDefaultTimeout(config.timeout);
```

> **Tip**
> You don't need to `await` `setDefaultTimeout` or `setDefaultNavigationTimeout` because they are not `async`.

The next option is the most interesting option in `goto`.

waitUntil

You might be thinking, "Wait until what?". Imagine if, when you do something like `await page.goto('https://www.packtpub.com/')`, Puppeteer resolves the `promise` as soon as the command is sent to the browser. The next command you run will get an empty page because it takes some time to be ready to be used. I bet you experience watching a white screen while waiting for a page to load. You have to **wait until** the page is ready.

Empty page

Waiting for the page to be ready is key in browser automation. Many of the questions I see on Stack Overflow are related to this question: How do you know the page is ready? I hope when you finish this book, you can master this topic. In *Chapter 5, Waiting for elements and network calls*, we will walk through many techniques to answer this question, but `page.goto` gives us this first tool: the `waitUntil` option.

`waitUntil` supports four options:

The first option, and the default option, is `load`. If you pass `load` (or no option), the `promise` will be resolved then the `load` event is fired. According to Mozilla, the load event is fired *when the whole page has loaded, including all dependent resources such as stylesheets and images.*

The second option is `domcontentloaded`, which relies on the `DOMContentLoaded` event. According to Mozilla, the `DOMContentLoaded` is fired *when the initial HTML document has been completely loaded and parsed, without waiting for stylesheets, images, and subframes to finish loading.*

The last two options are network-related. `networkidle0` will resolve the promise *when there are no more network connections for the past 500ms*. On the other hand, `networkidle2` will resolve the promise *when there are no more than 2 network connections for the past 500ms*.

Which one is better? Generally speaking, the default is good enough and pretty safe. You might need to switch to the network ones if you have many **AJAX** calls after the **DOM** is loaded, and you want to wait for the page to stop loading data from the server. We will see more about this in *Chapter 5, Waiting for elements and network calls*.

What is an AJAX call?

AJAX calls became so popular that many developers stopped calling them AJAX calls. You might also hear this referred to as "calling an endpoint" or "calling a (REST) API."

But, basically, it is an asynchronous call made to a server by the page to fetch more data or send data to the server. Don't worry, we'll go way deeper in *Chapter 5*, *Waiting for elements and network calls*.

What is the DOM?

The **Document Object Model (DOM)** is the object representation that the browser built based on the HTML sent by the server or created in JavaScript.

Remember that an HTML page is no more than a text file sent through the network. The browser loads that text, builds the model (DOM) representation, and then the browser engine renders that DOM. At that moment, the browser can say that **the DOM content was loaded**. Once the engine starts processing that DOM, it might find that it needs to fetch more resources, such as JavaScript, CSS, or image files. So, after all these resources are loaded, it fires the `load` event.

This takes us to the last option: the referrer.

Referrer

The referrer is an HTTP header that the browser sends to the server to inform it what page is requesting that resource.

You can see that if you go to `https://www.packtpub.com/`, open the developer tools, and check any CSS file under the network tab.

Referrer

Fun fact, the HTTP header is called `referer` due to a typo in the HTTP specification.

When would you use this? Well, this option is not so common, but some pages could change the behavior based on the referrer. Some sites might use them as a validation: *"This page only can be navigated when coming from this site."* You force that scenario using the `referer` option.

Early in this section, we mentioned that other types of navigation were the browser functions to go back, forward, and reload. Puppeteer provides an API for all those actions:

- `page.goBack(options)`
- `page.goForward(options)`
- `page.reload(options)`

These functions have the same behavior as `page.goto`. You don't need to pass a URL because it can be inferred from the action itself. `goBack` and `goForward` are based on the browsing history, and `reload` will use the same URL.

Another difference is that they don't support the `referer` option because it will use the same referrer used in the first navigation because these actions are repeating navigation performed in the past.

But that's not all; `goto` hides a nice surprise. Well, it's not hidden; it is documented. The next thing we need to know about `goto` is that it has a return value. It returns a `response` object.

Using the response object

The response is an important concept on the web. There is a corresponding **response** for every **request** the browser sends to the server.

It makes sense that the `goto` returns a `response`. It makes a `request`, and the result is the corresponding `response`.

There are many things we can do with the response. We won't cover all the functionality in this chapter. But these are the most relevant functions we can use as a response to a `goto` action.

Getting the response URL

Why would I want to know the URL if I know the URL I want to go to?

The server could redirect you to another page. For instance, if you open the browser in incognito/private mode and navigate to `https://mail.google.com/`, you will see that the server redirects you to `https://accounts.google.com/signin`.

I'm not saying that you should always check the response URL just in case, but you have to know that the site you are testing might behave like that. One common scenario is the login check. You navigate to a page, and if the response URL is the login page, you perform the login action, and then you can go back to the previous page and resume your test.

Getting the response status code

Every response has an HTTP status code. It tells you how the server reacted to your request. Status codes are grouped into five categories. These are the definitions according to Wikipedia (`https://en.wikipedia.org/wiki/List_of_HTTP_status_codes`):

1xx informational response: *the request was received, continuing process.* You won't need to deal with these.

2xx successful: *the request was successfully received, understood, and accepted.* There are some differences between all the 2xx codes, but what you have to know is that a 2xx code means that everything went well. The status code **200** is the most common.

3xx redirection: *further action needs to be taken in order to complete the request.*

When the server wants to redirect the user, that's not a server action but something that the browser needs to do. The server tells the browser: "You asked for `https://mail.google.com/`, but you have to go to `https://accounts.google.com/signin`." The browser needs to take the new URL and perform another request.

The most common status codes are **301 – Permanent Redirect** and **302 – Temporary Redirect**. 301 tells the browser that the old URL shouldn't be used anymore, and the browser should always use the new URL. 302 is the most commonly used. It tells the browser that it should temporarily go to the new URL. That's the case of the login scenario.

4xx client error: *the request contains bad syntax or cannot be fulfilled.*

4xx codes are known as *"it was your fault"* errors. There was something wrong with the request. The list of 4xx codes is huge. For these scenarios, the most common code that I think everybody knows is the world-famous **404**, which tells you that the resource was **not found**. The other errors you might face are **401 – Unauthorized** and **403 – Forbidden**, which are related to security issues.

5xx server error: *the server failed to fulfill an apparently valid request.*

5xx codes are known as *"it was the server's fault"* errors. The most common is the **500**, which means that the server has failed. I hope you never see this, but if you try to scrape a site and you get a **503**, that means that the **server is unavailable**, which means that the server started to reject your requests or that you took the server down.

The function `response.status()` will return the status code associated with the response.

If you just want to know whether the response was successful, there is a shortcut for that: `response.ok()`. This function will return true if the status code is between 200 and 299.

Let's test some of these features by implementing the following test: *"The admin page should redirect you to the login page"*. In the `test` directory you will find that we have an `admin.tests.js` file, where we can put our admin page tests. To test the redirection, we can do something like this:

```
it('Should redirect to the login page', async() => {
    const response = await pageModel.go();
    response.status().should.oneOf([200, 304]);
    response.url().should.contain('login');
});
```

The final status could be **200 (OK)** or **304 (Not Modified)** if the browser cached the redirection. Notice that we also used `response.url()` to get the URL of that response.

What if I wanted to check that I was effectively redirected from the admin page?

72 Navigating through a website

Well, that's trickier. We mentioned that every response is tied to a request. Puppeteer exposes that using the `response.request()` function. We won't get into the `request` object yet, but one thing you need to know now is that the request contains the list of all the redirections a request went through. Puppeteer represents them with the `redirectChain()` function. With this, we have the entire redirect map.

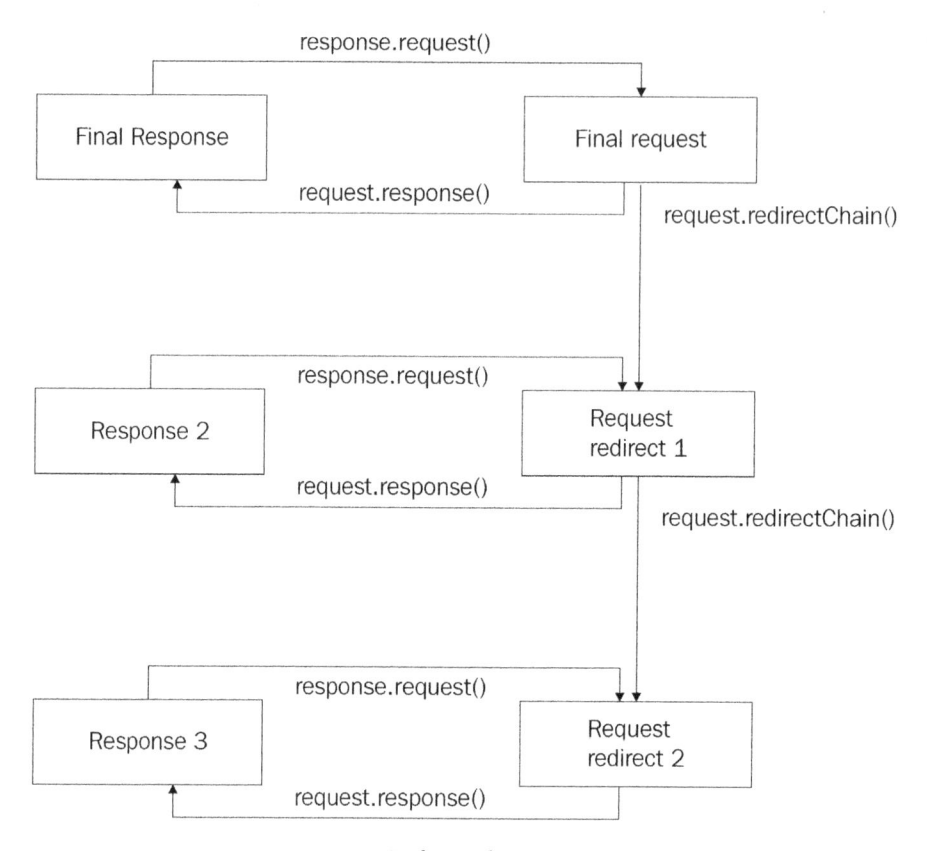

Redirect chain

It might sound complex, but you will get the idea once you start playing with it. The final code will look like this:

```
it('Should redirect to the login page', async () => {
  const response = await pageModel.go();
  response.status().should.equal(200);
  response.url().should.contain('login');

  response.request().redirectChain()[0].response().status().should.equal(302);
```

```
    response.request().redirectChain()[0].response().url().
should.contain('admin');
});
```

We learned a lot about the `launch` function and navigation with Puppeteer. As I mentioned at the beginning of this chapter, I also want to share some tools to add to your toolbox. Let's talk about continuous integration.

Introduction to continuous integration

Wouldn't it be great if a tool would guarantee that not a single line of code would break the functionality you are testing?

That's what **continuous integration** (**CI**) is about. CI is the practice of running test code before introducing a change into the code base. Atlassian wrote a great definition of CI (https://www.atlassian.com/continuous-delivery/continuous-integration): **Continuous integration** (**CI**) *is the practice of automating the integration of code changes from multiple contributors into a single software project. It's a primary DevOps best practice, allowing developers to frequently merge code changes into a central repository where builds and tests then run. Automated tools are used to assert the new code's correctness before integration.*

Let's review an ideal workflow:

1. We have our code base in a source control repository. It could be GitHub, Gitlab, Bitbucket, or a local server hosting a Git server.
2. A developer creates a new branch from that main code base.
3. We make some changes in that branch.
4. And then, it creates a Pull Request or Merge Request. The developer requests that their changes are reviewed and incorporated into the main code base.
5. Other developers will review the change, but the CI process will also run the tests on that branch.
6. If the developers approve the change and the CI runs successfully, the code will be ready to be merged into the main code base.

It sounds like an ideal world, right? Although life won't be that perfect all the time, we can achieve that. If you can implement this workflow when you start a new project, it will be easy to follow. Implementing all this in an ongoing project will be more challenging. My advice would be to make these changes little by little, not to affect productivity too much.

There are many CIs available on the market. Most of them have an entry-level free tier and then some paid tiers. The main differences you will see between them are the following:

- Support for private repositories: Some CIs offer free tiers only for public repositories.
- The number of parallel runs: This will be quite important if you have quite a big team with many Pull Requests opened simultaneously.
- Compute power: They could give you better virtual machines on higher tiers.
- Reporting: You will find different types of reports.

These are the most popular CIs in 2021; there are many others, but these are the ones you will see around:

- Travis CI
- Circle CI
- AppVeyor
- Jenkins
- GitHub Actions

We will test our code using GitHub Actions, just because we would only need a GitHub account, and we can do everything from our repository.

First, let's create a new repository on GitHub. If you don't have a GitHub account, you can create one at `https://github.com/join`. Once you have an account, you can create a repository at `https://github.com/new`.

Create a new repository

A repository contains all project files, including the revision history. Already have a project repository elsewhere? Import a repository.

Repository template
Start your repository with a template repository's contents.

No template ▼

Owner *   **Repository name ***

kblok ▼   /   ch3-demo   ✓

Great repository names are short and memorable. Need inspiration? How about upgraded-waddle?

Description (optional)

○ **Public**
    Anyone on the internet can see this repository. You choose who can commit.

◉ **Private**
    You choose who can see and commit to this repository.

Initialize this repository with:
Skip this step if you're importing an existing repository.

☐ **Add a README file**
    This is where you can write a long description for your project. Learn more.

☑ **Add .gitignore**
    Choose which files not to track from a list of templates. Learn more.

    .gitignore template: Node ▼

☑ **Choose a license**
    A license tells others what they can and can't do with your code. Learn more.

    License: MIT License ▼

This will set ⌥ master as the default branch. Change the default name in your settings.

[Create repository]

Creating a new repository

One important thing here is to pick **Node** as the `.gitignore` template, so we don't commit the `node_modules` folder.

Once you create the repository, you can get the Git URL using the **Code** button:

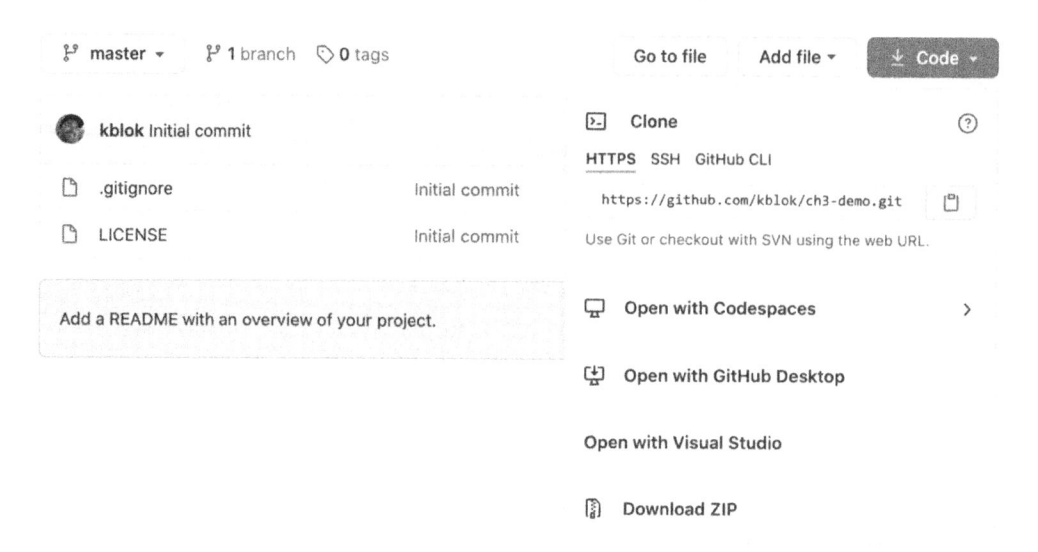

Git remote URL

We will now clone this Git repository into a new folder, copy our working code there, and **push** it to GitHub:

```
> git clone https://github.com/kblok/ch3-demo.git
> cd ch3-demo
```

Notice that you need to use **your** Git URL, not mine.

Next, we need to copy our current code to that folder. Make sure you delete any extra `git` folders when you copy these projects. After that, we need to run these three commands to commit our code and push it to GitHub:

```
> git add .
> git commit -m "First commit"
> git push origin
```

Now it's time to set up the CI. CI tasks in GitHub actions are YAML files inside the `.github/workflows` directory. This is what we need to do:

- Checkout the branch.
- Build the site.
- Build the tests package.

- Launch the site.
- Run tests.

The following example doesn't pretend to be the canonical way to run Puppeteer tests in GitHub actions. There many different ways to implement this. Let's create a YAML file inside the `.github/workflows` directory called `test.yml` (you can pick any name). The file will look like this:

```yaml
name: CI
on:
  push:
    branches:
      - master
  pull_request:
    branches:
      - master
jobs:
  test:
    name: Test
    runs-on: ubuntu-latest
    steps:
    - uses: actions/checkout@master
    - name: Install Web Dependencies
      working-directory: ./vuejs-firebase-shopping-cart
      run: npm install
    - name: Install Test Dependencies
      env:
        PUPPETEER_SKIP_CHROMIUM_DOWNLOAD: 'true'
      run: npm install
    - name: Run Site Test Code
      uses: mujo-code/puppeteer-headful@master
      env:
        TESTENV: 'CI'
        CI: 'true'
      with:
        args: sh ./.github/workflows/test.sh
```

- First, we are saying when we want to run this action. Then, we are setting up this action to run on every **Pull Request** created to be merged into the `master` branch. But also, it will run on every **push** to the `master` branch. This means that it will also run after the Pull Request is merged.
- `- uses: actions/checkout@master` will check out our code.
- Under `- name: Install Web Dependencies`, we build the site.
- Under `- name: Install Test Dependencies`, we build the test project.
- Under `- name: Run Site Test Code`, we run the site and the tests using the shell file `test.sh`, which is as simple as this:

```
cd ./vuejs-firebase-shopping-cart
npm run serve & npx wait-on http://localhost:8080
cd ..
npm test
```

As you can see, I'm waiting for `npm run serve` to print an `http://localhost:8080` before running the tests.

You will find that we are using `uses: mujo-code/puppeteer-headful@master`. Running a browser in a VM can be challenging. These VMs have many restrictions. You will need to find recipes that can help you launch a browser in a VM.

In this case, `mujo-code/puppeteer-headful` leaves us a browser ready to be used. That's why we use the environment variable `PUPPETEER_SKIP_CHROMIUM_DOWNLOAD: 'true'`, so when we run `npm install`, Puppeteer won't download a browser because we are going to use an existing one.

As we're going to use an existing browser, and we are going to run this in a restricted environment, we will need a new set of launch options. That's why a set the environment variable `TESTENV: 'CI'`, and I added a new setting in the config file:

```
CI: {
    baseURL : 'http://localhost:8080/',
    username: 'admin@gmail.com',
    password: 'admin',
    launchOptions: {
        executablePath: process.env.PUPPETEER_EXEC_PATH,
        headless: true,
        args: ['--no-sandbox'],
    },
```

```
        timeout: 5000,
    },
```

I'm setting as the executable path the environment variable `PUPPETEER_EXEC_PATH`, which is set by `mujo-code/puppeteer-headful`.

After setting up all this, you will start getting builds in your pull requests. Let's say that a developer comes and creates a Pull Request changing a color.

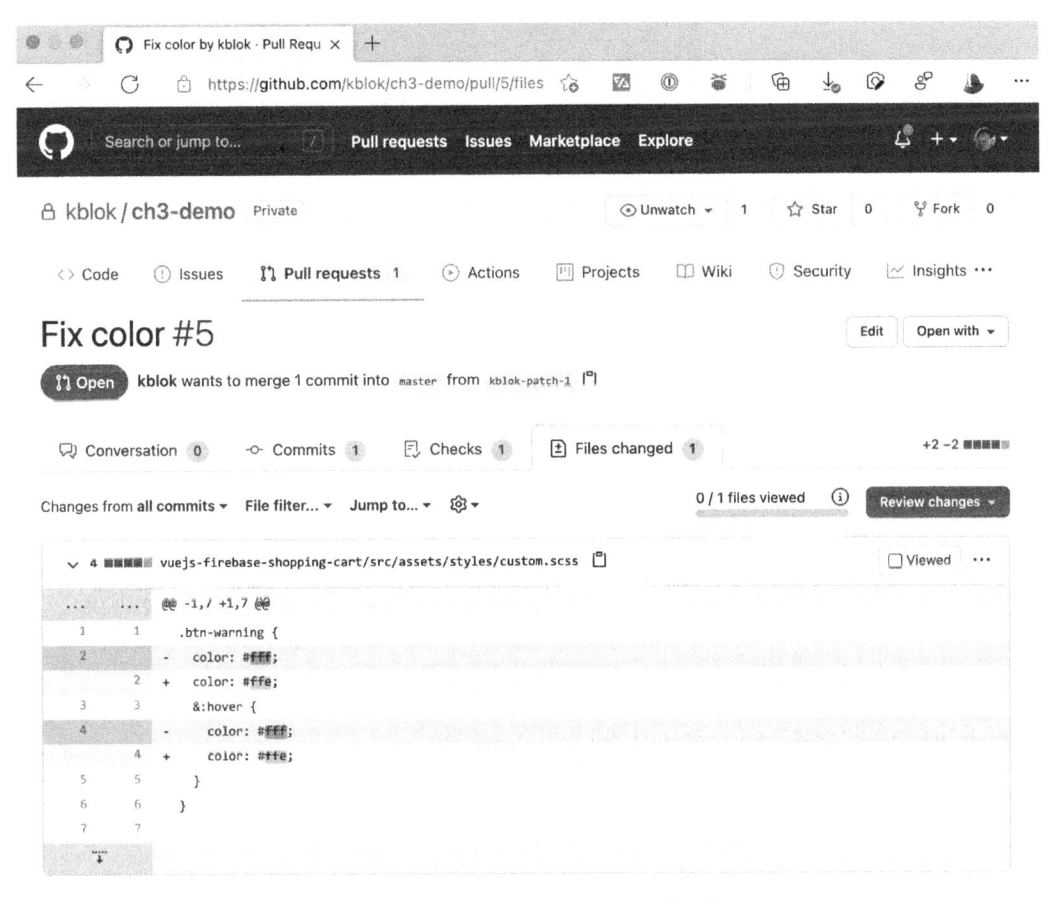

A Pull request changing a piece of code

If you go to the **Checks** tab, you will see all the actions and their status. In this case, we can see that our test runs correctly:

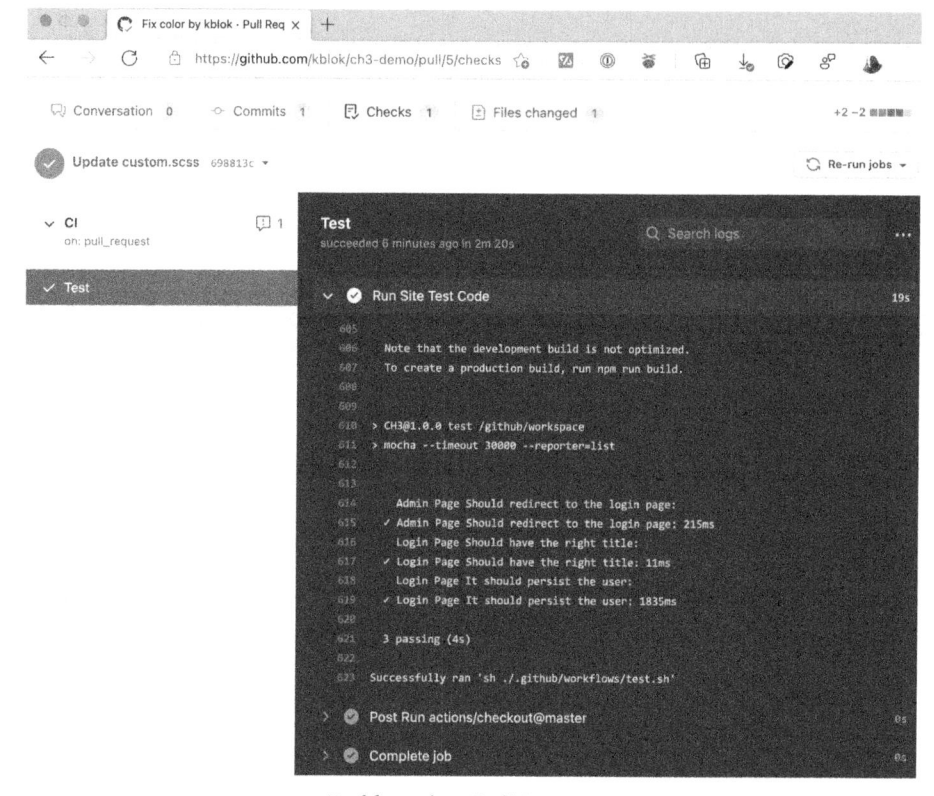

Build result in Pull Requests

There, you will find all the build details, with all the test results. But these results also propagate to other pages on GitHub. You will be able to see the build results on the main page of the Pull Request and even in the Pull Requests list.

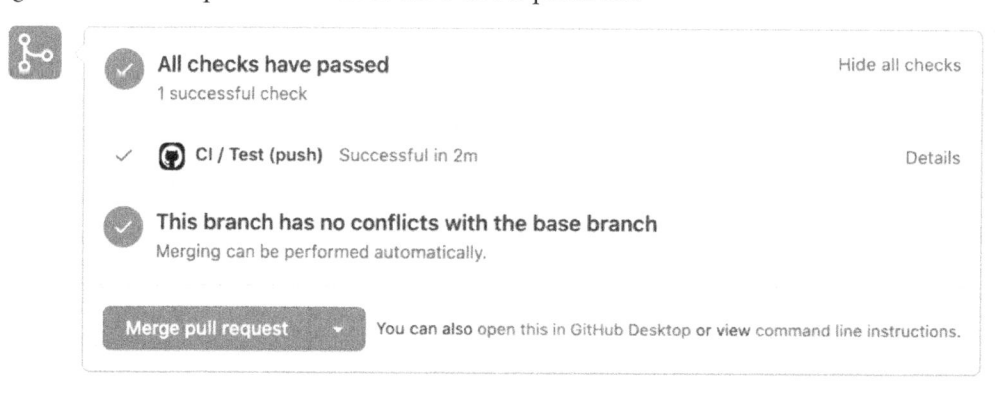

Build result on the Pull Request main page

There, you are not going to see the full details, but it will give you a quick view so you can know whether the Pull Request is ready to be merged or not.

I know that this might feel overwhelming. Take this as an idea about how that looks, what is possible, and the challenges you might find while setting up all this. It's not easy, but it is worth the effort.

Summary

As you can see, we started to go deeper into the Puppeteer API. We learned about all the different options we can use when launching a browser. We also learned how to navigate through a site and the different options we have to go from one page to another. We also saw new objects that weren't mentioned before, such as the `Response` and the `Request` class.

I hope you found the continuous integration section valuable. There are many tools and many different ways to run tests automatically in the cloud. This is an essential tool to add to your toolbox.

In the next chapter, we will get even more practical. We will see how to interact with the page, from CSS selectors to mouse and keyboard emulation

4
Interacting with a page

Thanks to *Chapter 3*, *Navigating through a website*, we now know how to open a browser and all the different options we have to launch browsers and create new pages. We also know how to navigate through other pages. We learned about HTTP responses and how they are related to a request.

This chapter is about interaction. Emulating user interaction is essential in UI testing. There is one pattern in unit testing called **Arrange-Act-Assert** (**AAA**). This pattern enforces a particular order in the test code:

- Arrange – Prepare the context.
- Act – Interact with the page.
- Assert – Check the page reaction.

In this chapter, we will learn how to find elements on a page. We will understand how the development team can improve their HTML so that you can easily find elements. But if you cannot change the page HTML, we will also look at another set of tools to find the elements we need.

Once we find an element, we will want to interact with it. Puppeteer provides two sets of APIs: One is action functions, such as click, select, or type. Then we have a set of emulation functions, such as mouse events or keyboard emulation. We will cover all those functions.

This chapter will introduce a new object we haven't mentioned yet: **The element handle**.

By the end of this chapter, we will have added another tool to our toolbox: The Visual Studio Code debugging tools.

We will cover the following topics in this chapter:

- Introduction to HTML, the DOM, and CSS
- Finding elements
- Finding elements using XPath
- Interacting with elements
- Keyboard and mouse emulation
- Interacting with multiple frames
- Debugging tests with Visual Studio Code

By the end of this chapter, you will be able to emulate most types of user interaction. But first, we need to lay the groundwork. Let's talk about HTML, the **Document Object Model** (**DOM**), and CSS.

Technical requirements

You will find all the code of this chapter on the GitHub repository (`https://github.com/PacktPublishing/UI-Testing-with-Puppeteer`) under the `Chapter4` directory. Remember to run `npm install` on that directory and then go to the `Chapter4/vuejs-firebase-shopping-cart directory` directory and run `npm install` again.

If you want to implement the code while following this chapter, you can start from the code you left in the `Chapter3` directory.

Introduction to HTML, the DOM, and CSS

You won't be able to find elements if you don't know CSS, and you won't understand CSS if you don't understand the **DOM** and **HTML**. So, we need to start with the basics.

I bet you've heard that you can build a site with HTML, CSS, and JavaScript. You might be using different server-side technologies. Your frontend might be implemented using cool technologies such as React or Angular. But in the end, the result will be a page based on HTML, CSS, and JavaScript.

HTML is the page's content. If you go to any website, open the **DevTools**, and click on the **Elements** tab, you will see the content of the page. You will see the page's title. If it's a news site, you will see all the articles there. If you visit a blog post, you will see the text of that post.

Without **CSS**, an HTML page would look like text written in Notepad. CSS not only brings color and fonts, but it's also the scaffolding that gives structure to a page.

> **Fun fact**
> Firefox has a built-in tool to disable all the styles on a page. If you go to **View | Page Style** and click on **No Style**, you will see how our life would be without CSS.

The last piece is JavaScript. JavaScript brings behavior to a page. Once the browser parses the HTML and builds the DOM, it allows us to manipulate and give life to a page.

But, as I mentioned before, we need to go to the basics, to the foundations of the web. Let's begin with HTML.

HTML

HTML stands for **HyperText Markup Language**: HyperText because the HTML is not content per se; HTML contains the content. Markup because it uses tags to give meaning to that content. And language because, although many developers disagree and they get mad about the idea, HTML is a language.

If we read an HTML file as a data structure, we can say that HTML is a **relaxed** version of XML. So, to better understand HTML, we need to look at the basics of XML.

These are the basic elements of XML content:

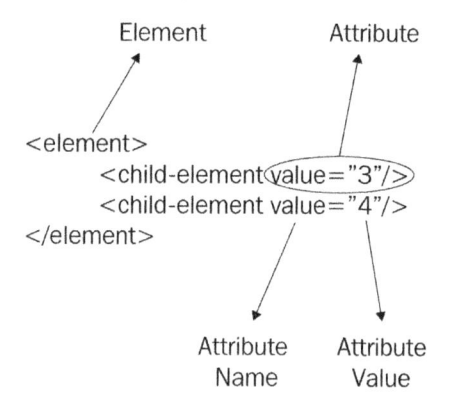

```
           Element              Attribute
              ↑                    ↑
              |                    |
        <element>
            <child-element value="3"/>
            <child-element value="4"/>
        </element>
                           |        |
                           ↓        ↓
                      Attribute  Attribute
                         Name      Value
```

XML Content

If you look at this figure, you already know almost everything you need to know about XML. Well, maybe I'm exaggerating. But this is the idea:

- You have elements, which are represented as `<ElementName>`. In our example, we have `<element>` and `<child-element>`.

- The element might have attributes, which are represented as `AttributeName="AttributeValue"`. We have `value="3"` and `value="4"` in our example.

- The element might contain other elements. You can see we have two **child-element** elements inside the main **element**.

- An element finishes (is closed) with `</ElementName>`, or with `/>` at the end instead of `>`.

XML parsers are very strict with these rules. If the XML content you are trying to parse breaks just a single rule, the parser will consider the entire XML invalid. Whether it's a missing closing element or an attribute without quotes, the parser will fail to evaluate the XML content.

But we will find that browsers are not that strict when parsing HTML content. Let's take a look at the following HTML:

```
<html>
    <body text="red">
        <div><span>hello world</span>
    </body>
</html>
```

A broken HTML

This simple HTML will print *Hello World* in red in the browser.

Is this valid XML? No. As you can see, the `<div>` element is not closed. But is this valid HTML? Yes.

> **Important Note**
> The fact that a browser would try to render *broken* HTML doesn't mean that you should take that lightly. It's possible you have heard a developer say that a particular bug was due to a *missing closing div*. If the HTML is broken, for instance, it has a missing closing `div`, the browser will try to guess the best way to render that HTML. The decision the browser makes when trying to fix broken HTML could end up with the page working as expected or with the full page layout broken.

Another interesting concept is that the XML specification doesn't give meaning to the elements. The names of the elements, the attributes, and the resulting information coming from that content depend on who wrote the XML and who is reading it.

HTML is XML with meaning. In *1993, Tim Berners-Lee,* who is known as the inventor of the World Wide Web, decided that the main element would be called HTML and that it would contain a BODY. He decided that images would be represented as IMG elements, paragraphs would be P elements, and so on. Over the years, browser and web developers followed and improved this convention, getting to what we today call HTML5. We, as a community, agreed on the meaning of HTML elements.

We agreed that if we add the `text` attribute with the value `red`, we will get the text in red, and so on. How many types of elements do we have in HTML? A lot! The good news is that you don't need to know all of them.

The more you know, the more productive you will be. However, these are the most common elements you will find on a page.

Document structure elements

Every HTML document will be contained inside an `<html>` element. That HTML element will have two child elements. The first element you will find is `<head>`. Inside that `<head>` element, you will find metadata elements, such as `<title>` with the page title, and many `<meta>` elements with metadata not supported by the standard HTML. Many sites use `<meta>` to enforce how the page should be shown on social media. The second set of elements you will find are **include elements**: `<link>` elements, including CSS files, and `<script>` files, including JavaScript code. Although the script elements are accepted in the header, most sites would add their script elements at the bottom of the page for faster rendering.

The second element you will find is the `<body>` element. The page itself will be inside this element.

Text elements

Then we have the basic text elements.

`<h1>`, `<h2>`, `<h3>`, `<h4>`, `<h5>`, and `<h6>` are headings. If you have a text editor, you might have seen that there are many levels of headings and subheadings.

`<p>` will denote paragraphs. Then you might find `<span>` elements, which help style part of the text in a paragraph.

Another type of text element is `<label>`. These labels are linked to an input control, such as a radio button, giving context to that control. For example, a radio button or a checkbox doesn't have text; it's just a check or a radio. You need a label to give them context:

Select a maintenance drone:
- ◉ Huey
- ○ Dewey
- ○ Louie

Radio buttons with labels

This HTML has three labels. *Huey* gives context to the first radio option, *Dewey* to the second, and *Louie* to the last one.

The last type of text element we will look at is list elements. Lists are expressed as a parent element, `<ul>` for unordered lists or `<ol>` for ordered lists, and `<li>` elements. You will see lots of these in menu bars.

Action elements

There are two main action elements in HTML. The `<a>` anchor, also known as a link, was designed to take you to another page, but these days it's not limited to that, and it could trigger actions inside the page.

The second element is <button>, which again, although it was designed to send data to the server using an HTTP POST request, is now being used for many other kinds of actions:

> **Important note**
> The days when you would only use buttons and links to perform actions are in the past. As most HTML elements support click events, you will find pages that show elements as buttons, but in fact, those buttons are HTML elements such as **DIVs**.

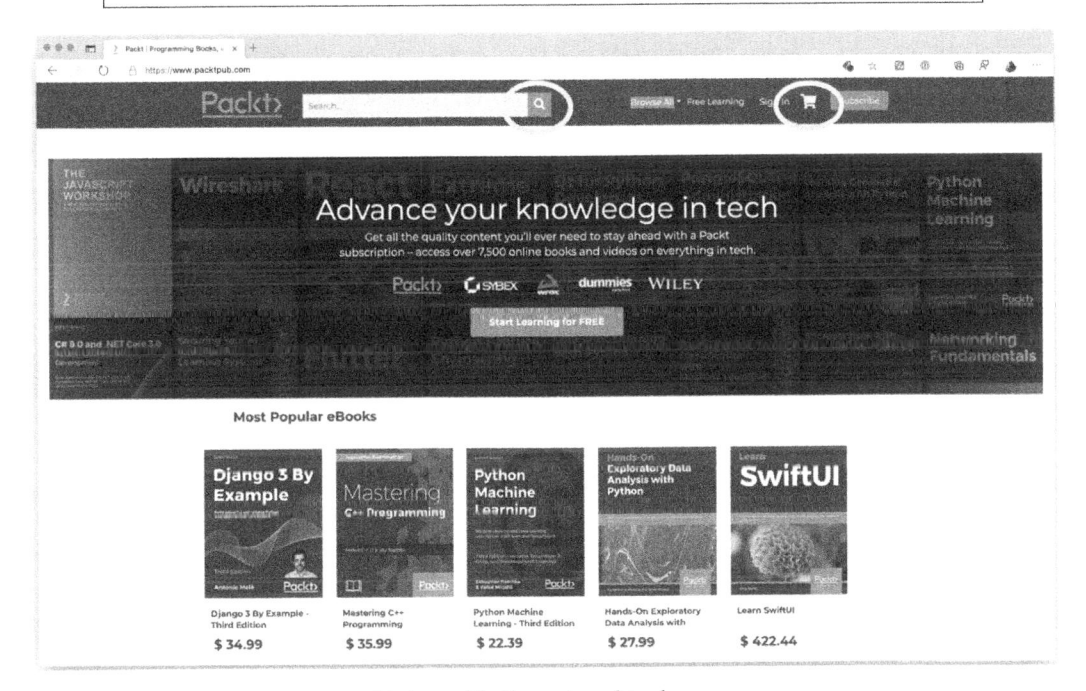

Links and buttons at packtpub.com

Many times, you won't notice the difference between a link and a button. For instance, in the `packtpub.com` site, the search button is a `button` element, whereas the cart button is, in fact, an `anchor`.

Most of your automation code will involve clicking on these action elements.

Container Elements

The role of container elements is grouping elements, mostly for layout and style purposes. The most popular element is `DIV`. What is `DIV`? It can be anything: A list of items, a popup, a header, anything. It is used to create groups of elements.

One element that was the king of the container elements was TABLE. As you can infer from the name, a table represents a grid. Inside a TABLE element, you can have TR elements representing rows, TH elements representing header cells, and TD elements representing a column inside a row. I mentioned that this *was* the king of containers because the community has now moved on from tables to DIVs due to performance issues, the need for more complex layouts, and responsiveness issues. But you might still see some tables on sites showing information using a grid style.

HTML5 brought a new kind of container element: The **Semantic Elements**. The goal of these semantic HTML elements is to communicate the type of content the element contains. So, instead of using DIVs for everything, developers should start using elements such as <header> for the site header, <footer> for the footer, <nav> for the navigation options, <articles> for blog posts, and so on. The purpose of these elements is to help external tools (such as screen readers, search engines, and even the same browser) to understand the HTML content.

Input elements

The last group of elements we need to know about are the input elements. The most common input element is the multifaceted input element. Depending on the type attribute, it can be "text", "password", "checkbox", "file" (upload), and so on; the list goes on to a total of 22 types.

Then we have select elements for drop-down lists and the option element to represent the items of a drop-down list.

Of course, we shouldn't forget the <IMG> element. It's impossible to picture a site without images.

> **Important note**
>
> Not every input you will see these days will be one of these elements. To make inputs more user-friendly or just nicer, you will find that developers might build inputs based on many other elements. For instance, you could find a drop-down list, which instead of being a select element would be an input element, plus an arrow button, which would show a floating list on clicking it. This kind of control makes sites prettier but automation more challenging.

HTML has not only a known list of elements but also a known list of attributes. These are the most common attributes you will find:

- `id`: Identifies a unique element. It's the element ID in the DOM (we will talk about the DOM in the next section).
- `class`: Contains the CSS classes applied to the element. It accepts more than one CSS class separated by a space.
- `style`: CSS style assigned to the element.

HTML won't limit the attributes you can add to an element. You can add any attribute you want, for instance, `defaultColor="blue"`. One convention is using **data- attributes** (pronounced data dash attributes). The browser will parse these attributes and make them available in the DOM. So, although `defaultColor` is a valid attribute, the general convention uses `data-default-color="blue"` instead.

The other set of attributes of interest to us is the **Accessible Rich Internet Applications** (**ARIA**) attributes. These attributes are being added to help accessibility tools, such as screen readers. Why would we be interested in those attributes? Because developers express things such as the *role* or the *state* of an element. If you find a site using ARIA, finding the selected menu item would be a matter of finding the element with `role="treeitem"` and `aria-expanded="true"`.

In the past few paragraphs, the DOM has been mentioned a few times. Let's talk about the DOM.

The DOM

The DOM is the interface you can use in JavaScript to interact with the HTML. According to the MDN (https://www.hardkoded.com/ui-testing-with-puppeteer/dom), it is *the data representation of the objects that comprise the structure and content of a document on the web*. Why should we care about that? Because we are going to use the same tools to automate our pages.

In the previous section, we mentioned that an element might have an ID. You'll find that the search input at https://www.packtpub.com/ has the ID search, so you will be able to get that element in JavaScript using `document.getElementById('search')`.

You might be wondering: How do I know the ID of a button? Or how do I check that the ID is valid? Remember we talked about the dev tools?

92 | Interacting with a page

The developer tools can be opened by clicking on the three dots in the top-right corner of Chrome and then going to **More Tools | Developer Tools**. You can also use the *Ctrl + Shift + J* shortcut in Windows or *Cmd + Option + I* in macOS:

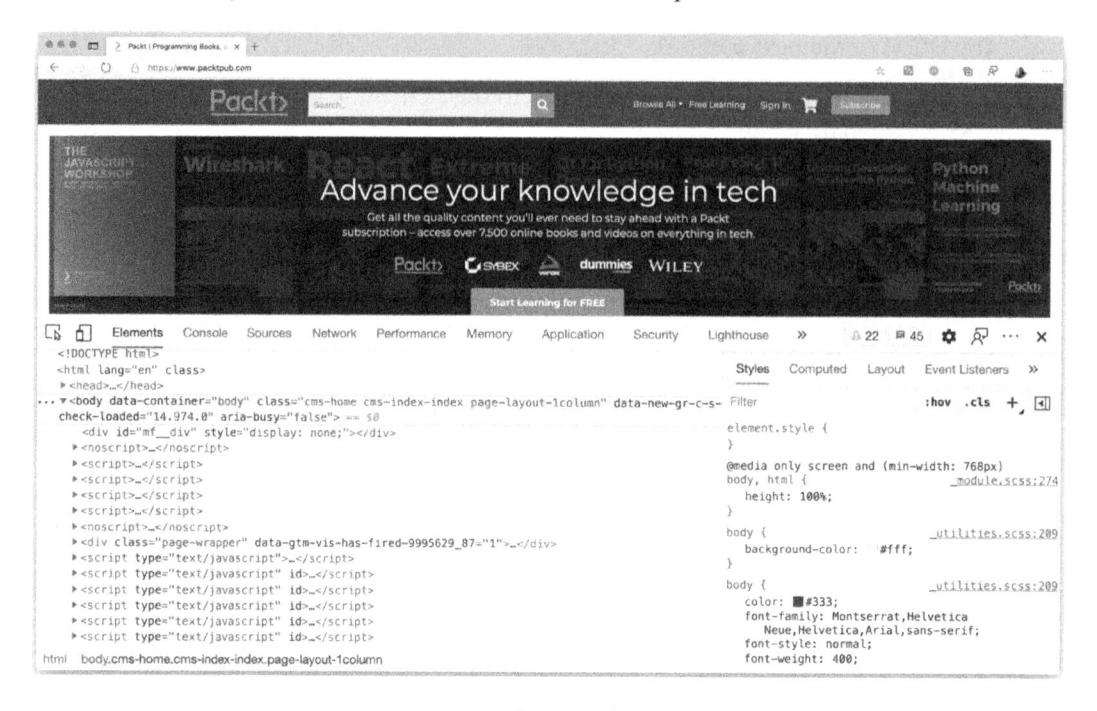

Developer Tools

If you right-click on any element on the page, for instance, the search button, you will find the **Inspect** option, which will select that element in the **Elements** tab. There you will be able to see all the attributes of that element:

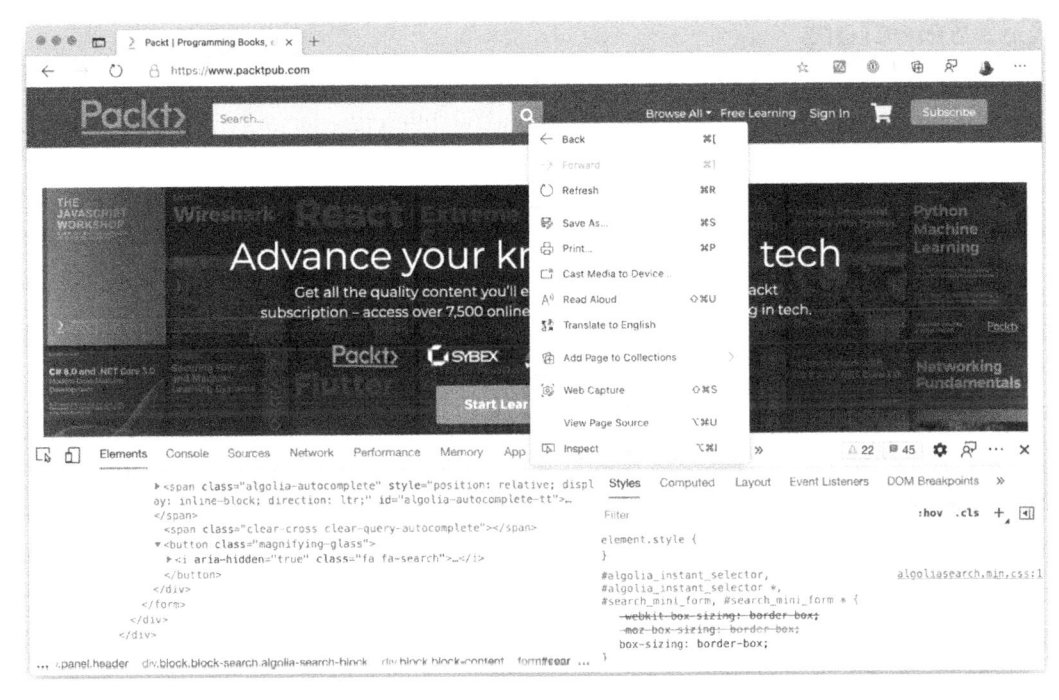

Inspect option

Another tab you will use a lot is the **Console** tab, where you will be able to run JavaScript code. If you are in the **Elements** tab and press the *Esc* key, you will get the **Console** tab below the **Elements** one. From there, you will be able to test your code:

Console tab

Another set of functions that you will use a lot are `document.querySelector` and `document.querySelectorAll`. The first function returns the first element matching a CSS selector, whereas the second function returns a list of elements matching a CSS selector. So, we need to learn about some CSS selectors next.

CSS Selectors

You don't need to learn CSS to understand how to style a page, but you should master how to find elements on a page. There are around 60 different selectors (https://www.w3schools.com/cssref/css_selectors.asp) we can use for finding elements. We won't cover all 60 here, but let's go through the most common selectors:

- Select by element name:

    Selector: `ElementName`.

    Example: `input` will select `<input>` elements.

- Select by class name:

    Selector: `.ClassName`.

    Example: `.input-text` will select any element that contains the `input-text` class.

    If you look at the search input in https://www.packtpub.com/, the class attribute is `class="input-text algolia-search-input aa-input"`. This selector won't check whether the class attribute is equal to `input-text`. It has to contain it.

- Select by ID:

    Selector: `#SomeID`.

    Example: `#search` will select the element with the `search` ID. In this case, it does check equality.

- Select by attribute:

    Selector: `[attribute=value]`.

    Example: `[aria-labelledby= "search"]` will select the element with the `aria-labelledby` attribute with the value `search`. This is an excellent example of the use of ARIA attributes for automation.

This selector is not limited by only the equality check (=). You could use only `[attribute]` to check whether the element contains the attribute, no matter the value. You can also use many other operators. For example, you can use `*=` to check whether the attribute contains a value or `|=` to check whether it begins with a value.

Combining selectors

What's great about CSS is that you can combine all these selectors. You could use `input.input-search[aria-labelledby=" search"]` to select an input with the `input-search` class and the `aria-labelledby` attribute with the value `search`.

You can also look for child elements. CSS allows us to "cascade" (that's what the C in CSS stands for) selectors. You can search for child elements by adding new selectors separated by a space. Let's take, for instance, the following selector:

```
form .algolia-autocomplete input
```

If you read it backwards, it will select an `input` inside an element with the `algolia-autocomplete` class, which is inside a `form` element. Notice that I said an input *inside* an element with the `algolia-autocomplete` class. That doesn't need to be the direct parent of the input element.

If you want to check strictly a parent-child relationship, you can separate selectors with a > instead of a space:

```
.algolia-autocomplete > input
```

This selector will look for an input whose direct parent element is an element with the `algolia-autocomplete` class.

Maybe you are thinking, why do I need to know all this information? I just want to get up and running with Puppeteer! Let me tell you something: You will spend half of your time inside the developer tools, and the most frequent element in your code will be a CSS selector. The more you know about HTML, the DOM, and CSS, the more proficient you will be at browser automation.

But now it's time to go back to the Puppeteer world.

Finding elements

It's time to apply everything we have learned so far. We need to master selectors because our Puppeteer code will be mostly about finding elements and interacting with them.

Let's bring back the login page from our e-commerce app:

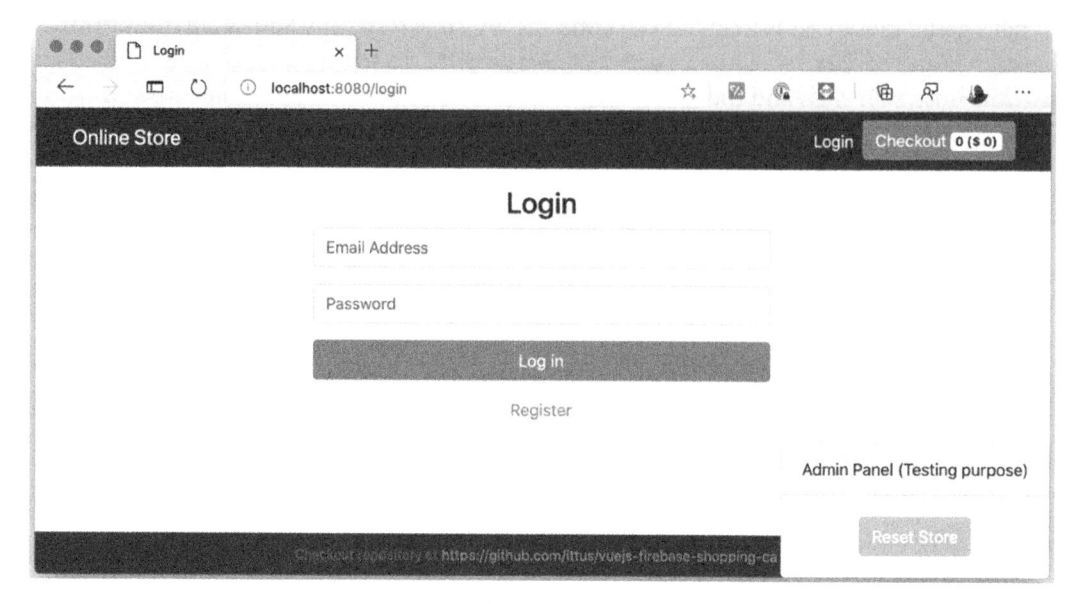

Login page

If we want to test the login page, we need to find these three elements: The **email input**, the **password input**, and the **login button**.

If we right-click on each input and click on the **Inspect element** menu item, we will find the following:

- The email has the ID `email`.
- The password has the ID `password`.
- The login is a `button` element, with the `btn` and `btn-success` CSS classes, and the `style=" width: 100%;"` style.

Puppeteer provides two functions to get elements from the page. The `$(selector)` function will run the `document.querySelector` function and return the first element matching that selector or `null` if no elements were found. The `$$(selector)` function will run the `document.querySelectorAll` function, returning an array of elements matching the selector or an empty array if no elements were found.

If we want to implement the `login` function in our `LoginPageModel` class using these new functions, finding the login inputs would be easy:

```
const emailInput = await this.page.$('#email');
const passwordInput = await this.page.$('#password');
```

> **Tip**
> To find the login button, you might think that you could use the `btn-success` selector, and you could, but you shouldn't use classes used to style a button because they might change in the future if the development team changes the style. You should try to pick a CSS selector to overcome a design change.

Let's re-evaluate our login button. If you look for `button` elements, you will find that you have five buttons on that page, so the `button` selector won't work. But, we can see that the login button is the only button with a `type="submit"` attribute, so we could use the `[type=submit]` CSS selector to find this element.

But the `[type=submit]` selector is too generic. The developers might, for instance, add a new button with the `submit` type in the toolbar, breaking our code. But we can see that the login button is inside a form with the ID `login-form`. So now, we can create a more stable selector. So, we could look for the login button in our login function in this way:

```
const loginBtn = await this.page.$('#login-form
 [type=submit]');
```

98　Interacting with a page

Now we have everything we need to test our login page. But we are not going to interact with the login page yet. Let's go to the home page and find some more complex scenarios:

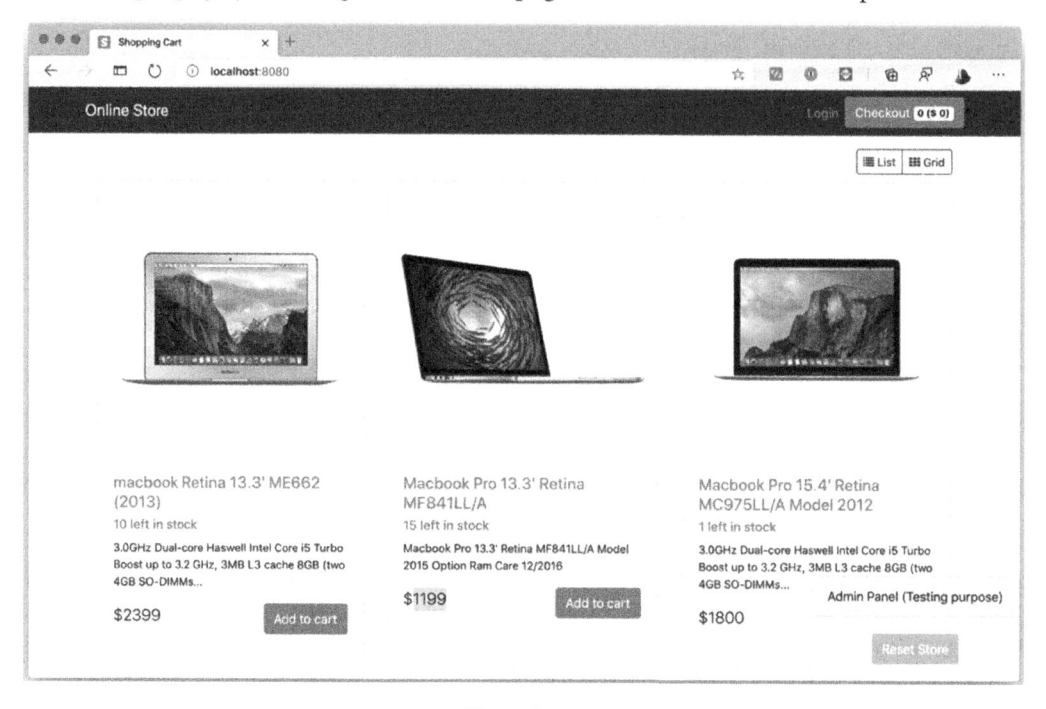

Home Page

Let's say we want to test that the **Macbook Pro 13.3' Retina MF841LL/A** product has 15 items left in stock, and the price is $1,199.

First, a piece of advice: It's better to code these kinds of tests down the testing pyramid. You could test the API that sends those values or the function that makes that query to the database.

But let's try to solve this as a UI test:

```
▼<div data-v-ae4ae6fc class="mb-3 col-sm-6 col-md-4 item"> == $0
  ▼<div data-v-ae4ae6fc class="thumbnail card">
    ▼<div data-v-ae4ae6fc class="img-event intrinsic">
        <img data-v-ae4ae6fc src="https://www.dropbox.com/s/6tqcep7rk29l59e/img2.jpeg?raw=1" alt class="grow thumbnail-image car
        tem p-3">
      </div>
    ▼<div data-v-ae4ae6fc class="card-body">
      ▶<h5 data-v-ae4ae6fc class="card-title">…</h5>
        <h6 data-v-ae4ae6fc class="card-subtitle mb-2 remain">15 left in stock</h6>
        <p data-v-ae4ae6fc class="card-text truncate">Macbook Pro 13.3' Retina MF841LL/A Model 2015 Option Ram Care 12/2016</p>
      ▼<div data-v-ae4ae6fc class="row">
          <p data-v-ae4ae6fc class="col-6 lead">$1199</p>
        ▶<p data-v-ae4ae6fc class="col-6">…</p>
        </div>
      </div>
    </div>
  </div>
```

Product HTML

If we take a look at the HTML, there is nothing that helps us find the product on the list, and if we were able to find the product, it's hard to find the elements inside that `div` element.

Here is where the collaboration between the development team and the QA team becomes valuable. How can developers help the QA team? Using data- attributes. Your team can use a `data-test-` attribute to help you find the elements you need:

```
<div data-v-ae4ae6fc class="mb-3 col-sm-6 col-md-4 item" data-test-product-id="2">
  <div data-v-ae4ae6fc class="thumbnail card">
    <div data-v-ae4ae6fc class="img-event intrinsic">...</div>
    <div data-v-ae4ae6fc class="card-body">
      <h5 data-v-ae4ae6fc class="card-title">...</h5>
      <h6 data-v-ae4ae6fc class="card-subtitle mb-2 remain" data-test-stock="15">15 left in stock</h6>
      <p data-v-ae4ae6fc class="card-text truncate">Macbook Pro 13.3' Retina MF841LL/A Model 2015 Option Ram Care 12/2016</p>
      <div data-v-ae4ae6fc class="row">
        <p data-v-ae4ae6fc class="col-6 lead" data-test-price>$1199</p>
        <p data-v-ae4ae6fc class="col-6">...</p>
      </div>
    </div>
  </div>
</div>
```

HTML with data-test attributes

As you can see in this HTML, it will be way easier to find elements with those new attributes. This is how we can get the values to test product ID 2:

```
const productId = config.productToTestId;
const productDiv = await this.page.$(`[data-test-product-id="${productId}"]`);
const stockElement = await productDiv.$('[data-test-stock]');
const priceElement = await productDiv.$('[data-test-price]');
```

With these four lines, we were able to find the three elements for our new test: The product container and the elements containing the stock and the price.

The are a few things to notice in this piece of code:

- First, remember not to hardcode values in your code. That's why we are going to grab the product ID from our config file.

- Second, notice that we are getting `stockElement` and `priceElement` using `productDiv.$` instead of `page.$`. That means that *the CSS selector you pass to that function will be processed in the element's context.*

  If we'd used `page.$$('[data-test-stock]')`, we would get many elements because each product has a `data-test-stock` element, but as we use `productDiv.$('[data-test-stock]')`, we'll get the element inside `productDiv`. This is an important resource.

- The last thing to highlight here is that our development team gave us the number of items in stock inside the `data-test-stock` element. This will come in handy when we need to test the stock but notice that we don't need to use the value of the attribute, in this case, 15, to get the element. Passing the attribute as a selector will be enough.

What if we don't have the chance to add these attributes? There is one more resource – trying to find those elements using XPath.

Finding elements using XPath

XPath is a language to query XML-like documents. Remember how we said that HTML was a relaxed kind of XML? This means that we could navigate through the DOM using some kind of XML query language such as XPath.

Before digging into XPath's selectors, if you want to try XPath queries, Chrome DevTools includes a set of functions you can use inside the developer tools **Console** tab (https://hardkoded.com/ui-testing-with-puppeteer/console). One of these functions is $x, which expects an XPath expression and returns an array of elements:

Testing XPath inside the Chrome Developer Tools

If you open the **Console** tab on any page, you can run `$x('//*')` to test the `//*` selector.

To better understand an XPath expression, you need to see your HTML as XML content. We are going to navigate this XML document from the very same root, the HTML attribute.

Select from the current node

Selector: `//`. This means "From the current node, bring me everything inside, no matter the position."

Example: $x('//div//a') will return, from the root, all the *divs* inside the document, no matter the position, and from those *divs* all a elements inside that div, no matter the position.

Are you confused about the "no matter the position" part? Well, let's now see the root selector.

Select from the root

Selector: /. This means "From the current node, bring me all the direct child elements."

Example: If we use $x('/div//a'), we'll get no results because there is no div as a child of the root object. The only valid root option would be $x('/HTML') because the HTML element is the only one under the main root object. But we could do something such as $x('//div/a'), which would mean "Bring me all the div elements, and from there all the a elements that are a direct child of those *divs*."

Select all the elements

Selector: *. This means "Bring me all the elements."

Example: When we say "all the elements," it will be based on the previous selector. $x('/*') will bring only the HTML element because that would mean "all the direct elements." But $x('//*') will bring you all the elements from the page.

Filter by attribute

Selector: [@attributeName=value].

Example: $x('//div[@class="card-body"]') will bring all the div elements where the class attribute is equal to card-body. This might look similar to the class selector in CSS, but it's not because this selector won't work if div has more than one class.

Up to this point, it seems just like CSS with another syntax. What's so powerful about XPath? Well, let's get to some power tools.

It turns out that the syntax we used to filter attributes is, in fact, expressions, also called predicates. This gives us the chance to not only use the @attributeName option but to also check for many other things.

Filter by text

Selector: `[text()=value]`.

Example: `$x('//div[text()="Admin Panel (Testing purpose)"]')` will bring all the `div` elements where its content is a the text *Admin Panel (Testing purpose)*. You could even make it more generic and use something like this, `$x('//*[text()="Admin Panel (Testing purpose)"]')`, so you wouldn't care whether it's a `div` or another type of element.

This function is by far one of the main reasons you would see people using XPath.

Contains a text

Selector: `[contains(text(), value)]`.

Example: *Filter by text* can be tricky. The text could have some space before or after the content. If you try to select the grid button on the page using this command, `$x('//*[text()= "Grid"]')`, you won't get any results because the element has some spaces after and before the word. This `contains` function can help us when we have spaces before or after the word, or when the word is part of a larger piece of text. This is how we can use this function: `$x('//*[contains(text(),"Grid")]')`.

There are many more functions. Mozilla has a good list of all the available functions (https://www.hardkoded.com/ui-testing-with-puppeteer/xpath).

We get to do really complex queries with XPath. Let's take a look our last example. We want all the elements with a price over $2,000:

`$x('//div[@class="row"]/p[1][number(substring-after(text(), "$")) > 2000]')`

Wow, let's see what we are doing there:

- With `//div[@class="row"]`, we grab `DIV`s with the `row` class.
- With `p[1]`, we take the first `p` element. We can use positional filters here.
- We get the text using `text()`.
- As the price begins with a dollar sign, we remove it using `substring-after`.
- We convert that text into a number using `number`.
- So then, we can check whether that number is greater than 2,000.

There is one more feature that makes XPath a powerful tool. Unlike CSS selectors, you can select the parent element with XPath using . . .

If we want to return the entire main `div` of the product with a price over $2,000, we can use the following:

`$x('//div[@class="row"]/p[1][number(substring-after(text(), "$")) > 2000]/../..')`

How do we use XPath expressions in Puppeteer? You already know how to do it: We have a `$x` function.

Let's go back to our test: *We want to test that the Macbook Pro 13.3' Retina MF841LL/A has 15 items left in stock, and the price is $1,199.*

What if the only way to find that product would be with the product name? We could do something like this:

```
const productName = config.productToTestName;
const productDiv = (await this.page.$x(`//a[text()="${productName}"]/../..`))[0];
const stockElement = (await productDiv.$('//h6'))[0];
const priceElement = (await productDiv.$('//div[@class="row"]/p[1]'))[0];
```

Remember that `$x` returns an array of elements. In this case, as we know that they will always return one element, we take the first one.

In the same way, we shouldn't rely on design classes for CSS selectors. We should try not to rely too much on the HTML structure in XPath selectors. We are assuming a couple of things in this code:

- We assume that the stock is an `h6` element.
- We assume that the price will be the first `p` element.

If the design team decides that the stock will look better using `div` instead of `h6`, if they wrapped the price inside a `div` element to improve mobile navigation, your test will break.

We learned how to get elements from the page, but it's important to know that the `$`, `$$`, and `$x` functions don't return an element from the DOM. They return something called **element handles**.

Element handles are a reference to a DOM element on the page. They are a pointer that helps Puppeteer send commands to the browser, referencing an existing DOM element. They are also one of the ways we have to interact with those elements.

Interacting with Elements

Let's go back to our login test. We already have the three elements we need: The user input, the password input, and the login button. Now we need to enter the email and the password and click on the button.

Typing on input elements

The `ElementHandle` class has a function called `type`. The signature is `type(text, [options])`. The `options` class is not big this time. It only has a `delay` property. The delay is the number of milliseconds Puppeteer will wait between letters. This is great to emulate real user interaction.

The first part of our test would look like this:

```
const emailInput = await this.page.$('#email');
await emailInput.type(user, {delay: 100});
const passwordInput = await this.page.$('#password');
await passwordInput.type(password, {delay: 100});
```

Here, we are looking for the email and password elements, and then emulating a user typing on those inputs.

Now, we need to click on the button.

Clicking on elements

The `ElementHandle` class also has a function called `click`. I bet you are already getting the pattern. The signature is `click([options])`. You can simply call `click()`, and that would do the job. But we can also use the three available options:

- `button`: This is a string with three valid options: "left," "right," or "middle."
- `clickCount`: The default is 1, but you could also have an impatient user clicking the same button many times, so you can emulate the user clicking on the element four times by passing 4.
- `delay`: This delay is not the time between clicks but the time (in milliseconds) between the mouse down action and mouse up.

Interacting with Elements

In our case, we don't need to use these options:

```
const loginBtn = await this.page.$('#login-form
[type=submit]');
await loginBtn.click();
```

With these two lines, we can finally finish our `login` function. We find the login button and then we click on it.

Selecting options in drop-down lists

The site now has a drop-down list, a `SELECT` element in HTML, to switch between the grid and the list view:

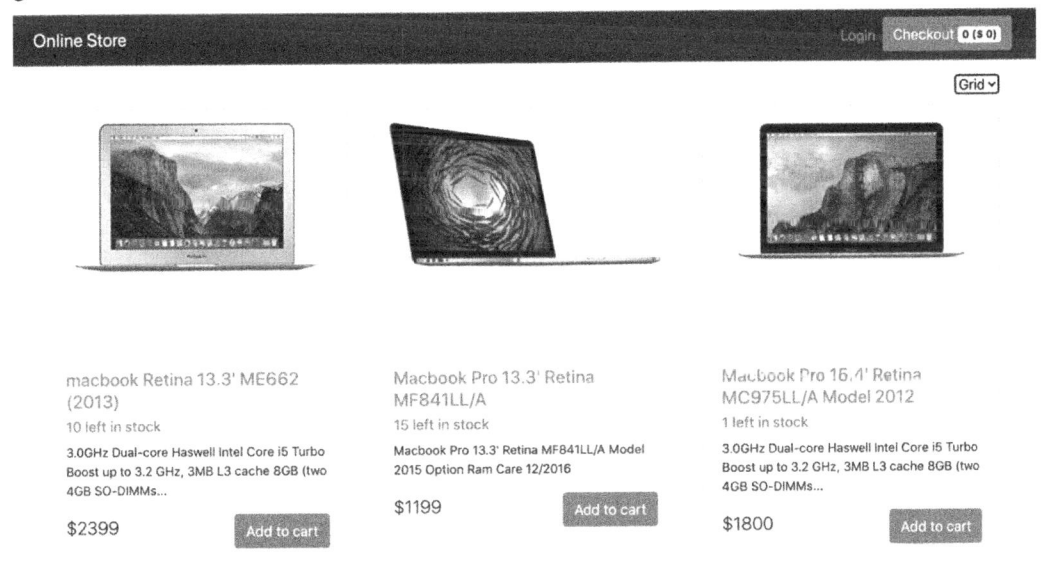

The site with a new switch option

As you might have guessed, the function to select an option is called `select`, and the signature is `select(...values)`. It's a list of values if the `select` element has the `multiple` attribute.

The next thing we need to know about this function is that the value `select` expects is not the text you see in the `option`, but the `option` of the value. We can see that by inspecting the element:

```
▼<div class="row action-panel">
  ▼<div class="col-12">
    ▼<div class="btn-group btn-group-sm pull-right">
      ▼<select id="#viewMode">
         <option value="list">List</option> == $0
         <option value="grid">Grid</option>
       </select>
     </div>
   </div>
 </div>
 ▶<div class="row">…</div>
</div>
```

Drop-down list options

In this case, we are lucky as the value is almost the same as the visible text, but it's not the same. If we want to select the Grid item, we need to use `grid`, instead of `Grid`.

If we switch the `option` to list mode, we can see that a `list-group-item` class is added to the elements:

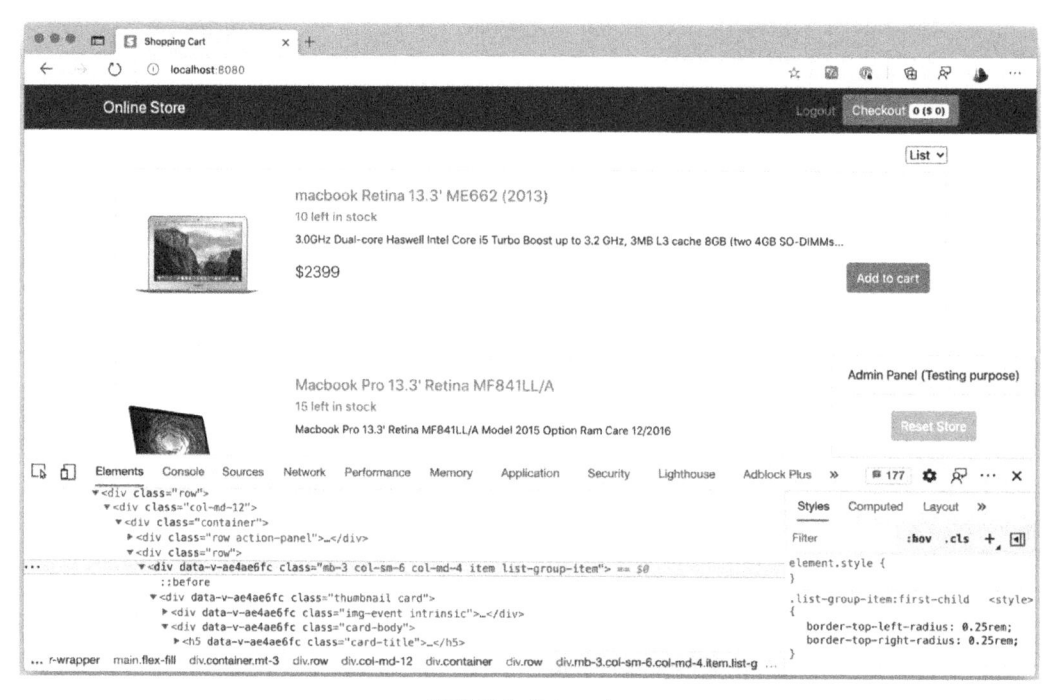

HTML in list mode

This is how we can test this functionality:

```
var switchSelect = await page.$('#viewMode');
await switchSelect.select('list');
expect(await page.$$('.list-group-item')).not.to.be.empty;
await switchSelect.select('grid');
expect(await page.$$('.list-group-item')).to.be.empty;
```

Using `await` and `page.$` every time we need to interact with an element requires a lot of boilerplate. Imagine if we had eight inputs to fill; that would be a lot. That's why both `Page` and `Frame` (if you are dealing with child frames) have most of the functions an element handle has, but they expect a selector as a first argument.

So, say we have this piece of code:

```
var switchSelect = await page.$('#viewMode');
await switchSelect.select('list');
```

It could be as simple as this:

```
await page.select('#viewMode', 'list');
```

You will find functions such as `page.click(selector, [options])`, `page.type(selector, text, [options])`, and many other interaction functions.

We have covered the most common user interactions. But we can go a little deeper and try to emulate how the user would interact with the page using their keyboard and mouse.

Keyboard and Mouse emulation

Although you will be able to test the most common scenarios by typing or clicking on elements, there are other scenarios where you would need to emulate how the users interact with a site using the keyboard and the mouse. Let's take, for instance, a Google spreadsheet:

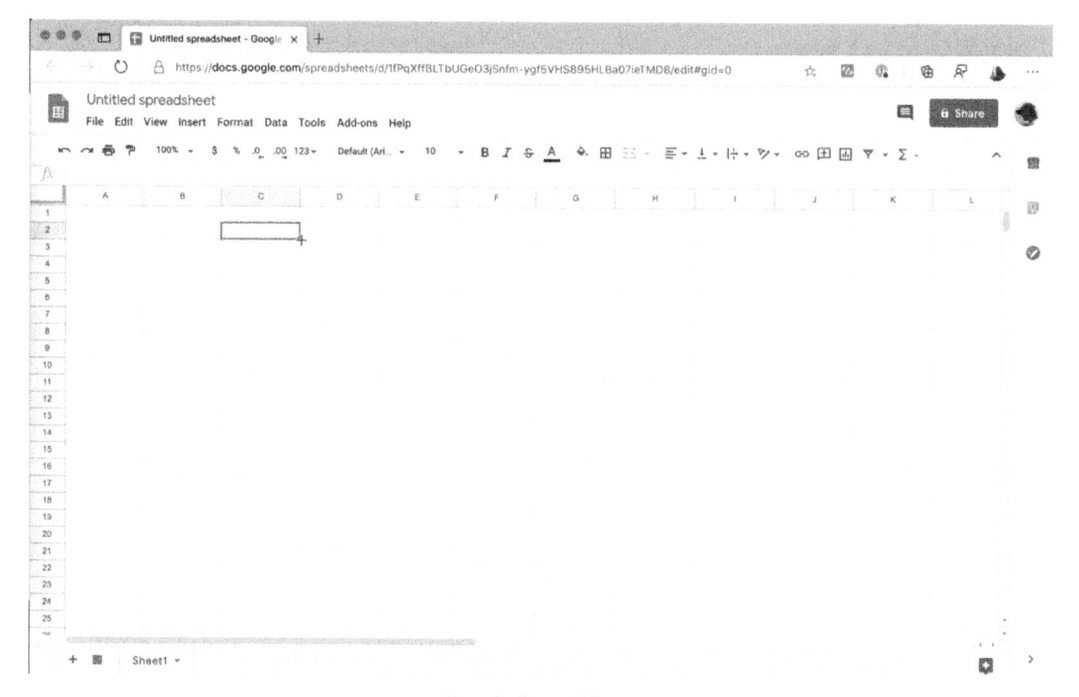

Google Spreadsheet

The Google spreadsheet page has a lot of keyboard and mouse interactions. You can move through the cells using your keyboard arrows or copy values by doing drag and drop with the mouse.

But it doesn't need to be that complicated. Let's say that you work in the QA team at `GitHub.com`, and you need to test the search box from the home page.

As `GitHub.com` is for developers, and developers for some weird reason hate using the mouse, the development team added many shortcuts on the site. We want to create a test to check that those shortcuts are working as expected:

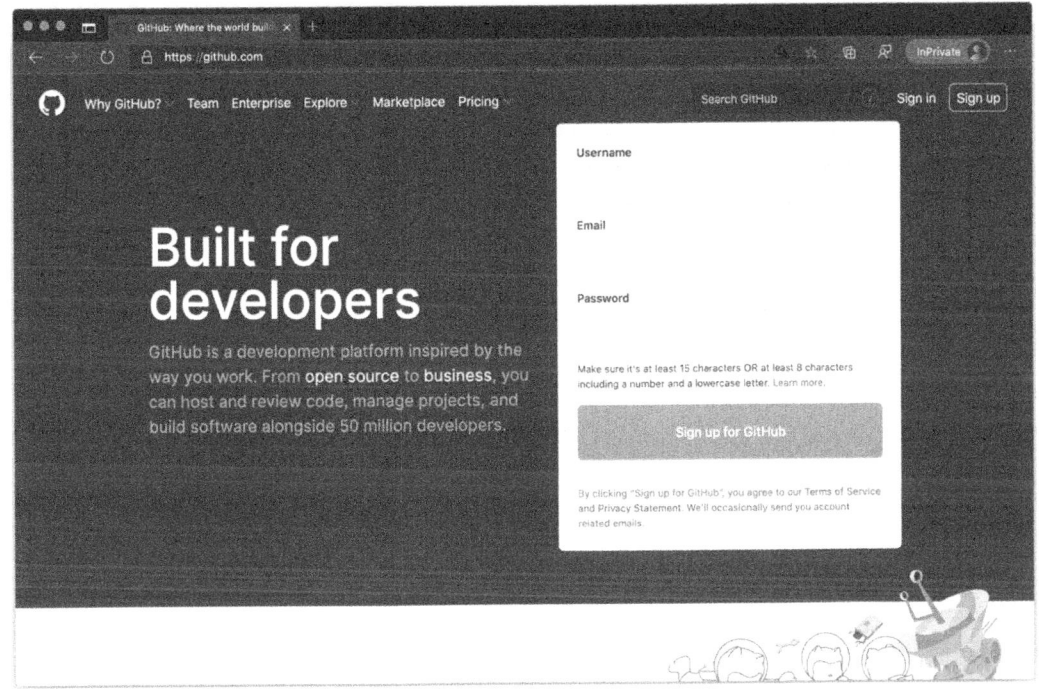

GitHub.com home page

As we can see there, the shortcut to the search input is a /. So, we need to do the following:

- Press slash.
- Type the repo name.
- And then press *Enter*.

We are going to use the `Keyboard` class that the `Page` class exposes as a property.

The first step is to press slash. To do that, we are going to use, you guessed it, the `press` function. The signature is `press(key, options)`. The first thing we need to know about press is that it's a shortcut to two other functions – `down(key, options)` and `up(key)`. As you can see, you can get an almost complete keyboard emulation.

Notice that the first argument is not `text` but `key`. You will find the full list of supported keys here: `https://www.hardkoded.com/ui-testing-with-puppeteer/USKeyboardLayout`. There, you will find keys such as *Enter*, *Backspace*, or *Shift*.

The `press` function has two options available: First, if you assign the `text` property, Puppeteer will create an input event with that value. It would work like a macro. For instance, if the key is p and the text is `puppeteer`, when you would press p, you would get `puppeteer` in the input element. I've never found a usage for that argument, but it's there. The `down` function also has this option. The second option is `delay`, which is the time between the key down and the key up actions.

The official Puppeteer documentation (`https://www.hardkoded.com/ui-testing-with-puppeteer/keyboard`) has a perfect example for this:

```
await page.keyboard.type('Hello World!');
await page.keyboard.press('ArrowLeft');

await page.keyboard.down('Shift');
for (let i = 0; i < ' World'.length; i++) {
  await page.keyboard.press('ArrowLeft');
}
await page.keyboard.up('Shift');

await page.keyboard.press('Backspace');
```

Let's unpack this code:

- It types **Hello World!**. The cursor is after the exclamation mark.
- It presses the left arrow key. Remember, `press` is `key down` and `key up`. So now the cursor is before the exclamation mark.
- Then, using `down`, it presses the *Shift* key, but it doesn't release the key.
- Then, it presses the left key as many times for the cursor to get to after the "Hello" word. But as the *Shift* key is still pressed, the "World" text got selected.
- Then, it releases the *Shift* key, using `up`.
- And what happens when you press *backspace* and we have text selected? You remove the entire selection, leaving the text **Hello!**.

Now we can go and test the `GitHub.com` home page:

```
const browser = await puppeteer.launch({headless: false, 
defaultViewport: null});
const page = await browser.newPage();
await page.goto('https://www.github.com/');
await page.keyboard.press('Slash');
await page.keyboard.type('puppeteer')
await page.keyboard.press('Enter');
```

If we go back to our login example, we could test that you should be able to log in by pressing *Enter* instead of clicking on the login button. Or if the navigation between controls is important, you can jump from the user input to the password and then to the login button by pressing *Tab*.

Do you want to play tic-tac-toe? Let's play it using the mouse.

In the `Chapter4` folder, you will find a `tictactoe.html` file with a small tic-tac-toe game made in **React**:

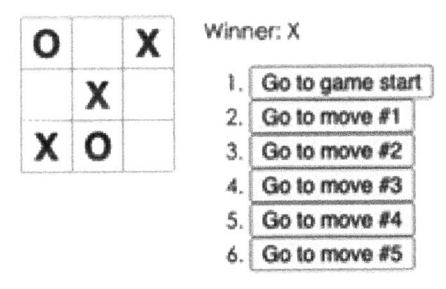

Tic-tac-toe game

If we consider the page as a canvas, where the top-left corner of the window is the coordinate **(0;0)** and the bottom right is the coordinate **(window width, window height)**, mouse interaction is about moving the mouse to an **(X;Y)** coordinate and clicking using one of the mouse buttons. Puppeteer offers the following functionalities.

Move the mouse using `mouse.move(x, y, [options])`. The only option available in this move function is `steps`. With `steps`, you can tell Puppeteer how many times you want to send `mousemove` events to the page. By default, it will send only one event at the end of the mouse move action.

In the same way as with the keyboard you have the up/down and `press` functions, with the mouse, you have up/down and `click`.

The mouse has one extra action that the keyboard doesn't have, which is `wheel`. You can emulate mouse scrolling using `mouse.wheel([options])`. This option has two properties: `deltaX` and `deltaY`, which can be positive or negative scroll values expressed in CSS pixels.

Let's go back to our tic-tac-toe game. We will do a simple test: Player 1 will use the first row and player 2 will use the second row, so player 1 will win after three moves. As this is a canvas, we need to know which coordinates we need to click.

We can use the style section of the developer tools to get those coordinates. If we look at the body, we will see a 20-pixel margin that will make `(20;20)` the starting point:

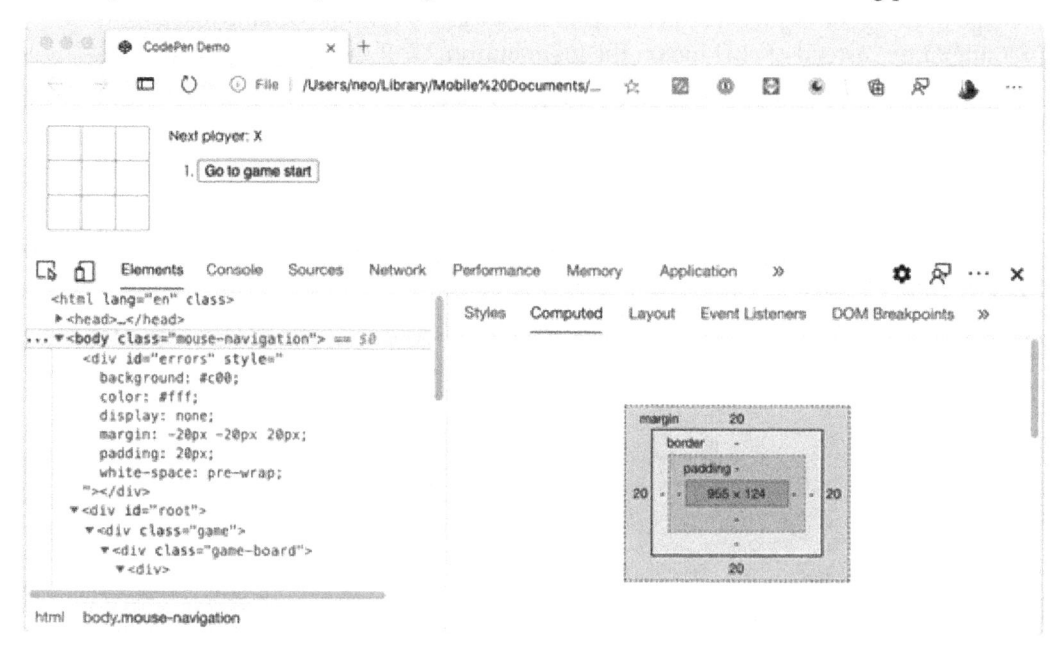

Body margin

We also know that each square is 32 px by 32 px, so the middle of the square should be *delta + (32 / 2)*. Let's test it:

```
const startingX = 20;
const startingY = 20;
const boxMiddle = 16;

// X turn 1;
await page.mouse.click(startingX + boxMiddle, startingY + boxMiddle);
// Y turn 1;
await page.mouse.click(startingX + boxMiddle, startingY + boxMiddle * 3);

// X turn 2;
await page.mouse.click(startingX + boxMiddle * 3, startingY + boxMiddle);
// Y turn 2;
await page.mouse.click(startingX + boxMiddle * 3, startingY + boxMiddle * 3);

// X turn 3;
await page.mouse.click(startingX + boxMiddle * 5, startingY + boxMiddle);
expect(await page.$eval('#status', status => status.innerHTML)).to.be('Winner: X');
```

So, here we know that the *tic-tac-toe* grid starts at the coordinate (20,20), and from there is simple math to find the right coordinates in our canvas. The first box will be clicked at the coordinate (startingX + boxMiddle; startingY + boxMiddle). If we want to click on the second row, it would be three middle squares, startingX + boxMiddle * 3, and so on until we know that we have a winner.

Don't worry about the last $eval. We'll get there.

But this is not just for games. Many modern UIs might require some mouse interactions, for instance, hoverable dropdowns or menus. We can see one example on the *W3Schools* site (`https://www.w3schools.com/howto/howto_css_dropdown.asp`):

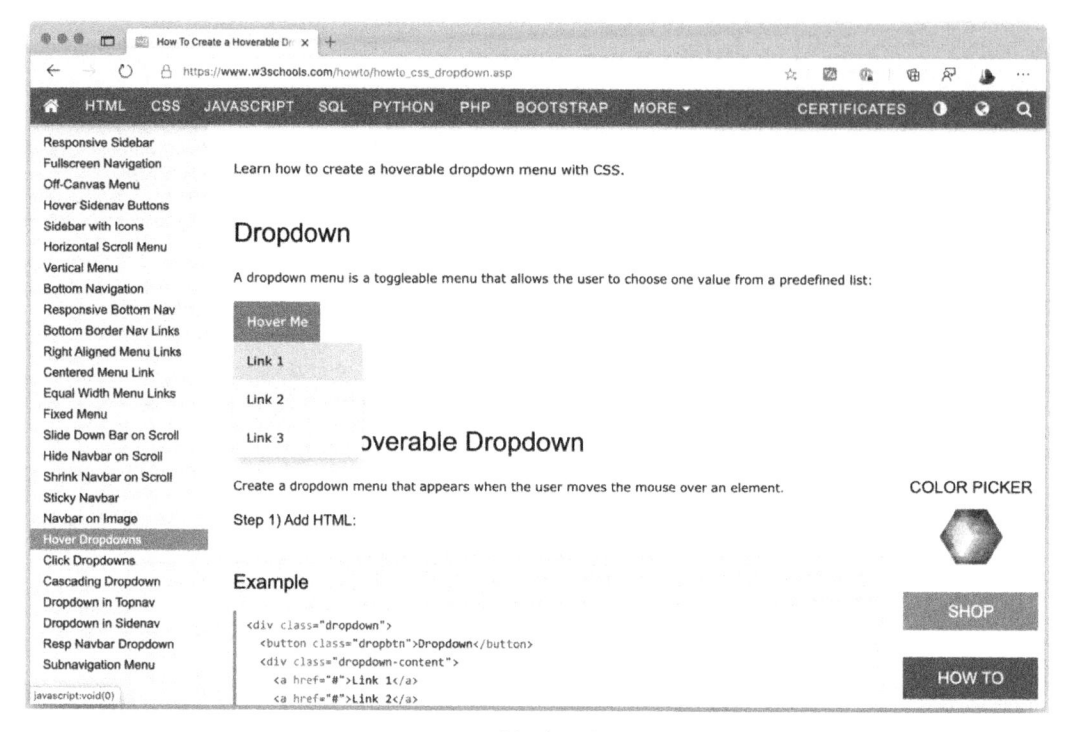

Hoverable dropdown

To be able to click on any item in that dropdown, we need to hover first on the button and then link on the option:

```
await page.goto("https://www.w3schools.com/howto/howto_css_dropdown.asp");
const btn = await page.$(".dropbtn");
const  box = await btn.boundingBox();
await page.mouse.move(box.x + (box.width / 2), box.y + (box.height / 2));
const  option = (await page.$x('//*[text()="Link 2"]'))[0];
await option.click();
```

As you can see, we don't need to guess the **Hover me** button's location. The element handle provides a function called `boundingBox`, which returns the position (*x* and *y*) and the element's size (width and height).

Is there an easier way? Yes, we can simply use `await btn.hover()`, which would hover on the element. I wanted to give you a complete example because sometimes UI components are quite sensitive to the mouse position, so you need to put the mouse in a precise location to get the desired result.

Time for a bonus track. Let's talk about debugging.

Debugging tests with Visual Studio Code

Many developers consider debugging a last resort. Others would flood their code with `console.log` messages. I consider debugging a productivity tool.

Debugging is trying to find bugs by running an application step by step.

We have two ways of launching our tests in debug mode. The first option is creating a **JavaScript debug terminal** from the **Terminal** tab. That will create a new terminal as we did before, but in this case, Visual Studio will enable the debugger when you run a command from that terminal:

Debugging from the terminal

116   Interacting with a page

The second option is going to the **Run** tab and creating a `launch.json` file. You could also create that file manually inside the `.vscode` folder:

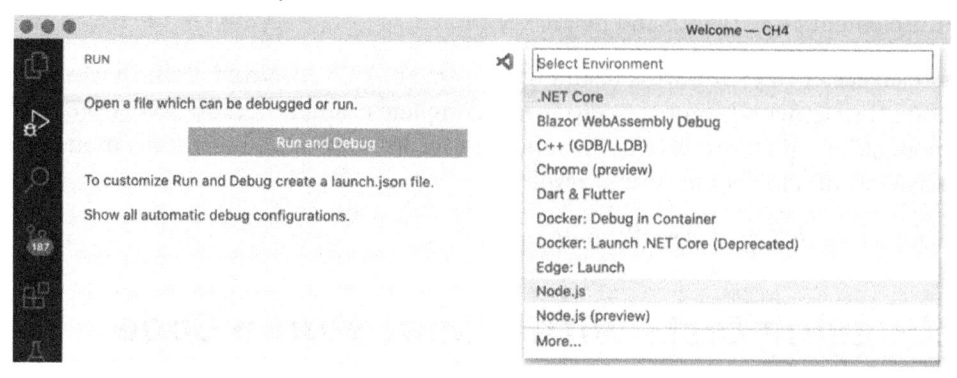

Create a launch.json from the run tab

Once we have the file, we can create a new configuration so that we can run `npm run test` in the terminal:

```
{
    "version": "0.2.0",
    "configurations": [
        {
            "name": "Test",
            "request": "launch",
            "runtimeArgs": [
                "run",
                "test"
            ],
            "runtimeExecutable": "npm",
            "skipFiles": [
                "<node_internals>/**"
            ],
            "type": "pwa-node"
        },
    ]
}
```

Which one is the best? Well, if you will work on this project for many days, creating the `launch.json` file is more productive; once created, you just need to hit *F5*, and you would be in debug mode. The terminal option is easier just to get running.

Once you have everything set up, it is about creating **breakpoints** in the line you want the debugger to stop, and from there it is about taking advantage of all the tools Visual Studio Code offers:

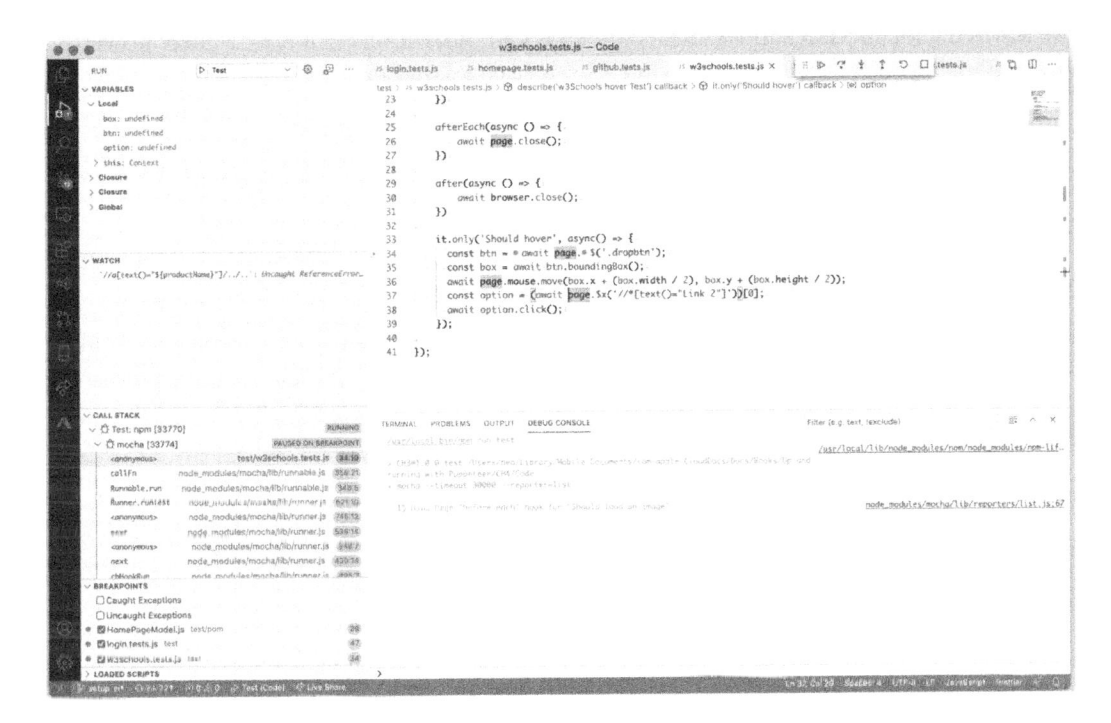

Visual Studio Code in debugging mode

There you will find the following:

- At the left of the line numbers, you will find the breakpoints. You can create or remove breakpoints by clicking at the left of the line number.
- You will find the full list of breakpoints at the bottom left of the window. From there, you will be able to disable breakpoints temporarily.
- At the top right of the window, you will find debug actions: Pause, play, step in/out, and stop buttons.
- In the left panel, you will find two useful sections: Variables, where you can automatically get the values of all the variables in the current scope. The next panel is Watch, and you can add there the variables or expressions you want to look at while running your code.

Summary

This chapter was massive. We began the chapter with a brief but complete introduction to HTML, the DOM, and CSS. These concepts are crucial to create top-notch tests. Then, we learned a lot about XPath, which is not a very popular tool, yet it is extremely powerful and will help you face scenarios where CSS selectors are not enough.

In the second part of this chapter, we went through the most common ways to interact with a page. Not only did we learn how to interact with elements but we also covered keyboard and mouse emulation.

I hope you enjoyed the tools section. Debugging with Visual Studio Code is a great tool to add to your toolbox.

In the next chapter, we are going to wait for stuff. Things take time on the web. Pages take time to load. Some actions on the page might trigger network calls. The next chapter is important because you will learn how to make your tests even more stable.

5
Waiting for elements and network calls

I won't say I'm old, but I started browsing the internet in the late 90s. So yes, I'm old. Back then, you would sometimes have to wait over a minute to get a page loaded. You might be thinking, "So if you had 10 tabs open, that would be impossible to use." Well, browsers didn't have tabs! Downloading one single MP3 file could take you an hour.

In the early 2000s, the web got into the corporate world, and we started developing business apps using websites. But that was a decision from an IT department. Old terminal apps were hard to update and introduce new features, and desktop apps were hard to distribute. Web apps were the IT department's solution, leaving users with slow and non user-friendly web apps.

Developers were trying to do their best with the tools they had back then. Pages were mostly generated on the server side using tools such as ASP 3.0 or PHP. AJAX was used for small tasks, such as loading the state's list based on a country selection without reloading the entire page.

In the late 2000s, Google launched *Gmail*, showing the world how the web should look. But the bar was too high for developers. Developing those kinds of apps was unthinkable for developers just trying to build CRUD pages.

Nowadays, our web looks different. Developers are now able to create rich experiences, even for more straightforward scenarios.

But there is a thing that didn't change in all these years: **You have to wait**.

You have to wait for the site to load, for the data to be refreshed, for the new page to be opened, for the form to be submitted. You have to wait.

Waiting for the right moment to act is key to avoid having flaky tests. A flaky test is a test that sometimes passes and sometimes fails. You have to consider flaky tests as a bug, not in the app but in your tests. Flaky tests bring many problems:

- They are a waste of time. Nobody wants to merge a pull request with the tests in red. So, they will repeatedly run the tests until they get all the tests green.

- Flaky tests are a false alarm. Suppose the developer doesn't know that the test is flaky. They might try to find a non-existent bug.

- Flaky tests hurt your tests' reputation. The loss of reputation begins by skipping one flaky test. If you have more flaky tests, the team might move your tests to a nightly process. If your tests keep being flaky, they might be removed from the CI process. You lose, and your team losses.

Waiting for the right moment to act is the key to making stable UI tests.

In this chapter, we will learn about the tools that Puppeteer provides to act at the right moment. We will also learn different techniques and approaches, so you can know how you can wait for the page to be ready, for an input to be visible, or for a request to be made, among many other things.

This chapter is about **waiting**, a key topic in web automation. I also want to show you a Puppeteer recorder so that you can add one more tool to your toolbox. We will cover the following topics in this chapter:

- Waiting for the page to load
- Waiting for elements
- Waiting for network calls
- Waiting for page events
- Bonus: Headless Recorder

Let's start at the beginning. How do you know that the page is already loaded?

Technical requirements

You will find all the code of this chapter on the GitHub repository (`https://github.com/PacktPublishing/UI-Testing-with-Puppeteer`) under the `Chapter5` directory. Remember to run `npm install` on that directory and then go to the `Chapter5/vuejs-firebase-shopping-cart` directory and run `npm install` again.

If you want to implement the code while following this chapter, you can start from the code you left in the `Chapter4` directory.

Waiting for the page to load

In *Chapter 3*, *Navigating through a website*, we talked about navigation through a site. We covered functions such as `goto`, `goBack`, `goForward`, and `reload`. One of the options these functions have is the `waitUntil` option. This option will help us determine when the function we are calling will be resolved. Let's do a quick recap. We have four options there:

- `domcontentloaded`, which relies on the `DOMContentLoaded` event.
- `load`: If you pass this option, the `promise` will be resolved when the `load` event is fired.
- `networkidle0` will resolve the promise *when there are no more network connections for the past 500 ms*.
- `networkidle2` will resolve the promise *when there are no more than 2 network connections for the past 500 ms*.

Let's see how these options work with a site full of content such as `https://shop.mango.com/gb`. We are going to see what content is ready, depending on which `waitUntil` is used:

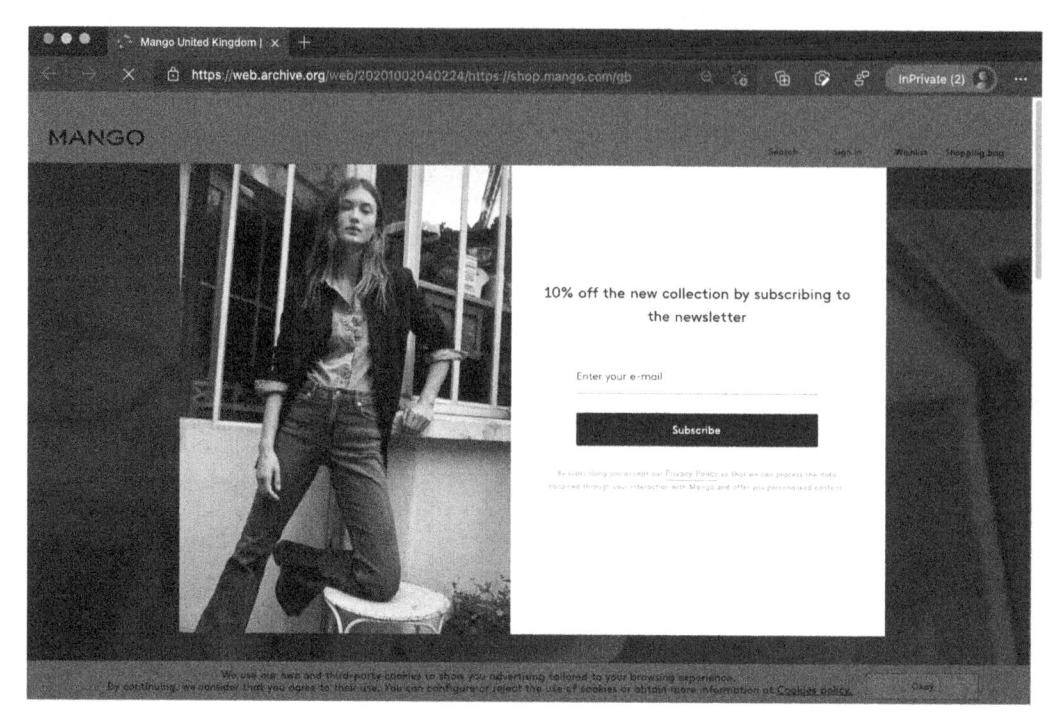

Mango home page

The earliest option to be resolved is `DOMContentLoaded`:

![every(wear) page screenshot with cookie banner]

DOM content loaded

124   Waiting for elements and network calls

That page is not ready at all. Does that mean that `DOMContentLoaded` is useless? Well, it is useless in this case. If you do the same with Wikipedia, the page is so straightforward that it will be ready to automate:

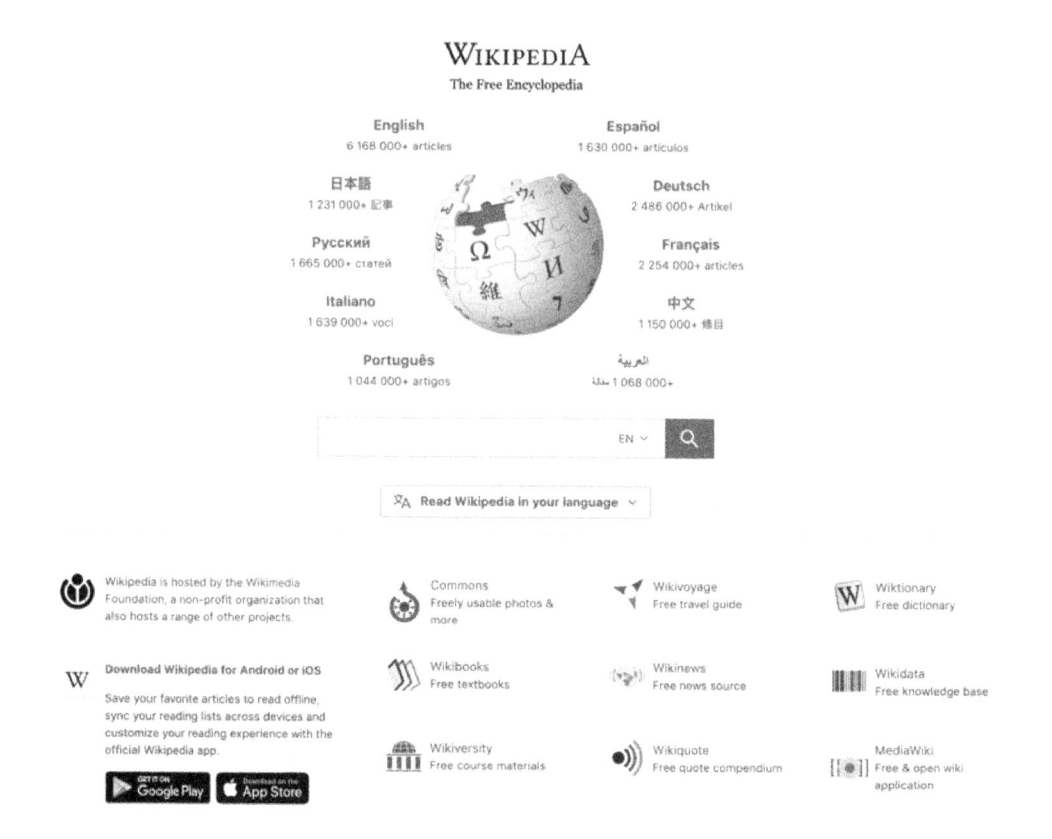

DOM content loaded in Wikipedia

Going back to the Mango page. Waiting for the `load` event gives us all the content from the page:

Page after load

The background video is not there yet. And the subscribe popup didn't show up. But if we want to interact with the menu bar, use the login action, or test the cookies banner, the page is ready.

It would be hard to find a page where `networkidle0` and `networkidle2` behave differently that you have to pick between one or the other. In this case, we'll get an almost complete page:

Page using networkidle0 and networkidle2

The video is not being played yet, so if you want to take screenshots or generate PDF files, as we will see in *Chapter 7, Generating Content with Puppeteer*, this won't be enough. But we could say it's ready to be tested.

So, which one is better? Should we play safe and use `networkidle0` all the time? Shouldn't that be the default then?

Here's where we need to find a balance. We could just wait 10 seconds between actions, and we wouldn't have any flaky tests. But, if you have 1,000 tests (remember, you will have over 1,000 tests) with 10 actions each, that would mean that the entire test suite would take almost 14 hours to run.

To reduce flakiness, we need to find a balance between waiting for too long and going too fast.

Sometimes getting the DOM from the server will be enough. If we were testing Wikipedia, our links would be ready for us on the DOMContentLoaded event. If we want to test our home page and we wait for DOMContentLoaded, images won't be ready yet, but we will get the stock and price values from the server. We don't need more than that.

Setting the right waitUntil will make your code less flaky, but unless you test a simple site such as Wikipedia, that won't be enough.

The most effective way to make your code stable is by waiting for the element we want to interact with.

Waiting for elements

Before acting on an element, you need to make sure of two things: first, that the element is there, it exists in the DOM; and second, you can act on that element. In other words, it's visible to the user. Let's see how we can wait for our element to be ready.

You should wait for a selector after some kind of network call. You goto a page, wait for a selector, and then you act. You click on a button, wait for a selector, and then you act.

In some cases, the selector you need to wait for is easy to find. On our login page, we need to wait for the user name input. In other cases, such as our home page, we would need to wait for the div element containing all the products. It's just a little bit more complicated but still straightforward.

But what if we want to test Mango's newsletter popup? Maybe the pop-up HTML is on the page, but it's not visible. Here's where I start to consider waiting as a kind of art. It's not just about automating a page. It's not only about the tool. You need to find the right selectors to make your automation code stable.

We have two functions that will help us wait for elements: waitForSelector and waitForXPath. Both functions have a similar signature. waitForSelector(selector, [options]) expects a CSS selector and an options object. waitForXPath(XPath, [options]) expects an XPath expression and an options object.

These are the available properties you will be able to set in the options argument:

- timeout: We will find this option in all wait functions. We don't want our tests to get stuck. This is another cause of flaky tests. If the timeout is reached, the promise will be rejected. If we don't pass a timeout, the function will use the timeout set using page.setDefaultTimeout(timeout). If setDefaultTimeout wasn't used, it will default to **30 seconds**.

- `visible`: If `visible` is set to true, Puppeteer will not only check that the element exists in the DOM but that it is also visible. We would need to use that in our newsletter popup. This check won't be performed by default. And, again, it's something you might want to check or not, depending on your scenario.
- `hidden`: If `hidden` is set to true, Puppeteer will check if the element is not visible or if the element is not in the DOM. This option is useful when you need to deal with loading animations. You know that the page is reading when the loading animation is hidden. `Twitter.com` is a great example:

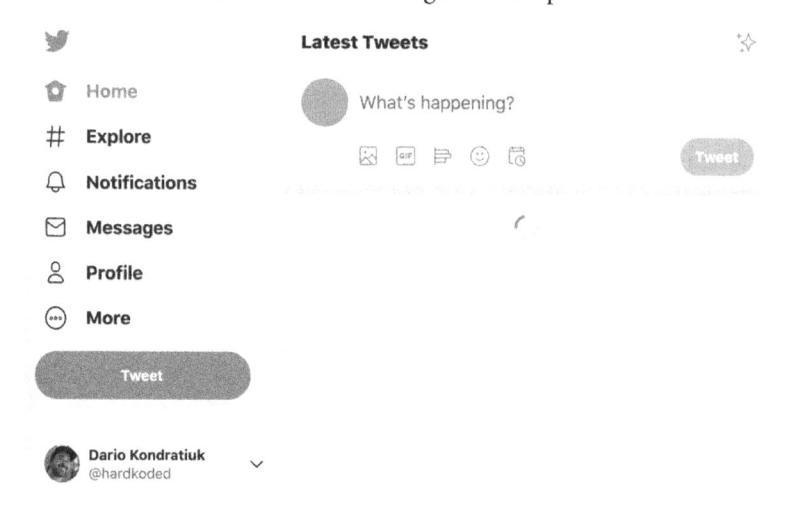

Loading animation on Twitter.com

Both `waitForSelector` and `waitForXPath` will return a promise that can resolve to the following:

- An `ElementHandle`: This element handle will be the element that eventually matches the CSS selector or the XPath.
- Null: When `hidden` is set to true, and the element was not found in the DOM.

There are four approaches to waiting for elements. It's not about which one is the best. These approaches will help you in different scenarios.

Await a wait function

You will find the code used in this section in the `stackoverflow.tests.js` file.

If we go to Stack Overflow (https://stackoverflow.com/questions), we will find that there are job postings on the right of the page. But as we can see, that's loaded after the page.

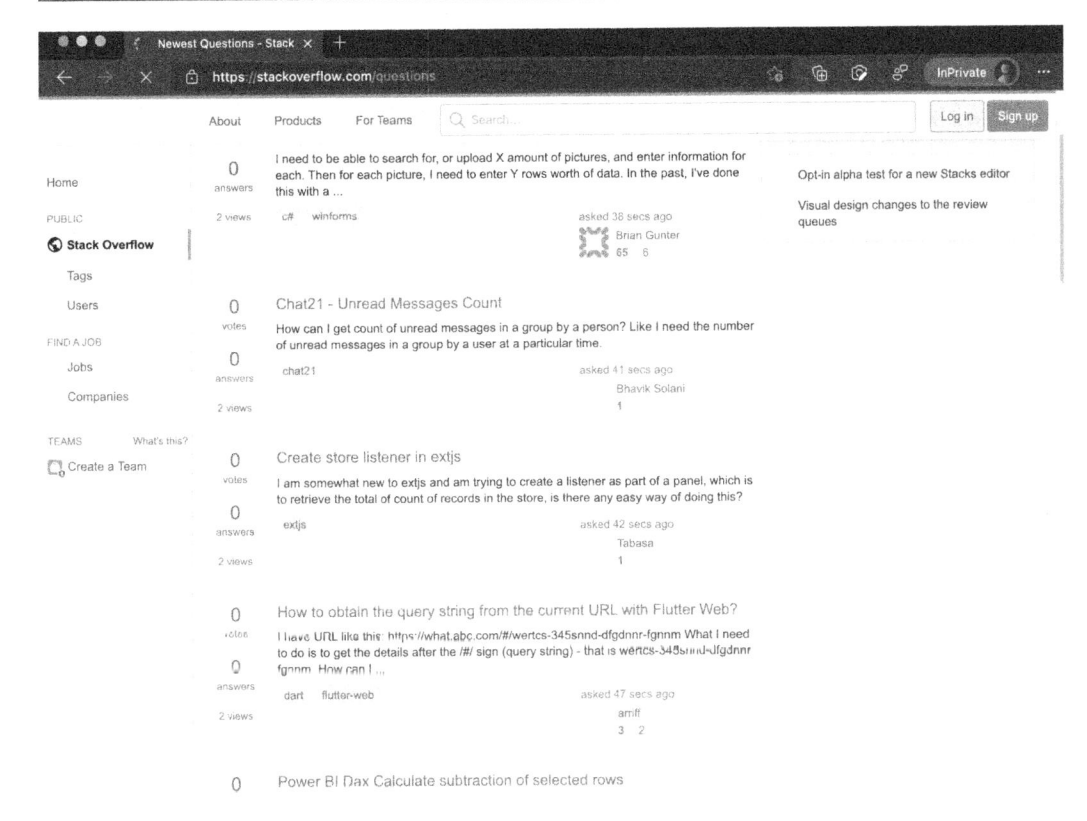

Listing while loading and list once loaded

Let's say that we want to test that the page has a list of jobs by default.

We could just grab the `LI` elements using `$$` and then check whether the list is empty or not:

```
const jobs = await page.$$('.jobs li');
expect(jobs).not.be.empty;
```

Honestly, this will work most of the time using a decent network, but it could also get flaky. What we need to do is wait for the elements to be loaded before checking that list. What we could do is call the `waitForSelector` function before calling `$$`.

```
await page.waitForSelector('.jobs li');
const jobs = await page.$$('.jobs li');
expect(jobs).not.be.empty;
```

As I mentioned before, `waitForSelector` returns an `ElementHandle`. It uses `document.querySelector`. That's why we can't use the result of `waitForSelector`.

But if we wanted to check whether the title is **"jobs near you"**, we could use the result of the `waitForSelector` function:

```
const title = await page.waitForSelector('#hireme .header .grid--cell.fl1');
expect(await title.evaluate(e => e.innerText))
.to.contain('job');
```

I think that's the second time I have used the `evaluate` function. Patience – that will come in the next chapter.

In case you are wondering why we didn't use the result of `waitForSelector` in the job listing example, it turns out that `waitForSelector` uses `document.querySelector` to evaluate the CSS expression. That will make `waitForSelector` return only one item.

The same happens with `waitForXpath`. Unlike `$x`, that returns an array of elements. `waitForXpath` will return only one element.

`waitForSelector` and `waitForXPath` will save your day most of the time, but there are other scenarios we might want to consider. For instance, we might need to check network calls. We might want to wait for a request to be made or for a response to be received. Let's see how to accomplish that.

Waiting for network calls

In *Chapter 3, Navigating through a website*, we talked about **requests** and **responses**. Every page navigation begins with a request to a page. The server then processes that request and sends a response. That response generally is an HTML page, which has resources declared that need to be requested. The server will process each of those requests again and send many responses.

But that's not all. Modern apps will send requests to the server based on user actions. Take *Google Maps*: the user moves the mouse, and the page will need to request a new picture of the map without reloading the entire page.

We don't work on the *Google Maps* teams, but many users have reported that the home page sometimes doesn't load the product image after login. So, we could write a test to check that *it should load an image*. Oh… you thought we were going to test *Google Maps*? Not this time, sorry.

In this case, we can use `waitForResponse(urlOrPredicate, [options])`. Let's unpack these arguments:

- `urlOrPredicate` can be a string with the URL we want to wait for. But it can also be a function. This should be a function expecting a response, which will be the response you will want to check and return a truthy value.

- The only option we have in this function is `timeout`. This property has the same conditions as the one in `waitForSelector`: If not passed, Puppeteer will use `page.setDefaultTimeout(timeout)`, and if that function wasn't used, the default will be 30 seconds.

Let's write our test. We need to log in and wait for the product image. To accomplish this, we are going to use the **Arrange, Act, Await** approach.

Arrange, Act, Await

This name comes from the arrange, act, assert pattern we talked about in *Chapter 4, Interacting with a page*.

With this pattern, we try to prevent **race conditions**, a common issue in async programming, and a cause of flakiness. A race condition in async programming is when you are trying to do two or more tasks simultaneously, and the speed of one task (too fast or too slow) causes another task to never complete.

Let's take, for instance, this test:

```
await loginModel.go();
await loginModel.login(config.username, config.password);
await page.waitForResponse(config.productImage);
```

First, notice something. We are not using asserts. The fact that the `waitForResponse` promise resolves is enough for us to know that the test was successful.

Another important concept here is that `waitForReponse` doesn't behave in the same way as `waitForSelector`. When we use `waitForSelector`, the function will resolve when the element we are waiting for is already in the DOM. But with `waitForResponse`, if the response we are waiting for has already happened, our `waitForResponse` will time out.

Our code there has a risk of flakiness. If our server is too fast serving the page after login, the image might have already been served before we wait for it. To solve that, we need to get the promise first, and then await it. This is how we could change our code:

```
await loginModel.go();
const promise = page.waitForResponse(config.productImage);
await loginModel.login(config.username, config.password);
await promise;
```

Notice that instead of awaiting the promised returned by `waitForResponse`, we are assigning that promise to a variable. We call `waitForResponse`, we keep that promise, then we act (log in). After that, we await that promise, hoping that it will be resolved at one point after the login action is complete. You can find this test in the `login.tests.js` file. There, the test is called `Should load image after login`.

In the same way that we use `waitForResponse`, we can use `waitForRequest`.

We would use `waitForRequest` instead of `waitForResponse` if we wanted to check whether the browser is sending a request to the server. As this function also expects a `predicate`, a function, as an argument, we can check not only for the URL but also the content of the request.

Let's say that we work at The Weather Channel (`https://weather.com/`). We want to check that the browser is sending our location. We found that the page is calling `redux-dal`. We want to wait for that request, parse the **payload** (the data sent to the server), and validate that it has a geocode object inside the `params` object.

Waiting for network calls   133

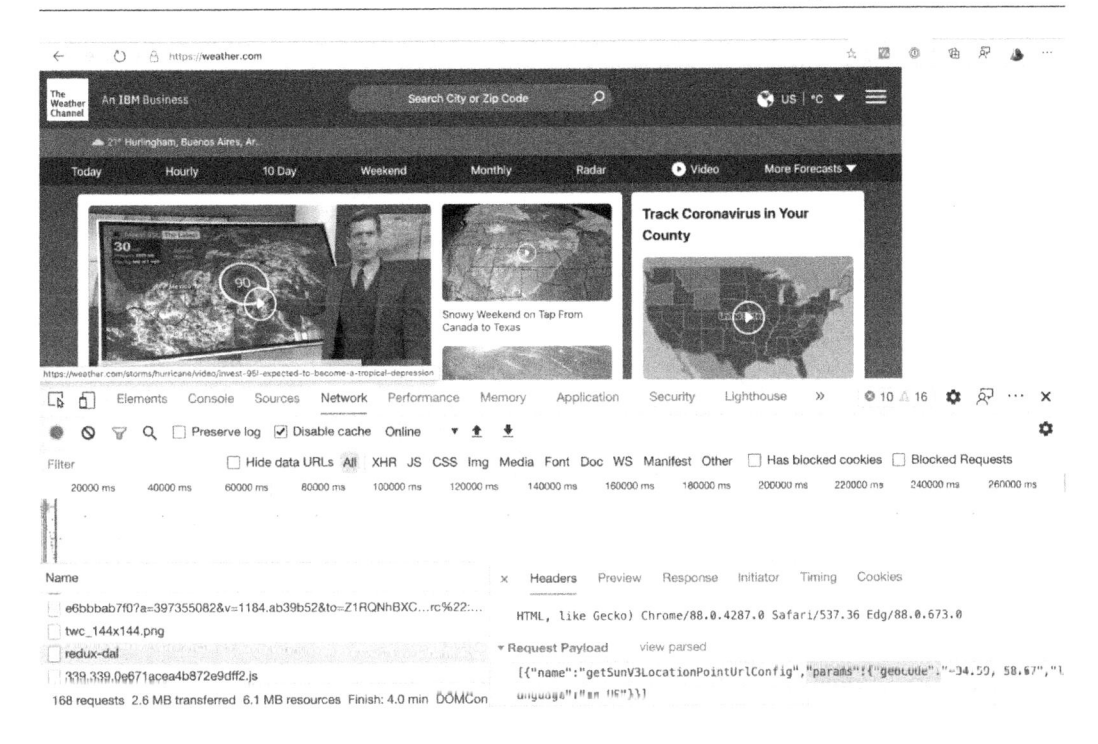

The weather channel

We are going to solve this using the **fire and forget** approach.

Fire and forget

You will find the code used in this section in the `weather.tests.js` file.

We call it a "fire and forget" when we call a function that returns a promise but we don't await that promise, and we don't even care about the result of that promise. "Fire and forget" is a military term that refers to a type of missile that does not require further guidance after launch. In our case, our missiles are Promises that we launch, but we don't care about the outcome of them.

Let's see how a fire and forget approach would look:

```
const promise = page.waitForRequest(r => r.url().includes('redux-dal'));
page.goto('https://weather.com/');
const request = await promise;
const json = JSON.parse(request.postData());
expect(json[0].params.geocode).not.be.empty;
```

There are many new things to learn here.

We fire and forget the `goto` action. We call `goto`, but we don't wait for it to finish. Doing a fire and forget means that we won't care if the promise resolves or fails. In this case, we care about the `request` promise. If `goto` fails, the `waitForRequest` will fail, and the test will fail.

The second new feature we can see here is that we are waiting for a request using a predicate, a function that expects a request and returns a truthy value: `r => r.url().includes('redux-dal')`.

The last thing we can learn here is that we are working with the request resolved by the `waitForRequest` promise. Once we get the request, we extract the payload using `postData`, parse it, and evaluate the content.

The last feature we have to handle network calls is `waitForNavigation`. Imagine `waitForNavigation` as the `goto` function without the URL argument. It's `waitForNavigation([options])`. The options are the same options `goto` has. We can use this function to wait for navigation triggered by one action we perform.

Let's take, for example, the Packtpub site (https://www.packtpub.com/). We want to search for a book, press *Enter*, and wait for the page to be redirected to the results page.

For this test, we are going to use our fourth approach: `Promise.all`.

Promise.all

You will find the code used in this section in the `packpub.tests.js` file.

Depending on the scenario, `Promise.all` could be a shortcut for Act, Arrange, Await. In fact, I would keep the latter for more complex scenarios and use `Promise.all` if I need to wait for two tasks at the same time.

Our test code would look like this with a `Promise.all`:

```
await page.goto('https://www.packtpub.com/');
const search = await page.$('#search');
await search.type('Puppeteer');

await Promise.all([
    page.waitForNavigation(),
    search.press('Enter')
]);
const textResult = await page.$eval('[data-ui-id="page-title-
```

```
 wrapper"]', e => e.innerText);
 expect(textResult).to.be.equal(`Search results for:
 'Puppeteer'`);
```

The first part is pretty straightforward. We go to the site, get the search input, and type "Puppeteer." But then, we wait for two Promises in the same `await` statement. We wait for navigation to be completed and the `press` function.

Although it would be quite weird getting a race condition inside a `Promise.all`, I feel safer adding the `wait` function as the first argument of the `all` function.

As I mentioned in *Chapter 1, Getting started with Puppeteer*, `Promise.all` will wait for all promises to finish. It will also resolve as soon as one promise fails.

Now we know how to wait for elements and network calls. But let me tell you a little secret: `waitForRequest` and `waitForResponse` are just wrappers around the request and response events the page offers. Puppeteer would create a Promise, start listening to an event, and then resolve the Promise when a condition is met. The good news is that we can use this same approach to wait for many other events.

Waiting for page events

Events are messages that a class sends when something happens. As a consumer, you can **attach** a function to those events, so you can listen to those events and react accordingly. You can find the code examples of these demos in the `page-event-demos.js` file inside the `Chapter5` directory. To run that demo, you just need to run `node page-event-demos.js`.

This is how you could listen to responses without the `waitForResponse`:

```
 page.on('response', response =>
   console.log('Response URL: ' + response.url()));
 await page.goto('https://www.packtpub.com/');
```

In the first line, we say that we want to listen to the `response` event, and when a new response arrives, we want to print the URL in the console. Then, we call the `goto` function, and all the responses will start being written in the console.

Using the arrow (=>) is a simple way to write single-line functions. But, if you open a bracket, you can write more complex functions, like the following:

```
page.on('response', response => {
  if(response.request().resourceType() === 'image') {
    console.log('Image URL: ' + response.url());
  }
});
await page.goto('https://www.packtpub.com/');
```

If you want to reuse a function, you can pass a function there:

```
const listenToImages = response => {
  if(response.request().resourceType() === 'image') {
    console.log('Image URL from function: ' + response.url());
  }
};
page.on('response', listenToImages);
```

As you can see, we can create a function, assign it to a variable – in this case, `listenToImages` – and then pass it to the `page.on` function. If you pass a function, you will be able to remove that listener:

```
page.removeListener('response', listenToImages);
```

The `removeListener` function will detach the `listenToImages` function from the `response` event.

There is one more feature to add to your toolbox. You can listen to an event only once, using – you guessed it – `once`:

```
page.once('response', r => console.log(r.url()));
```

`once` will attach your function to an event and remove it as soon as the first event arrives. Notice that `once` won't evaluate the result of your function. You won't be able to prevent `once` from removing your listener as soon as the first event arrives.

We can now try to make our own `waitForResponse` function. We will use the approach we mentioned in *Chapter 1, Getting started with Puppeteer*: *Fulfill our own promises*. We can create a promise, and then we will resolve it when the condition we are waiting for is met:

```
await loginModel.go();
const promise = new Promise(resolve =>
   page.on('response', r => {
      if (r.url() === config.productImage) {
         resolve(r);
      }
   }));

await loginModel.login(config.username, config.password);
await promise;
```

In this code, we created a promise that will be resolved when the `resolve` function is called. Inside that function, we attached to the response event and, when the URL matched, we called `resolve` passing that response.

In this case, using the `waitForResponse` function will be easier. But there are events that don't have a `waitFor` function, and you will need to use this approach to wait for them. Let's see what page events we have available.

The close event

The `close` event is triggered when the page is closed. These days, it's not so common to have popups, mainly because they are not mobile-friendly. But we can still find some cases. For instance, when you want to add an account to your existing *Gmail* account.

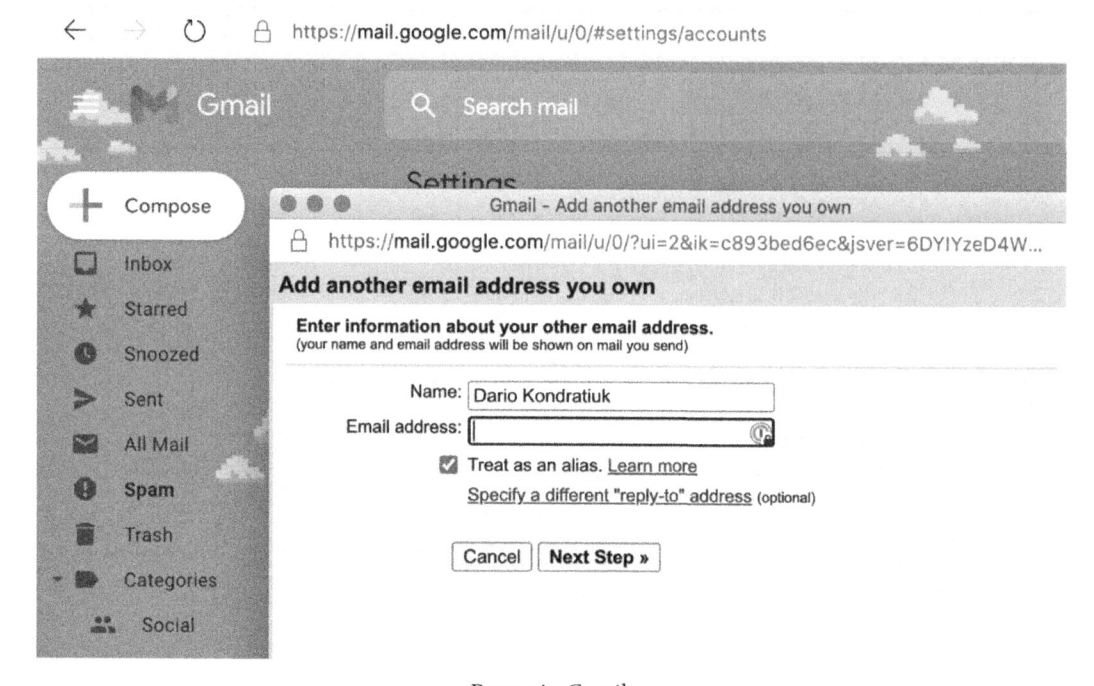

Popup in Gmail

You will need to listen to that page's `close` event to know that the wizard process has finished.

But that leaves us with another question. How do you get to that page? If we are testing the *Gmail* page and click on the **Create account** link, how do we get the popup?

The popup event

The page will trigger a `popup` event when it opens a new tab or window. We could do something like this:

```
const [newPage] = Promise.all([
  new Promise(resolve => page.once('popup', resolve)),
  page.click('someselector')
]);
```

One new thing we can learn here is that `promise.all` returns an array of all the responses. As we only care about the response of the first promise, we create an array with only one element `[newPage]`.

If you want to listen to new pages regardless of what triggered that new page, you can also listen to browser events.

Target created event

The `targetcreated` event is triggered when a new target (page) is created inside the browser. We could do something like this:

```
const [newPage] = Promise.all([
  new Promise(resolve => browser.once('targetcreated', resolve
)),
  page.click('someselector')
]);
```

In most scenarios, this will work in the same way as the popup event. But it's good for you to know that you also have this tool available.

Let's go back to page events.

The console event

The `console` event will be triggered every time a new line is printed on the browser console. In the same way the `response` event gives us a `response` object with all the information, the `console` event will give us a message class with the following functions:

- `text()` with the text message.
- `type()`, which will help us identify the type of the message. The most common types are: 'log', 'debug', 'info', 'error,' and 'warning'.
- `location()`, giving us the source of the message.
- As `console.log` can expect objects as arguments, we can access those element handles with `args()`.

You can use this event to check that there are no JavaScript errors during the test.

The dialog event

The `dialog` event is important because dialogs stop the execution of a page. There are many types of dialogs, and each of them will require us to react differently. We can know the dialog type using the `type()` function. Let's take a look at the different dialog types and how we can react to them.

The alert type

`Alert` is a dialog with only an **OK** option. You can resume the execution by calling `dialog.accept()`:

Alert

Confirm type

`Confirm` is a dialog with an **OK** and a **Cancel** option. You accept the dialog with `dialog.accept()` or `dialog.dismiss()` to cancel it:

Confirm

The prompt type

The `prompt` dialog is not common these days. It's like the `confirm` dialog but it prompts an input that you can pass by passing a string to the `accept` function:

www.google.com says

How old are you?

Cancel   OK

Prompt

The beforeunload type

You will see `beforeunload` these days, asking you if you want to leave the site without saving your changes. It works as a `confirm` dialog. You can interact with this dialog in the same way you would interact with the `prompt` dialog:

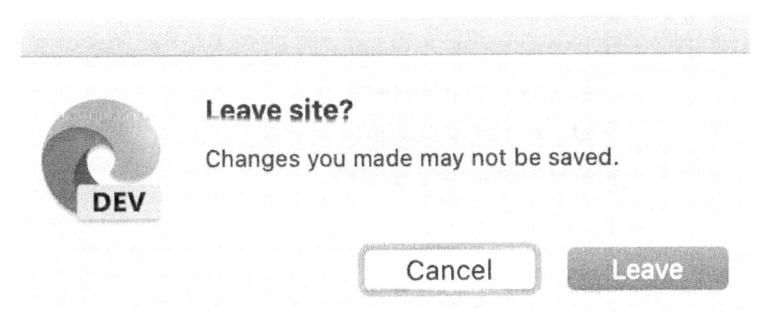

Before unload dialog

Let's wrap up this chapter with a new tool for our toolbox: **the headless recorder**.

The headless recorder

The headless recorder is a Chrome extension developed by *Checkly* (https://www.checklyhq.com/). This extension will record the actions you perform on a page and generate Puppeteer code based on those actions. I think it's a great tool to get a first draft of a Puppeteer test, and from there, start working on the final code.

You can download this extension by going to the Chrome Web Store (`https://chrome.google.com/webstore`) and searching for `Headless Recorder`:

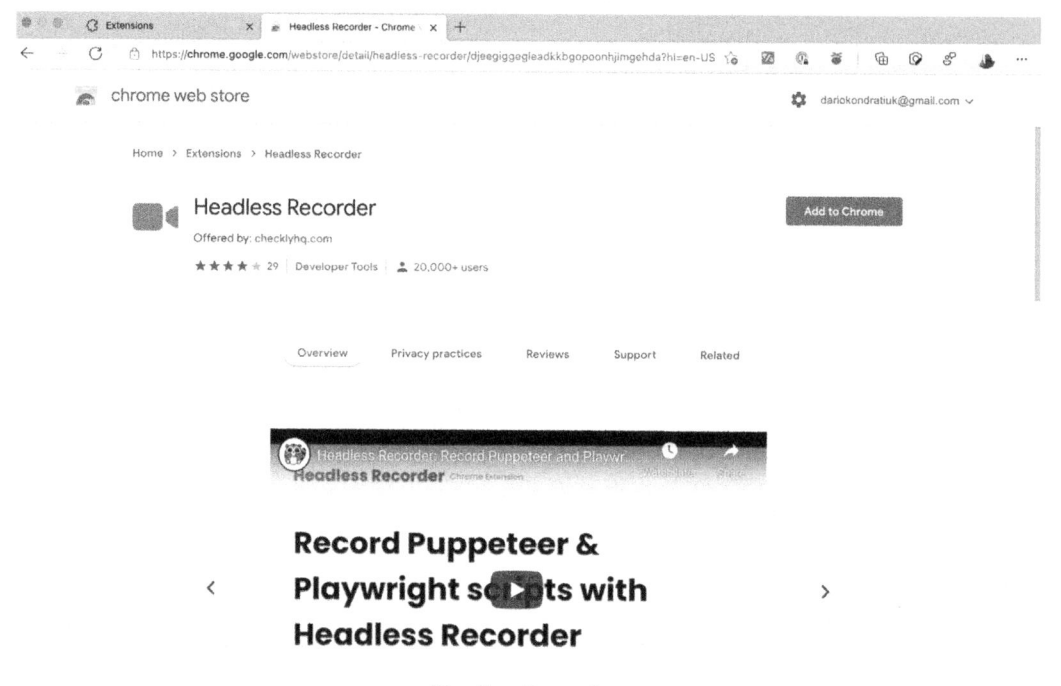

Headless Recorder

Once installed, you will find a **recorder icon** at the top right of your browser. From there, you will have the **record button**, which will start to capture all the actions you perform on a page:

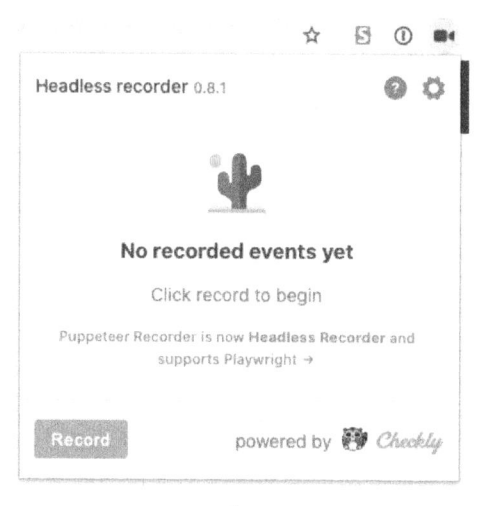

Record option

Once you finish performing your test actions, you click **stop**, and you'll get the code almost ready to be used:

```
const puppeteer = require('puppeteer');
(async () => {
  const browser = await puppeteer.launch()
  const page = await browser.newPage()

  await page.goto('http://localhost:8080/')

  await page.setViewport({ width: 1760, heig

  await page.waitForSelector('.mb-3:nth-chil
  await page.click('.mb-3:nth-child(1) > .th

  await page.waitForSelector('.flex-fill > .
  await page.click('.flex-fill > .message-ba

  await page.waitForSelector('.mb-3:nth-chil
  await page.click('.mb-3:nth-child(2) > .th

  await browser.close()
})()
```

Headless Recorder result

I say almost ready because the recorder can't guess your real intentions. It's just a guide. As you can see there are selectors such as `.mb-3:nth-child(1) > .thumbnail > .card-body > .row > .col-6 > .btn`. The recorder doesn't know what your intentions are behind clicking on a certain link. But it's a good start, and it can help you when your test requires many steps.

Summary

In this chapter, we learned the concept of flaky tests, and we saw many techniques and tools to prevent having flaky tests in our test suites.

While we were learning about these wait tools, we saw many page events without even noticing them. Now you can not only wait for selectors and network calls but you can also deal with dialogs and popups.

The last section was short, but as promised, we now have another tool in our toolbox, a headless recorder.

In the next chapter, we will get into more advanced tools and learn how to execute JavaScript in the browser.

6
Executing and Injecting JavaScript

In the past few chapters, we learned about most of the basic Puppeteer features, from creating a browser and a page correctly, to finding elements and interacting with them.

Now it's time to get into more powerful tools. In this chapter, we will see how Puppeteer gives us the ability to execute JavaScript code in the browser.

It might sound like a hack or a last resort tool. Sometimes it is. But it is also a tool that will help us perform actions that are not provided by the Puppeteer API.

The communication between the code being executed on the Node side and the code being executed in the browser can sometimes be tricky. We will learn how to communicate with both sides efficiently.

As we did in the previous chapter, we will add another tool to our toolbox. We are going to run our code on *Checkly*.

We will cover the following topics in this chapter:

- Executing JavaScript code
- Manipulating handles with JavaScript code

- Waiting for functions
- Exposing local functions
- Running our checks with Checkly

By the end of this chapter, you will be able to get more out of the page you are automating by executing JavaScript code.

Technical requirements

You will find all the code of this chapter in the GitHub repository (`https://github.com/PacktPublishing/UI-Testing-with-Puppeteer`) under the `Chapter6` directory. Remember to run `npm install` on that directory and then go to the `Chapter6/vuejs-firebase-shopping-cart` directory and run `npm install` again.

If you want to implement the code while following this chapter, you can start from the code you left in the `Chapter5` directory.

Let's get started.

Executing JavaScript code

The first question you might ask is: "Why would I need to run JavaScript code? Shouldn't Puppeteer give me all the APIs I need?" Well, yes and no.

Before getting into the different possible use cases, let's see how this feature works.

Variable scopes in JavaScript

One thing that makes JavaScript so flexible is that functions are first-class citizens. You can declare functions, assign them to variables, and pass them as an argument. You could even return functions from other functions, like in this example:

```
function getFunc() {
    let word = 'world';

    return function() {
        console.log('Hello ' + word);
    }
}
getFunc()();
```

That code is pretty fun. getFunc returns another function. When we do getFunc()(), we are calling the function returned by getFunc.

This piece of code will print 'Hello world' in the console. The interesting part is that the function returned by getFunc is able to keep the variable word in its scope.

You could even do more complex things, for instance, passing an argument to getFunc, and then using that argument inside the function that getFunc will return:

```
function getFunc(name) {
    return function() {
        console.log('Hello ' + name);
    }
}
getFunc('world')();
getFunc('mars')();
```

That piece of code will print 'Hello world' and 'Hello mars'. This is called a **closure**. According to MDN (https://www.hardkoded.com/ui-testing-with puppeteer/closures), *A closure is the combination of a function bundled together (enclosed) with references to its surrounding state (the lexical environment). In other words, a closure gives you access to an outer function's scope from an inner function.* When we call getFunc, the returned function will be bundled together with the string 'world' in the first case, or 'mars' in the second case.

We won't get into the internals of this feature. But you need to know that **this is not how functions work in Puppeteer**.

Let's try to use closures in Puppeteer:

```
const browser = await puppeteer.launch({headless: false, defaultViewport: null});
const page = await browser.newPage();
const name = 'world';
await page.evaluate(() => alert('Hello ' + name));
browser.close();
```

In this case, we have a function that we are passing to the `evaluate` function, and that function is using the variable `name`, which is in the scope of the function we just created. But this is what we get:

Variable scopes in Puppeteer

As you can see, the name didn't get to the alert. For us as developers, the big issue is that the code looks good. If you look at the code, the code is perfect. It's not very different from our previous examples. But something works differently there. Once you understand this, you will be able to answer lots of questions on Stack Overflow.

First, the signature of `page.evaluate` is `page.evaluate(pageFunction[, ...args])`, where `pageFunction` can be a string or a function. The second argument is an optional list of values to pass to `pageFunction`.

You can pass **expressions** as strings to the `evaluate` function. An expression is a statement like the ones you can write inside the DevTools console. For instance, a simple string returning the URL property of the `document` object:

```
console.log(await page.evaluate('document.URL'));
```

`page.evaluate` will send the expression `document.URL` to the browser and the browser will evaluate it. Once the browser evaluates the expression, it will send that back to Puppeteer, and `page.evaluate` will return the result. In this case, `about:blank`.

Expressions are perfect when you want to evaluate simple expressions. But you could accomplish the same result using a JavaScript function:

```
console.log(await page.evaluate(() => document.URL));
```

As you can see, passing an expression is more straightforward, but you will be able to write more complex code using functions, and, no less important, you will get the autocomplete features of your code editor.

The key concept here is that `page.evaluate` **will send the expression to the browser**. How can Puppeteer send a function to the browser? It will serialize it. As I mentioned before, functions are first-class citizens in JavaScript, which means that you can call `toString()` to function inside a variable. Let's try that out:

```
console.log((() => alert('Hello ' + name)).toString());
```

This will print the function as a string value in the console:

```
() => alert('Hello ' + name)
```

If Puppeteer takes that function, converts it to a string using `toString`, and sends it to the browser, the value of the `name` variable will be lost in the process.

When you send a function to be evaluated inside the browser context, you need to make sure that all the values the function uses are already in the browser or are being passed as an argument. This is how we can fix our code:

```
const browser = await puppeteer.launch({headless: false, defaultViewport: null});
const page = await browser.newPage();
const name = 'world';
await page.evaluate((n) => alert('Hello ' + n), name);
browser.close();
```

As we can see, we are passing the `name` variable as part of the `args` argument of `evaluate`. Now Puppeteer knows that it has to serialize that function and also send `args`. The browser will now be able to execute that function, passing those arguments.

> **Tip**
> Notice that I renamed the variable name to `n`. It's not required, but this practice will help you avoid these kinds of scope mistakes. Now you, and your IDE, know that the n variable being used in the `alert` function is an argument being passed to that function.

This `evaluate` function is available not only in the `page` and `frame` classes but also in the `JSHandle` and `ElementHandle` classes. Let's explore how we can execute JavaScript code once we've got an `ElementHandle` or a `JSHandle` in Puppeteer.

Manipulating handles with JavaScript code

We talked about `ElementHandle` in *Chapter 4, Interacting with a Page*. Let's recap this concept. `ElementHandle` is a variable in our code pointing to a DOM element inside the page we are automating. Now it's time to know that an `ElementHandle` is, in fact, a **JSHandle**.

In the same way that `ElementHandle` is a variable pointing to an element in the browser, **a JSHandle is a variable pointing to a variable on the page we are automating**. If we think about that, the only difference between a JavaScript variable like, for instance, `document.URL`, and a DOM element, like `document.activeElement`, is that a DOM element has a visual representation, that's all. So, we can say that an `ElementHandle` (a DOM element) is also a `JSHandle` (a JavaScript variable). Inheritance 101.

We were using functions like `$` or `$x` to get `ElementHandles`. Now we can also use `evaluateHandle`, which works like `evaluate`, but as Puppeteer knows that we want a pointer to a variable in the browser, a handle, it will return an object that will represent that variable in the browser.

Let's go back to our login test. The way we were getting the password input was straightforward:

```
const passwordInput = await this.page.$('#password');
```

But, let's imagine that the developers want to create a super-secure login creating elements dynamically. But, they tell us that they are storing the password input in the `window.passwordInput` variable. We could get that input using an `evaluateHandle`:

```
const passwordInput = (await page.evaluateHandle(() => window.passwordInput)).asElement();
```

There, `evaluateHandle` will return a `JSHandle`, which we can convert to an `ElementHandle` using the `asElement` function. If you have to find an element that you cannot find using a CSS selector or an XPath selector, you now have a third tool: you can use a JavaScript function.

The `evaluateHandle` function is not limited to DOM elements or simple variables. You can also return, and even create, objects for later access. You will find this code in the `Chapter6/demos.js` file:

```
const counter = await page.evaluateHandle(() => {
    window.counter = { count: 2 };
    return window.counter;
});
await counter.evaluate((c, inc) => c.count += inc, 3);
await page.evaluate(() => alert(window.counter.count));
```

If you run this, you will see this result:

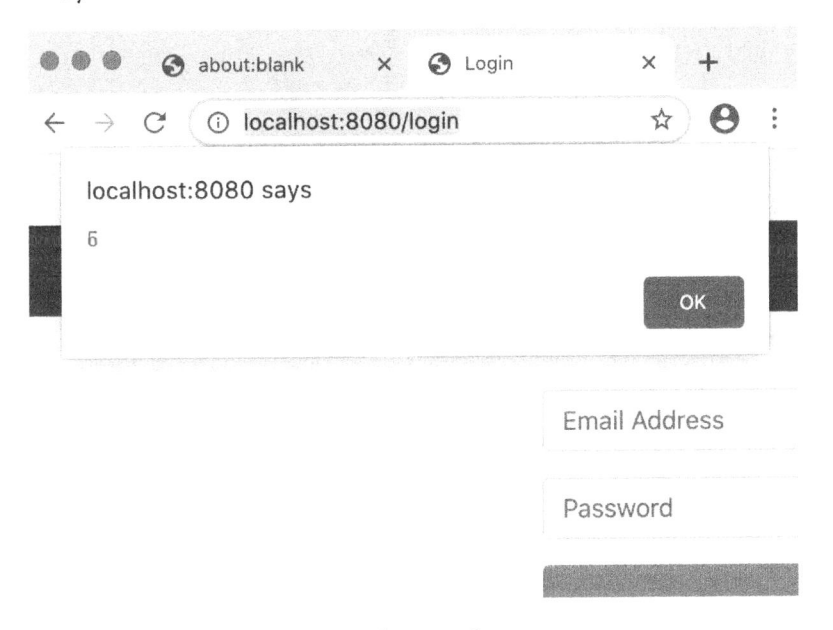

Evaluate result

In the first `evaluateHandle`, we create an object with a property `count`, assign it to a property `counter` in the `window` object, and then return that object.

By using the `window` object, we make it clear that we are using a global variable. If we declare a variable inside that function, we will lose it after executing the function. Although it is not considered a good practice, we could declare `counter` as a global variable by changing `window.counter` with just `counter`:

```
const counter = await page.evaluateHandle(() => {
    counter = { count: 2 };
```

```
        return counter;
});
```

In the second step, we are learning how to use the `evaluate` function, but in the context of a `JSHandle`. The function works in the same way as the `evaluate` function in the `page` class. But here, it will pass the `JSHandle` as the first argument:

```
await counter.evaluate((c, inc) => c.count += inc, 3);
```

As you can see there, the function expects two arguments: `c` and `inc`. But we are only passing 3, which is the second argument, `inc`, because the first argument, `c`, is our `JSHandle`.

We could also have a function with no extra arguments. For instance, we could hardcode that 3 inside the function:

```
await counter.evaluate(c => c.count += 3);
```

You can also pass `JSHandle` objects as arguments to the `evaluate` function of the `page` class. So, this would be the equivalent of the previous example:

```
await page.evaluate(c => c.count += 3, counter);
```

This opens the door to many new things we can do with Puppeteer. Let's see some examples.

Getting information from the elements

Checking how the page reacts to an action is quite essential. For instance, if you add an item to the cart, you would like to check whether the number of items count was increased.

If we take a look at our `HomePageModel` class, this is how we solved the `getStock` function, which helped us check the stock prices:

```
async getStock(productName) {
    const productDiv = (await this.page.$x(`//a[text()="${productName}"]/../..`))[0];
    const stockElement = (await productDiv.$x('./h6'))[0];
    return await stockElement.evaluate(e => e.innerText);
}
```

We used that code to learn the XPath expression. In the first two lines, we were getting the product `div`, and from there, the `stock` element. After that, we used the `evaluate` function to get the text of that element.

I believe these kinds of functionalities should be part of the Puppeteer API. But in the meantime, you can start building your utility functions. We can start with a generic function to return the `innerText` value:

```
async getInnerText(el) {
    return await el.evaluate(el => el.innerText);
}
```

This function will expect an element as an argument and return the `innerText` property. The `innerText` property returns the text content of a DOM element, including all its descendants. But you could also create new utility functions for other common properties:

- `innerHtml` returns the HTML content inside an element.
- `outerHTML` returns the HTML content, including the HTML of the element itself.
- If you want to get the value of an input element, you will need to use `value` instead of `innerText`.

You can check the MDN site for a complete list of element properties (https://www.hardkoded.com/ui-testing-with-puppeteer/element). You will also find that some elements have specific properties. For instance, an input box has properties such as `disabled` or `checked` when the type is a checkbox.

If you don't want to mess with `ElementHandle`s, you can also use `page.$eval`. The signature of this function is `page.$eval(selector, pageFunction[, ...args])`. The page will get the `ElementHandle` using the selector, and then execute `evaluate`, passing the `pageFunction` and the `args`.

With this in mind, we can replace this line we can find in the `logState` function inside the `LoginPageModel.js` file:

```
return await this.page.evaluate(() => document.querySelector('#navbarTop .nav-link').innerText);
```

With this simpler line of code:

```
return await this.page.$eval('#navbarTop .nav-link', el => el.innerText);
```

This line of code is easier to read because you have the selector on one side and the function to execute on the other side. Notice that the `pageFunction` must always have the element as the first argument.

But using the `evaluate` function is not only about getting information. We can change the page behavior, acting on elements.

Acting on elements

You can use the `evaluate` function to get values from elements and act on those elements so that you can **force** specific scenarios.

This might sound hacky, but sometimes all the steps required to get to a particular scenario aren't worth the effort. It's like those cooking TV shows, where they are baking a cake, and suddenly, they come up with an already baked cake, and they show you how to add the cream.

These kinds of shortcuts not only save you time, but reduce potential flakiness that could come up during a long process, where you need to wait for many things to happen before you can act.

The first action we will learn about is forcing a `click` action. Wait, don't we have a `click` function in Puppeteer? We do have a `click` function. The good thing about the `click` function is that it emulates a user click. But to be a real emulation, the element being clicked needs to be visible and actionable (clickable). Sometimes we don't want to run the risk of getting a fail because the element was hidden. We can take a shortcut and force a click using the `click` function:

```
await el.evaluate(el => el.click());
```

Here, instead of calling `el.click()`, we call the `click` function inside the browser.

In the same way as with properties, this method is not only for the `click` function. You can use it to force the `blur` event or select a text in an input with the `setSelectionRange` function.

You can act on elements not only through functions. You can also set properties. For instance, you could disable the email input on the login page programmatically. Let's see that in action:

```
const emailInput = await page.$('#email');
await emailInput.evaluate(e => e.disabled = true);
```

Here, we get the element, and then we set the disabled property. With this recipe, you could also set the `innerText` of an element. For instance, you could change a product description with a very long text to see how the page reacts to long product titles.

Sometimes, being "hacky" is what we want to test. Is our site ready for clever users?

Enforcing server rules

With the rise of rich web applications, a new type of bad practice emerged: **writing business rules only on the client side**.

We need important business rules on the server first, and then on the client. Let's say that in our cart application, we need to validate that the user has been authorized to make purchases. We wrote that business rule, but the only thing we did was add an "`is-disabled`" CSS class in the checkout button. If I'm a clever user, I could open the developer tools, remove that class, and then click on the button. If we don't have the same rule on the server, the user might have easily bypassed our business rule.

We can write our own "should validate on the server" test. Let's grab the checkbox, remove the CSS class, and try to click on it:

```
const checkoutBtn = (await page.$x('//
button[contains(text(),"Checkout")]'))[0];
checkoutBtn.evaluate(el => el.classList.remove('is-disabled'));
await checkoutBtn.click();
```

Here, we are getting the checkout button, and then we remove the `is-disabled` CSS class programmatically. That would enable the button, so then we can click it. After that, we should do some validation to check that the business rule was enforced on the server side.

The `evaluate` function can also help us when we can't find elements using CSS selectors or XPath expressions.

Finding elements using JavaScript

We can find DOM elements using CSS selectors in over 90% of cases, even more if we use attribute selectors. XPath expressions help us cover another 9% of the cases. But there is that 1% where we need something more elaborated. For instance, there are properties that are not exposed in a way for a CSS selector to work. Let's take the case of input text.

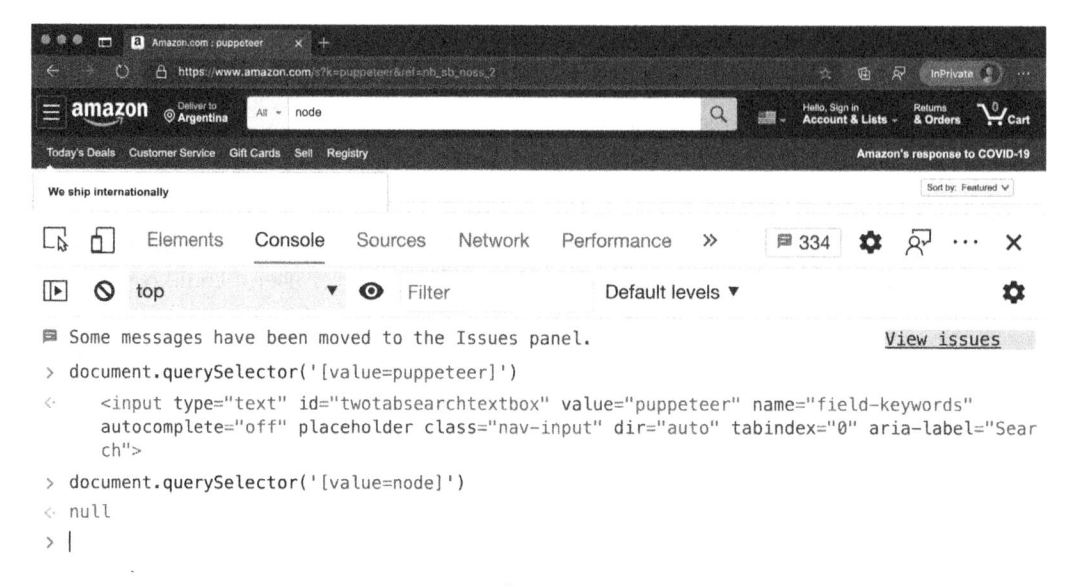

An input box in Amazon

If the input box is rendered with the word puppeteer (by rendered, I mean that it has the value in the HTML content), the attribute selector `[value=puppeteer]` will work. But if the value changes to, for example, *node*, the `[value=node]` selector won't work, and the first selector, `[value=puppeteer]`, would still return a DOM element.

Some properties are not exposed as HTML attributes, so we won't be able to use them on CSS selectors or XPath expressions. For instance, the IMG element has a property called `naturalWidth`. This property will return the original size of the image. With this property, we could write a test to check that all the images on our home page are being loaded. If the `naturalWidth` of an image is 0, it means that the image was not loaded. You can find this code in the test called `'Should load all images'` inside the `Chapter6/test/homepage.tests.js` file:

```
const images = await page.evaluateHandle(() =>
  Array.from(document.querySelectorAll('IMG')).filter(e =>
!e.naturalWidth));
(await images.evaluate(e => e.length)).should.equal(0);
```

In this test, we are getting all the IMG elements with `document.querySelectorAll('IMG')`. Then we need to wrap it inside an `Array.from`, so we can filter those elements. And then, we call the `filter` function, asking for elements with a `naturalWidth` value: `!e.naturalWidth`.

Here is something important for you to notice. The function we are executing using `evaluateHandle` returns a list of elements. But `evaluateHandle` will return one element handle. It will return a pointer to that array in the browser. So, if we need to get the `length` of that array, we need to call `evaluate` and request the `length` property.

Situations like these are when you need to find a balance. Sometimes it's simpler to have a big `evaluate` function but evaluate everything in one trip. In this case, this could have been solved in only one async call:

```
(await page.evaluateHandle(() =>
  Array.from(document.querySelectorAll('IMG')).filter(
    e => !e.naturalWidth).length)).should.equal(0);
```

Now we are doing everything in one hit. We query the images, we filter them, and check for the length.

We've learned how to execute JavaScript code and how to manipulate elements, but there is more. We can also use JavaScript code as wait functions.

Waiting for functions

We learned about many wait functions in *Chapter 5, Waiting for elements and network calls*. We learned to wait for network events, for DOM elements to be visible or hidden. We also covered many page events we can wait for. But in the same way that a CSS selector won't cover 100% of cases, and an XPath expression cannot cover all other scenarios, the same happens with wait functions.

There are some scenarios where we need something more. Now we have the `waitForFunction`.

This is the signature of the `waitForFunction` function: `page.waitForFunction(pageFunction, options, ...args)`.

The first argument is the `pageFunction`. It works in the same way as in the `evaluate` function. It can be a JavaScript function; it could also be a string; it can expect arguments, and so on.

The third argument, `args`, is the arguments that can be sent to the function. This is an optional list of values.

I didn't forget about the second argument. The second argument is the `options` argument. The `options` object has two settings:

- The first property is, you guessed it, `timeout`. It has the same defaults as we saw in the different wait functions in *Chapter 5, Waiting for elements and network calls*: defaults to 30 seconds, and then you change or overwrite the value with `page.setDefaultTimeout(timeout)`.

- The second property is the interesting one: the `polling` option. This option determines the frequency at which Puppeteer will execute our function. We have three possible options:

  a) The default option is `raf`. **Raf** is short for `requestAnimationFrame`. According to Mozilla, the *requestAnimationFrame method tells the browser that you wish to perform an animation and requests that the browser calls a specified function to update an animation before the next repaint. The method takes a callback as an argument to be invoked before the repaint* (https://www.hardkoded.com/ui-testing-with-puppeteer/raf). It is the most frequent polling you can use.

  b) The second option available is `mutation`. This option will use a `MutationObserver`. According to Mozilla, *The MutationObserver interface provides the ability to watch for changes being made to the DOM tree* (https://www.hardkoded.com/ui-testing-with-puppeteer/MutationObserver).

  c) The last option is a `number`. This number will be an interval in milliseconds at which the function will be executed.

When we talked about finding elements using JavaScript, we mentioned that there are many scenarios where CSS selectors or XPath expressions won't be enough. But I also think that sometimes an `evaluateHandle` or a `waitForFunction` call will be easier to read than a complex XPath expression.

Let's take, for instance, the Packt cart:

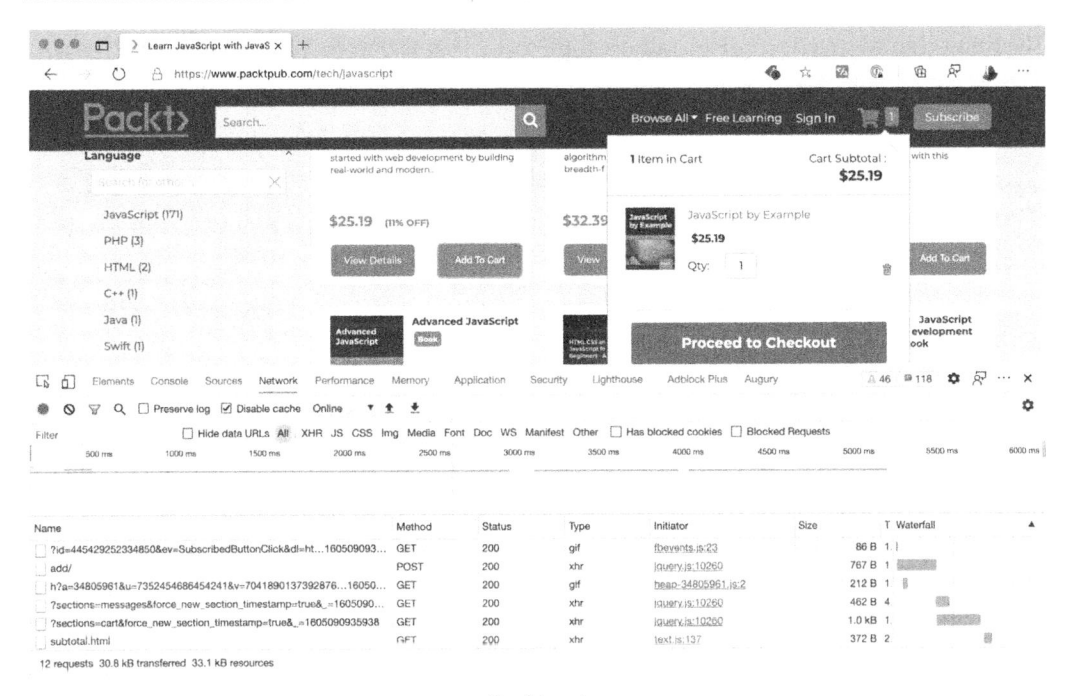

Packt cart

When we add a new book to the cart, the cart number is not updated immediately. If we look at the **Network** tab, there is a network call to an "**add**" endpoint, and after that, the cart is updated.

We can wait for that item number to be updated in many ways. We could wait for the items list to be updated using a CSS selector. We could also wait for a network response with the URL "**add**". But we could also do something as simple as wait for the number to change.

There is one more challenge there. When we add an item to the cart, we need to dismiss it. But the popup is moving. The good news is that **we can use a** `waitForFunction` **to wait for animations to finish**.

> **Important note**
> I thought this would be a simple example, and it turned out to be quite complicated. But I think it's great. You will find these kinds of issues in real life, and you need to resolve them.

I'm going to explain the test piece by piece. You will be able to see the entire test in the `packpub.tests.js` file.

The first thing we need to solve, and it's something that we, unfortunately, see a lot these days, is the cookies notification. Let's see how we can wait for a notification banner using Puppeteer:

```
await page.goto('https://www.packtpub.com/tech/javascript/');
const cookieLink = await page.waitForSelector('.accept_all', {
timeout : 1000}).catch(e => e);
```

```
if (cookieLink) {
    await cookieLink.click();
}
```

The first thing we do is go to the page we want to test. Then we might, or might not, get the cookies banner. The problem is that the cookies banner might take a little while to be shown. So, we wait for the `'.accept_all'` selector, which is the **Accept cookies** button. We give it a second, 1000 ms. If we don't get that button, that's why we swallow the exception using `.catch(e => e)`. If we finally get that cookie button, we click on it.

Once the cookies banner is dismissed, we need to wait for the page to be ready to act. We don't care which client library the page is using, but it seems that it takes a little bit to be ready to act. One of the things I found is that it will set the class `empty` to the cart button when the cart is ready. Another thing we know is that the **Add to cart** buttons have the `add-to-cart` class. We can add a `Promise.all` and wait for those two conditions:

```
await Promise.all([
    page.waitForSelector('.counter.qty.empty'),
    page.waitForSelector('.add-to-cart')
]);
```

This step was easy. We need to wait for the selectors, `.counter.qty.empty`, which is the empty cart button, and `.add-to-cart`, which is the **Add to cart** button.

Next up, we need to set up our wait promises:

```
const cartIsOnePromise = page.waitForFunction(() => document.querySelector('.counter.qty .counter-number').innerText.trim() === '1');
const cartIsTwoPromise = page.waitForFunction(() => document.querySelector('.counter.qty .counter-number').innerText.trim() === '2');
```

This looks complex, but it's not that complex. We are setting up two promises. The first promise will resolve when the text (using the `innerText` property) of the cart counter, which has the selector `.counter.qty .counter-number`, is equal to 1. We hope it will be resolved at one point in time after we click on the first product. There, I added a `trim` function, so we remove any extra spaces.

The second promise is the same as the first one. But it will resolve when the cart number is equal to 2.

Now that we have our wait promises, it's time to click on the first product:

```
const addToCartButtons = await page.$$('.add-to-cart');
await addToCartButtons[0].click();
```

Here, we are grabbing all the **Add to cart** buttons and clicking on the first one.

Now we get to the fun part. We need to wait for the checkout popup to show up and finish its fancy animation:

```
await page.waitForFunction(async () => {
    const element = document.querySelector('.block-minicart');
    let currentHeight = element.getBoundingClientRect().height;
    let stopMovingCounter = 0;
    await new Promise((resolve) => {
        const stoppedMoving = function() {
            if (element.getAttribute('style') !== 'display: block;') {
                setTimeout(stoppedMoving, 20);
            }
            if(element.getBoundingClientRect().height > 0 &&
currentHeight === element.getBoundingClientRect().height) {
                stopMovingCounter++;
            } else {
                stopMovingCounter = 0;
                currentHeight = element.getBoundingClientRect().height;
            }
            if(stopMovingCounter === 10) {
                resolve();
            }
            setTimeout(stoppedMoving, 20);
```

```
            };
        stoppedMoving();
    });

    return true;
});
```

Pretty scary, right? Let's analyze this function because it's a handy method.

Our `wait for` function needs to be resolved when the checkout popup is visible and has stopped moving. How do we know that it stopped moving? Well, we could check the element height every 20 milliseconds, and if the height is the same after 10 checks, we can assume it stopped moving.

The first thing we do is get the element, grabbing the initial height using `getBoundingClientRect`, and set a counter to 0.

Once we have that, we will `await` a `promise`, but it will be resolved inside the browser. Inside that `promise`, we will create a function called `stoppedMoving`, and we will call it.

The first thing we will check inside that function is whether the element is visible. If it's not, we will call the function again after 20 milliseconds.

Then we check the current height. If the height has changed, we reset the counter, and we start over. If it didn't change for the past 10 times, we resolve the promise by calling `resolve()`.

The last thing we do there is to call the same function after 20 milliseconds. Eventually, that function will be resolved, or it will fail due to the `waitForFunction` timeout.

The numbers here are relative. You don't need to wait 20 milliseconds or wait 10 times. You can pick the numbers that will suit you in your example.

Once we know that the popup is opened and is not moving, we can close it using the following code:

```
await page.click('#btn-minicart-close');
```

As simple as calling `click`, we are passing the close button selector.

Now we can wait for the cart number to be updated to 1:

```
await cartIsOnePromise;
```

Here, we are awaiting the promise we built before. The promise might have already been resolved by the time we get here; we don't care. If the promise is resolved, the `await` will resolve immediately. If not, we will wait.

Lastly, we click on a second product and await the second promise:

```
await addToCartButtons[1].click();
await cartIsTwoPromise;
```

Here, we grabbed the second product on the list, clicked on it, and waited for the cart number to change to 2. Again, we don't care if that promise was already resolved or not.

If all promises were resolved, there is nothing to assert. We know that everything worked as expected.

I bet you will need a break after this section. Once you are ready, we will see one more thing we can do with functions. We are going to make the browser call functions on the Node side.

Exposing local functions

With Puppeteer, you can not only execute code inside the browser but also make calls from the browser back to your Node app. The `exposeFunction` function allows us to register Node functions inside the browser.

This is the `exposeFunction` signature: `page.exposeFunction(name, puppeteerFunction)`:

- The first argument is `name`. This will be the function name inside the browser.
- `puppeteerFunction` is a function that follows the same style and functionality as all the functions we have learned about in this chapter.

This feature is perfect when it is called from a `MutationObserver`.

For instance, instead of executing a function over and over, waiting for the checkout counter to change, we could create a `MutationObserver` to let us know when the value has changed in the HTML Node. Let's see how the code would look:

```
let observer = new MutationObserver(list => console.
log(list[0].target.nodeValue));
observer.observe(
  document.querySelector('.counter.qty .counter-number'),
  {
    characterData: true,
    attributes: false,
    childList: false,
    subtree: true
  });
```

In this piece of code, we are declaring an observer, which expects a `callback` function. The first argument of that `callback` function will be a list of mutations. That mutation has the `target` object, and we can get the `nodeValue` from there. You can go to the Mozilla documentation (https://www.hardkoded.com/ui-testing-with-puppeteer/MutationRecord) if you want to know the full list of properties of the mutation records.

That observer won't do much. We need to tell it to observe changes in a particular element, in our case, an element with the selector `.counter.qty .counter-number`. So, we call `observe`, passing the `counter` element, and, as a second argument, we will tell the `observe` function what changes we want to listen to. In this case, we only care about `characterData` changes, and we also want to listen to changes in the `subtree` (child elements). That means text changes.

So now, we could make a copy of our previous test and replace `cartIsOnePromise` and `cartIsTwoPromise` with something like this:

```
const reachedToTwo = new Promise((resolve) => {
    page.exposeFunction('notifyCartChange', i => {
        if(i ==='2')
            resolve();
    })
});
await page.evaluate(() => {
    let observer = new MutationObserver(list =>
notifiyCartChange(list[0].target.nodeValue));
```

```
    observer.observe(
        document.querySelector('.counter.qty .counter-number'),
        {
            characterData: true,
            attributes: false,
            childList: false,
            subtree: true
        });
});
```

We create a promise, `reachedToTwo`. Inside the promise constructor, we will expose a function named `'notifyCartChange'`. The function we will expose there will expect one argument, and we will resolve the promise if the argument is equal to `'2'`.

That `exposeFunction` function will allow us to call a `notifiyCartChange` inside the `MutationObserver` we declared using an `evaluate` call.

For the last step, we replace our old awaits with the new promise:

```
 await reachedToTwo;
```

If everything goes as expected, `notifyCartChange` will be called twice, once with the value `'1'` and then with the value `'2'`, and the second call will resolve the `reachedToTwo` promise we added at the end of the test.

This might sound like silly, overcomplicated code, but picture all you could do with `exposeFunction` and `MutationObserver`. You could test chat apps by listening to incoming changes and many other complex scenarios.

Before wrapping up this chapter, it is time to add another tool to our toolbox.

Running our checks with Checkly

This is an extra tool that I want to show you, and you shouldn't miss the chance of trying it out. *Checkly* (`https://www.checklyhq.com/`) is a platform that will help you monitor your website. The following screenshot shows the *Checkly* website:

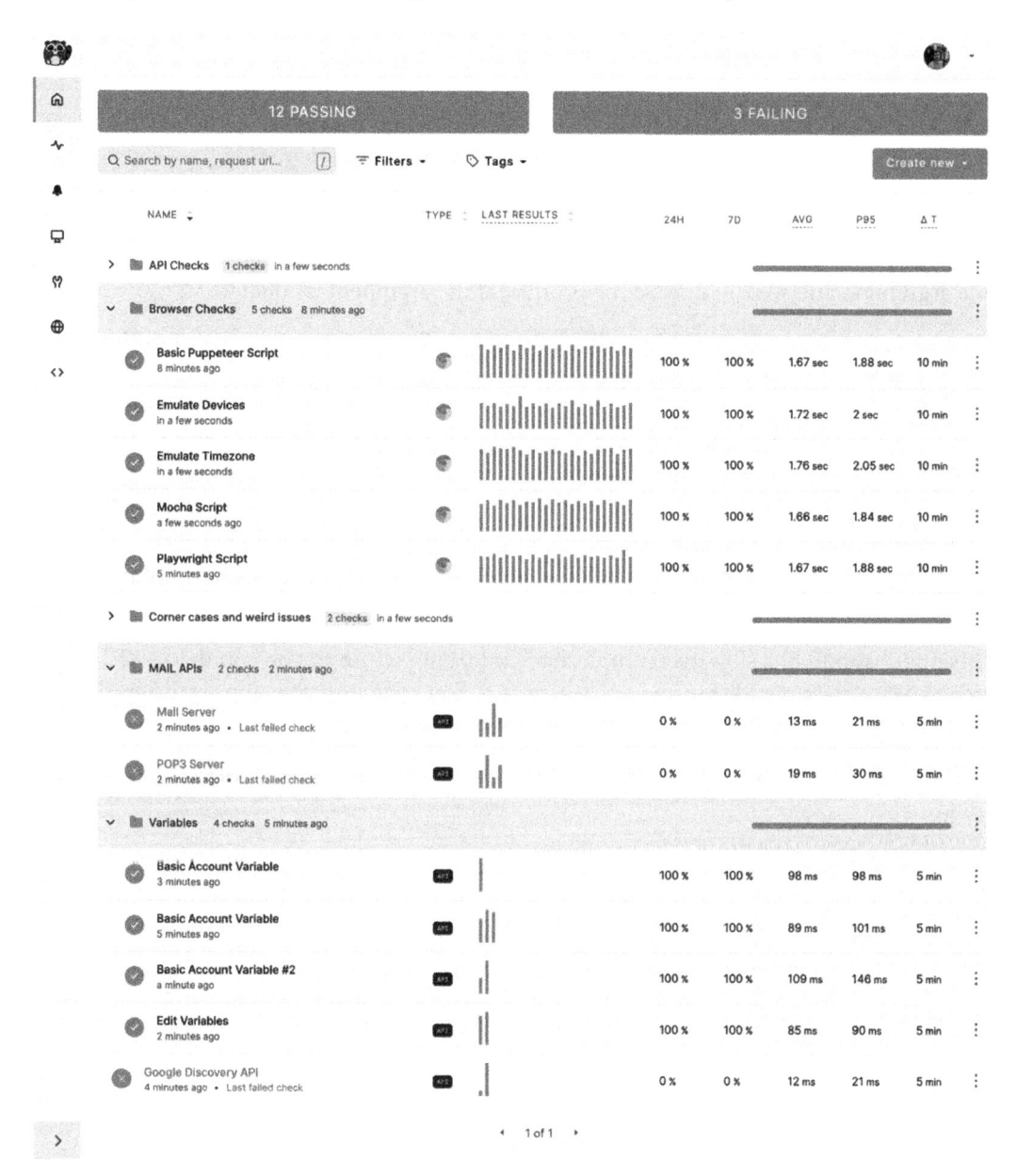

Checkly website

Once you create an account in *Checkly*, you will be able to upload your tests (or checks), and *Checkly* will run those checks every certain number of minutes, reporting back. Firstly, it will report whether the check is passing, and secondly, it will report the time it took to run.

You will also be able to test your website's API without running a browser. This is huge. It's like having your own, personal quality guard.

Let's go to `https://www.checklyhq.com/` and start our trial. Follow these steps to start using *Checkly*:

1. Once you enter your email, phone number, and account name, you will get the first dashboard with a few examples, as shown here:

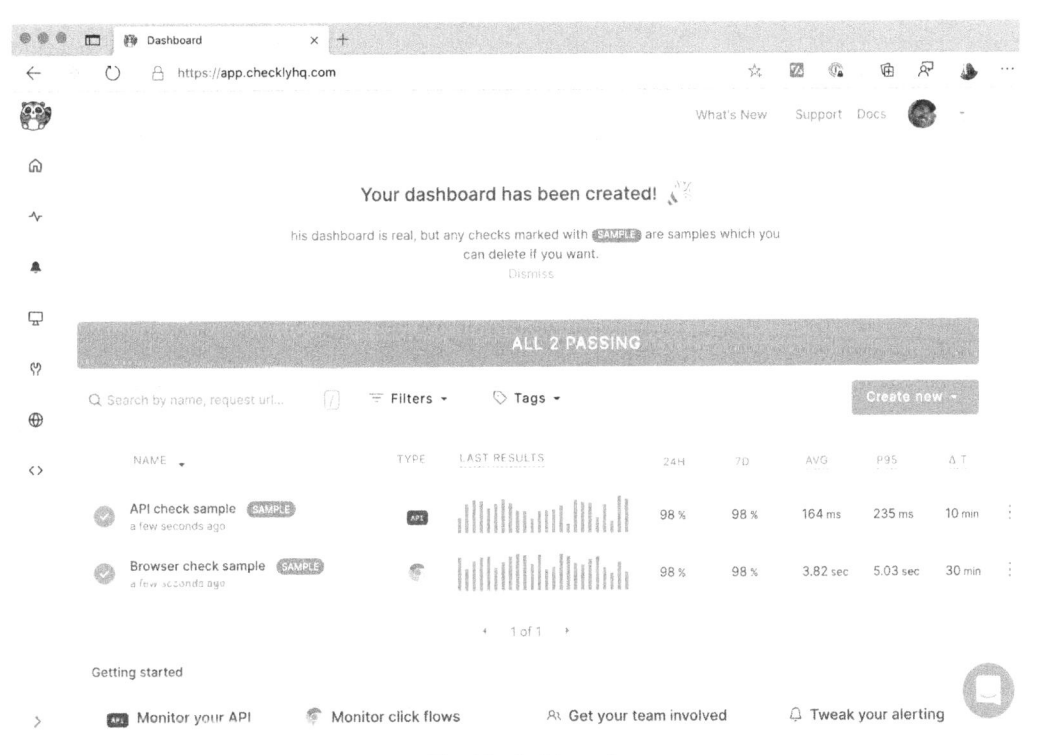

Checkly dashboard

2. You can now delete those two examples and create your own cart test. We can create a browser test:

...hmm, seems empty here.

Add your first check, this will be your dashboard.

API check
Check the speed and validity of API endpoints.

Browser check
Check your crucial browser click flows.

New test dialog

3. Now, name your check `Cart number check`. You can copy the code from the `Chapter6/checkly.js` file:

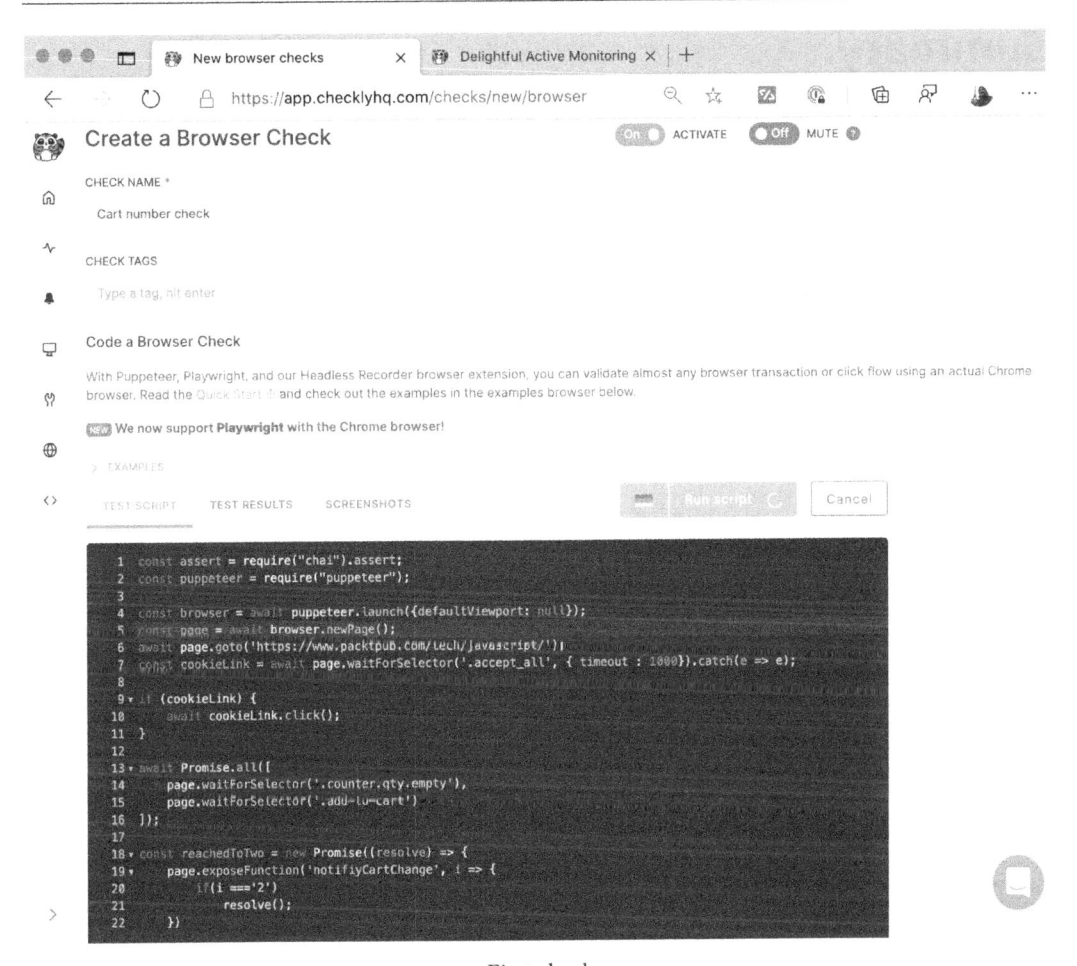

First check

Notice that we have left the browser and the page creation there. Once we have copied the code, we can click on the **Run Script** button to check that the code is correct. Finally, we will need to pick our data center locations, hit **Save Check**, and we will have a platform checking our website's health automatically.

If your team can afford it, *Checkly* will take you to the next level. Now it's time to wrap up.

Summary

We covered one of the most powerful features of Puppeteer in this chapter. Most web automation tools let you run JavaScript code somehow, but Puppeteer makes it super easy to implement.

We started this chapter by talking about some basic JavaScript concepts. We learned about variable scopes and closures. That helped us understand how variables and closures work (or don't work) in Puppeteer. If you learned those differences, you will be able to answer 20% of the Puppeteer questions on Stack Overflow.

Then, we learned about `JSHandles` and `ElementHandles`. You don't see these classes being used a lot by the community, but they are very helpful if you know how to use them, and now you know.

The `waitForFunction` completed our "wait" toolbox. You will use that wait function a lot. We also learned how to expose functions and listen to HTML changes using `MutationObserver`. Exposing functions and listening to HTML changes is not used much in UI testing, but it is an excellent tool for web scraping, a great topic we will cover in *Chapter 9, Scraping tools*.

With this chapter, we have completed the basics of Puppeteer. You now have most of the tools you need to start doing end-to-end testing.

I hope you are as excited with *Checkly* as I was when I saw this platform for the very first time. *Checkly* is a dashboard that will help not only the QA team but also the development team. It will help your team find issues and even find new opportunities to improve your site's performance.

In the next chapter, we will see some features you wouldn't expect from an automation tool. We are going to see how to generate content using Puppeteer.

7
Generating Content with Puppeteer

When I launched Puppeteer-Sharp (https://github.com/hardkoded/puppeteer-sharp) back in 2019, I was surprised to see that the two main use-case scenarios were content generation and web scraping.

Things are not too different in the Node.js world. Lots of developers use Puppeteer in Node.js for content generation and web scraping as well.

If you are a QA analyst, you will learn how to use screenshots to create regression tests. But, please, don't stop there; the other sections will give you a complete picture of everything you can do with Puppeteer on this topic. If you are not much into web development, share this chapter with your development team. No, don't share it – ask them to buy the book. That will be better.

Web developers will love this chapter. We will see how to use Puppeteer as a content generator tool for your website.

We will cover the following topics in this chapter:

- Taking screenshots
- Using screenshots for regression tests

- Generating PDF files
- Creating HTML content

By the end of this chapter, you will have gotten to a new level. You will have learned how to use Puppeteer as a testing tool and as a content generator.

Let's get started.

Technical requirements

You will find all the code of this chapter in the GitHub repository (`https://github.com/PacktPublishing/UI-Testing-with-Puppeteer`) under the `Chapter7` directory. Remember to run `npm install` on that directory and then go to the `Chapter7/vuejs-firebase-shopping-cart` directory and run `npm install` again.

Taking screenshots

Taking screenshots is the first feature I mention when I give talks about Puppeteer or Puppeteer-Sharp. Don't ask me why, maybe because I find it fun to use, or perhaps because it's hard to explain why we would need to take screenshots.

As a web developer, there are many things you can accomplish using screenshots. The first popular use-case you'll find is to improve your **Open Graph** information.

According to their website (`https://ogp.me/`), *"The Open Graph protocol enables any web page to become a rich object in a social graph. For instance, this is used on Facebook to allow any web page to have the same functionality as any other object on Facebook."*

Open Graph is what will make social media posts (on Twitter or Facebook) look pretty when people share the URL of your site. We are not going to talk about product positioning on social media in this book. But what you need to know is that if you are working on a public site with users wanting to share your content on social media, someone will ask you to improve the open graph information:

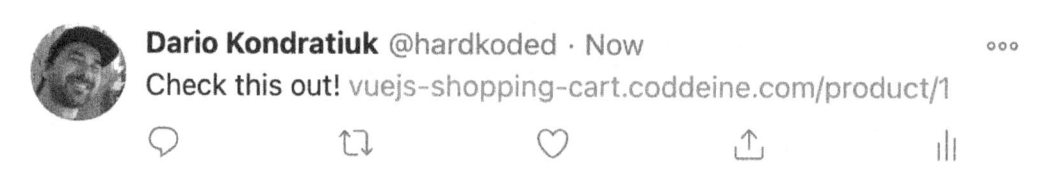

A post with no Open Graph information

You don't want your site to look like the preceding screenshot when you share your products on social media. You want your links to be like Amazon, with a nice description and a big image, as shown in the following screenshot:

Amazon posts on social media

Adding an image to your posts is as easy as adding a meta property called `og:image` in the html head of your product page:

```
<head>
<title>The Rock (1996)</title>
<meta property="og:title" content="The Rock" />
<meta property="og:type" content="video.movie" />
<meta property="og:url" content="https://www.imdb.com/title/tt0117500/" />
<meta property="og:image" content="https://ia.media-imdb.com/images/rock.jpg" />
</head>
```

Those few lines will make your post look prettier on social media.

What does this have to do with taking screenshots? Well, sometimes getting the image for a post is simple. In a shopping cart, the image would be the product image – a piece of cake. But sometimes, getting the image for a URL is not that easy. Let's take, for instance, this post from the great HolyJS conference:

HolyJS post

If you go to that post (`https://www.hardkoded.com/ui-testing-with-puppeteer/holyjs-post`), you won't find the image used in that tweet. You will see Roman's photo, but you won't find the image with the photo, the conference logo, or the talk title. They might have created that image manually. You don't need great Photoshop skills to do that. But if you created hundreds of tweets for all the talks at the HolyJS conference, I bet it would be more productive to code a Puppeteer script in a few minutes.

We could have an internal page that we would navigate by passing a talk ID. Once loaded, we take a screenshot, and we save that image in some kind of storage.

But before getting into Puppeteer's code, let me show you a new tool. Do you know that you can take full-page screenshots using Chromium?

If you open up the Developer Tools in *Chrome* and then press *Cmd + Shift + P* in macOS or *Ctrl + Shift + P*, a **command menu list** will pop up, just like in VS Code:

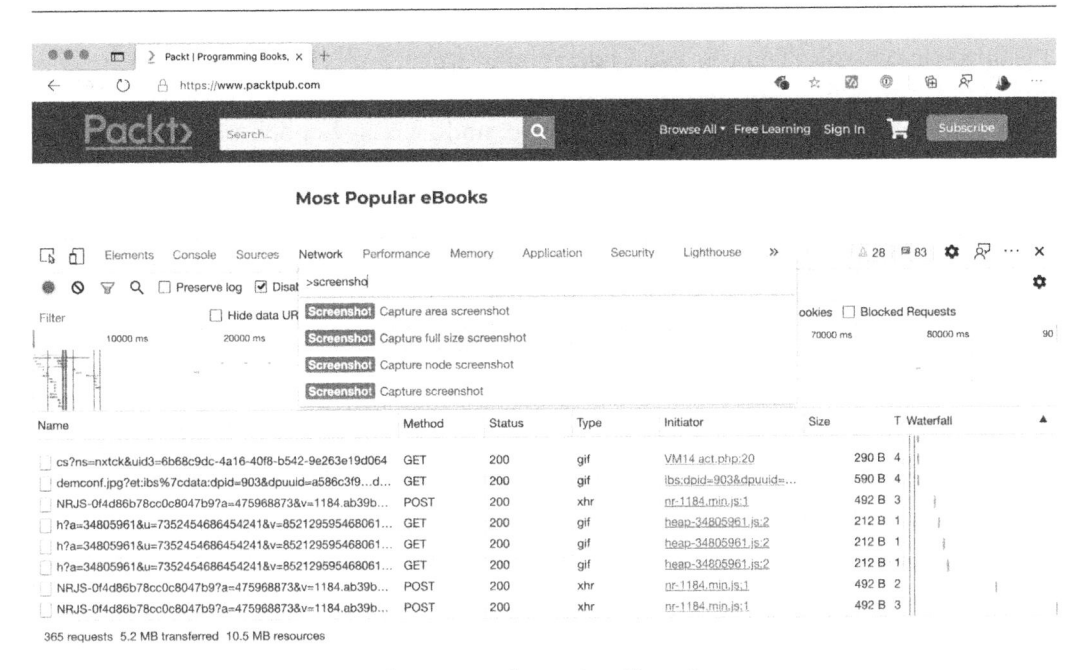

Taking screenshots using Chromium

You will find tons of commands there. Do you want to have some fun? Open the 3D Viewer. I'll give you 3 minutes.

OK, back to work. If you type `screenshot` in the **command menu list**, you will get four options.

The first option is **Capture area screenshot**. This option works like the take screenshot area you have in macOS by pressing *Cmd + Shift + 4* or the **Rectangular snip** in Windows's snipping tool. When you select that option, the cursor turns into a cross. You select the area you want to take a screenshot of, then you release the mouse and get an image download.

The second option is **Capture a full size screenshot**. This feature is so cool that I would put this option in a huge font size, in bold, red, and italics, but I don't think my editor would let me. **Capture a full size screenshot** will take a screenshot of the entire page, even the parts off the screen. I remember other tools trying to accomplish this by taking several screenshots while scrolling the page, and the results were terrible. To be honest, I have heard of people having issues with this option, but generally speaking, the results are pretty good. You can use this tool for marketing purposes or for reporting bugs so that you can show the entire page.

The third option is also fantastic. Now I don't know which one is my favorite. **Capture node screenshot** works with the **Elements** tab. You go to the **Elements** tab, select an element by clicking on it, then select the **Capture node screenshot** option, and you will get a screenshot of that element. This is way better than trying to select a section of the page with the capture area option.

The last option is just **Capture screenshot**. It will capture the visible part of the page. Yes, I know, it sounds boring compared with the others, but it's still useful.

I don't think I need to tell you the good news because you already know. We can do all these things with Puppeteer using the `screenshot` function.

Both the `Page` class and the `ElementHandle` class have this function. If you call the `screenshot` function on an `ElementHandle`, you will use the **Capture node screenshot** option in Chrome.

The function's signature is quite simple, just `screenshot([options])`, which means that just calling `screenshot()` would be enough. But the `options` object has many interesting properties. Let's take a look at them:

- `path` is one of the most common properties you will use. If you pass a path, your screenshot will be saved there. Whether you pass the path or not, the resulting image will be returned by the `screenshot` function.
- With the `type` option, you can determine whether you want a **jpeg** or a **png** image. If you don't pass a `type`, Puppeteer will infer the type from the `path`. If you pass neither the `type` nor the `path`, it will default to **png**.
- If you set the type (whether using the `type` option or the `path` options) to **jpeg**, you can also pass a `quality` option. It has to be a value from 0 to 100. It will determine the quality of the **jpeg** image.
- Then we have `fullPage`. This option is a boolean option that will help us perform the **Capture a full size screenshot** action.
- The `clip` property is an object that will help us perform the **Capture area screenshot** action. It represents a square, an area, using four properties: `x` for the x-coordinate, `y` for the y-coordinate, and then `width` and `height` to determine the area's size.
- With the `omitBackground` property, you will be able to change the page's default (white) background to transparent.

> **Important Note**
> `omitBackground` changes the default background of the page. If the page has a custom background, even a white background using `background-color: white`, or an image, this option won't work.

- The last property available is `encoding`, which will determine the return type of the `screenshot` function. If you pass `base64`, it will return a base64 string. If you pass `binary` or don't set any value, it will return a Node.js `Buffer` object.

Time to see some code. Let's create a script and try to replicate the four options that Chrome offers. You will also be able to see this code in the `screenshots.js` file:

```
const browser = await puppeteer.launch({headless: false,
defaultViewport: null});
const page = await browser.newPage();
await page.goto('https://www.packtpub.com/');

await page.screenshot({ path: 'normal-only-viewport.png'});
await page.screenshot({ path: 'full-page.png', fullPage:
true});
await page.screenshot({
    path: 'clip.png',
    clip: {
        x: 300,
        y: 150,
        width: 286,
        height: 64
    }
});
const firstBook = await page.$('.tombstone');
await firstBook.screenshot({ path: 'first-book.png'});
```

We can see the four actions expressed in the code. If we pass only the `path`, we **Capture screenshot**. Then, if we set `fullPage` to true, we will get **Capture full size screenshot**. If, instead of passing `fullPage`, we pass a `clip`, we'll get **Capture area screenshot**. Finally, based on the `ElementHandle` we get from `page.$('.tombstone')`, we get **Capture node screenshot**.

> **Tip**
> Finding the right `clip` will be quite tricky. Pages change their layout based on the window size, which might break the fixed position you are trying to use. I would recommend trying to capture node screenshots instead of using a `clip`. If there is no element you can use, I would try to build the `clip` based on other elements' positions.

I bet web developers will find more use cases for the screenshot feature. But if you are a QA analyst, we will now learn how to use screenshots to perform UI regression tests.

Using screenshots for regression tests

We briefly talked about UI regression tests in *Chapter 2, Automated Testing and Test runners*. Now it's time to get practical. First, let's recap the concept of **regression**. Regression is something you hear a lot when you see bug reports. If a user says something like "I found a regression in X feature," they mean that something that was working before in a certain way has now changed. It might be a bug, an error in the app, or an unreported change of behavior.

We can say that a UI regression is when we detect that a page or component has changed visually. I want to be emphatic again. It might have changed due to a bug or an unreported change of style.

To prove a regression, you need evidence. Until now, we were testing behavior, and our evidence was the code: "If I input the user, the password, and then I click on the login button, I should get logged in."

To prove a UI regression, our evidence will be **screenshots**. A UI regression test would consist of the following steps:

1. The first thing we need to do is take a screenshot of the current state.
2. The first time we run a test, we have nothing to compare our screenshot to. We have no history, no evidence. We have nothing to test. But now, we have the evidence for the next run.
3. If we have evidence, we will compare our current screenshot with the baseline, and we will fail if the images are different.

That's it. Simple. But what happens when we have a difference? When we get a test fail in end-to-end tests, we would first see if it's an error in our test. If our tests are working as expected, that failure will end up in a bug report.

But with UI regression tests, that's a little bit different. We would need to evaluate the results to check if we found an error or if **the baseline has changed**. We get UI changes in pages all the time, so we need to see if they are desired changes or not. If a change was desired, we would need to delete our baseline and create a new baseline image.

That's our cake. Now, what tools do we need to bake that cake? And also, what are our requirements for those tools? We need four elements:

- A **test runner**. We already talked about what we need from a test runner, and we saw that Mocha and Jest meet our expectations.
- A **screenshot taker**. The screenshot taker needs to be stable. By stable, I mean that it needs to return the same screenshot under the same circumstances all the time. It sounds obvious, but UI regression tests are the king of flaky tests. We need a tool that provides the same screenshots consistently. Puppeteer is great for this.
- A **place to store baselines**. We are not talking about a tool here. But we need files to be organized so that it's easy to find and remove baselines and find the resulting comparisons.
- A **tool to compare images**. This tool is as important as the screenshot taker. We don't want false alarms. We don't need a tool that tells us that everything is wrong just because one pixel is not the exact same white as the baseline. This tool should allow us to pass some kind of threshold to determine how sensitive we want it to be to changes. It should also need to support anti-aliased pixels to reduce the difference in the image rendering. *Pixelmatch* (https://www.hardkoded.com/ui-testing-with-puppeteer/pixelmatch) is the most popular image comparison package for Node.js.

As you can see, it shouldn't be that hard implementing that. But many tools on the market solve all that boilerplate for us. Again, it's not about me telling you what's the best tool. You have to look for the right tool for you. I found that *Project Awesome* (http://www.hardkoded.com/ui-testing-with-puppeteer/awesome-regression-testing) has a huge list of regression testing tools. On that site, I found *differencify* (https://www.hardkoded.com/ui-testing-with-puppeteer/differencify). I like it because it's simple and covers all the requirements mentioned in the preceding list. I don't like much that it's a layer between Puppeteer and us, but it does the job; I can live with that.

We can create a test called "Should visually match", and use differencify there. You can find this test in the homepage.tests.js file. Let's see how to implement it:

```
it ('Should visually match', async() => {
  const target = differencify.init({
    chain: false,
    testName: 'Home' });
  await target.launch();
  const page = await target.newPage();
  await page.setViewport({ width: 1600, height: 1200 });
  await page.goto(config.baseURL);
  const image = await page.screenshot();
  const result = await target.toMatchSnapshot(image);
  await page.close();
  await target.close();

  expect(result).to.be.true;
});
```

It looks pretty much like a normal Puppeteer test. But there are some differences. Let's take a look at them:

It begins by declaring a variable named `target` and assigning to it the result of `differencify.init`. We won't get into the internals of *differencify*, because we don't care about the internals. The only thing important in that `init` call is that we are setting the test name there, which, as we will see later, will be used to name the images.

After that, it looks like pure Puppeteer code, except that we call `target.launch();` instead of `puppeteer.launch();`.

One important thing we need to do when taking screenshots is setting the **viewport**. The viewport will determine the size of the screenshot we will use. Even if you take a full-page screenshot, the viewport will determine that image's width.

Unless you want to check a page's style after specific actions, UI regression tests will just go to a page, wait for the page to be loaded and stable, and take a screenshot. By stable, I mean that you don't want to take a screenshot with half of the resources, for example, images still loading.

Once the page is loaded, we take a screenshot using `page.screenshot()` and then call `await target.toMatchSnapshot(image)`. This function will be responsible for creating a baseline image if it doesn't exist, and if it exists, make the image comparison.

When we run the test for the very first time, the test will pass because, again, there is no baseline. One important thing we will notice is that *differencify* created the baseline inside a `differencify_reports` directory. You can see the complete directory structure inside the `Chapter7/differencify_reports` directory.

Now we have our baseline. Hopefully, this test will be green unless something changes on that page. Let's try to break it. We will open the `vuejs-firebase-shopping-cart/src/components/Header.vue` file and change the `color` `.navbar-btn` elements to blue:

```
.navbar-btn {
  color: blue;
}
```

This is a typical scenario of a UI regression test. Maybe you wanted to change the color of a button on the login page, and you didn't realize that the `navbar-btn` class was also being used on the home page.

If we run the test, we will get the following output, telling us that the test has failed:

```
1) Home Page
    Should visually match:

    AssertionError: expected false to be true
    + expected - actual

    -false
    +true
```

That doesn't say much. It just simply says that the image is not the same. But if we go to the `differencify_reports` directory, we will see that *differencify* created two new files: `Home 1.current.png` under `differencify_reports/__image_snapshots__/__current_output__`, which shows the latest screenshot. The second image is `Home 1.differencified.png` under `differencify_reports/__image_snapshots__/__differencified_output__`. You can see the differencified image inside the directory mentioned above or following the link https://www.hardkoded.com/ui-testing-with-puppeteer/differencified will show us where the changes were detected. In this case, you will see that it highlighted the word "**Checkout**". We can now compare the baseline image with the one created in the `__current_output__` directory and evaluate what went wrong.

To wrap up this section, UI regression tests are not for every project. If you use CSS frameworks like **bootstrap** or **tailwindcss** the chances of UI regressions are low. There are also projects where the page style is not considered a bug. Stakeholders won't care if a box is a few pixels below.

I do think it's an excellent tool for frontend developers working on custom CSS. With UI regression tests, a frontend developer can measure the impact of their changes. It's like unit tests for CSS.

In the next chapter, we are going to talk about device emulation. With device emulation plus UI regression tests, you will be able to check how your site looks on mobile devices.

Now it's time to learn another way to generate content with Puppeteer. Time to generate PDF files.

Generate PDF files

We are out of QA land, and we'll go into the development world again.

When I talk about PDF generation, I get the same question I mentioned in the screenshot section: "Why would I need to generate PDFs using Puppeteer?"

The first scenario to mention is using PDFs as an output format for your website. I don't know if you've lived what I lived once. I had to build an e-commerce app. I built the product list, the checkout process, and even the receipt page. Then the requirement came out: "We need to send an email with that receipt as a PDF." That's an estimation breaker. There is no easy way to create PDF files just from scratch.

Then you find a library that generates PDFs, and you are happy with it. But the stakeholders tell you that it needs to look exactly like the receipt page. Your estimation goes to the trash again. There should be an easy way to generate PDF files.

Maybe it's not a receipt. Haven't you ever got a request to send a daily report by email as a PDF? You would end up using some huge, complex, and expensive reporting tool, just for that daily email.

The second scenario is PDF files as a product by themselves. Do you sell documents? Finance reports? You can autogenerate that content using PDF generation tools.

I bet you already know that you can save any page as a PDF file using Chrome's print tool:

Generate PDF files   183

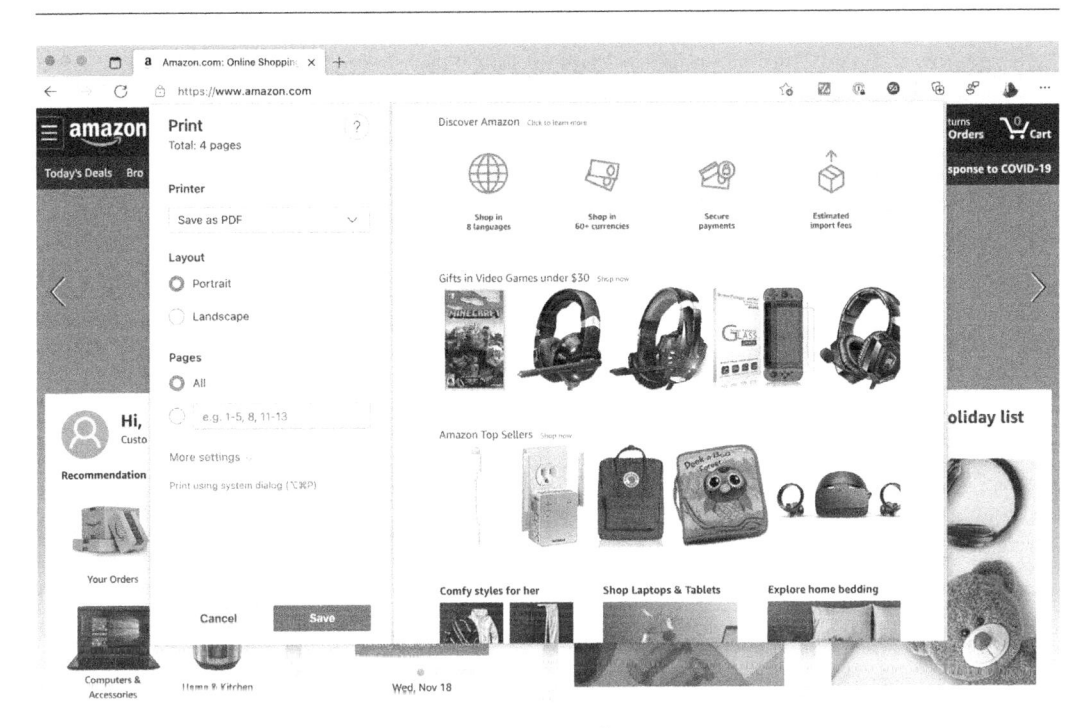

Save as PDF in Chrome

You can go to any page, hit *Cmd + P* or *Ctrl + P*, and instead of selecting a real printer, you choose **Save as PDF**. Then you click **Save**, and you get your PDF.

I think I don't need to tell you this, but as you might have guessed, Puppeteer uses this same utility to generate PDF files.

There is something essential you need to know. If you know this, you will be able to answer lots of questions in Stack Overflow. Here goes: **PDF generation doesn't work as a screenshot but as a print action**.

It might sound obvious, now that we've seen that **Print** dialog. But it's important for you to know that the viewport (the window size) won't determine how the PDF will be generated. The page size will determine that.

Designers and frontend developers can determine how a page should be printed using the media query print (https://www.hardkoded.com/ui-testing-with-puppeteer/mediaqueries).

Let's see how you can change a page style using `@media print`:

```html
<html>
    <head>
        <style>
            body {
                color: blue;
                font-size: 16px;
            }
            @media print {
                body{
                    color: black;
                    font-size: 32px;
                }
            }
        </style>
    </head>
    <body>
        Hello world;
    </body>
</html>
```

As we can see, if you browse this HTML content (you will find this code as `mediaprint.html` in the repository), you will find that "`Hello world`" is rendered in blue with a size of 16px. But if you hit `print`, the browser will add all the CSS style from the `@media print` section, changing the font size to 32px and the color to black. In the next section, we will learn how to add print styles if the page has none. For now, what you need to know is that we are printing content.

If the `@media print` style used in the page doesn't work for you, there is a way to bypass this functionality. You can force the media type `screen` using the following code:

```
page.emulateMediaType('screen')
```

If you call `emulateMediaType` before generating the PDF, `@media print` will be ignored by the browser.

I don't think I need to tell you that the function we will use to generate PDF files is called `page.pdf`. Unlike `screenshot`, there is no `elementHandle.pdf` because you can't print just an element.

The signature is simple, just `page.pdf([options])`, but we have many available options. Let's begin with the options that map the settings you would find in the print dialog.

The first option you will see in the print dialog after selecting **Save as PDF**, is the **Layout**. The option to set the layout is `landscape`. It's a boolean that will tell the browser if you want to generate the PDF with a landscape orientation or not.

The next option is **Pages**. In Puppeteer, the property is `pageRanges`. It's a string where you can pass things like `'1-5, 8, 11-13'`. If you don't set this property, it will work as if you had set **Pages** to **All** in the print dialog.

If you click **More settings** in the print dialog, the next option available will be **Paper size**. In Puppeteer, it will be `format`, which is a string that accepts the following options:

- `Letter`: 8.5 in x 11 in
- `Legal`: 8.5 in x 14 in
- `Tabloid`: 11 in x 17 in
- `Ledger`: 17 in x 11 in
- `A0`: 33.1 in x 46.8 in
- `A1`: 23.4 in x 33.1 in
- `A2`: 16.54 in x 23.4 in
- `A3`: 11.7 in x 16.54 in
- `A4`: 8.27 in x 11.7 in
- `A5`: 5.83 in x 8.27 in
- `A6`: 4.13 in x 5.83 in

Puppeteer also offers two extra options: `width` and `height`. If none of those formats suit you, you can set custom dimensions with these two properties. These properties accept a number or a string. If you use strings, you can pass values in units, such as **px** for pixels, **in** for inches, **cm** for centimeters, or **mm** for millimeters.

Next up is **Scale**. The property is `scale`, and it's the zoom that will be used to print the page. You will see it in the print dialog as a percentage from 10% to 200%. Here, it will be a decimal value from 0.1 to 2.

After **Scale**, you will find **Pages per sheet**. We don't have that setting in Puppeteer.

The next option in the **Print** dialog is **Margins**. The **Print** dialog offers a few fixed options. In Puppeteer, the `margin` option is an object with four properties:

- `top`
- `right`
- `bottom`
- `left`

All these properties accept a number or a string, supporting units as `width` and `height` do.

After the margins, the print dialog offers an extra set of options. The first one is Headers and footers. This is a really fun feature in Puppeteer. Puppeteer not only provides a `displayHeaderFooter` boolean property, but it also provides a `headerTemplate` property and a `footerTemplate` property. That means that you can set what you want the header and the footer to look like. Puppeteer will even populate elements with the following classes:

- `date`: Formatted print date
- `title`: Document title
- `url`: Document location
- `pageNumber`: Current page number
- `totalPages`: Total pages in the document

The next option is **Background graphics**. You can turn this option on with the `printBackground` property. It will tell the browser that you want to print background graphics. This is `false` by default because this option is intended for printers, and you don't want to waste your toner on a background. But you should consider whether this is something you need to turn on. Let's consider Wikipedia:

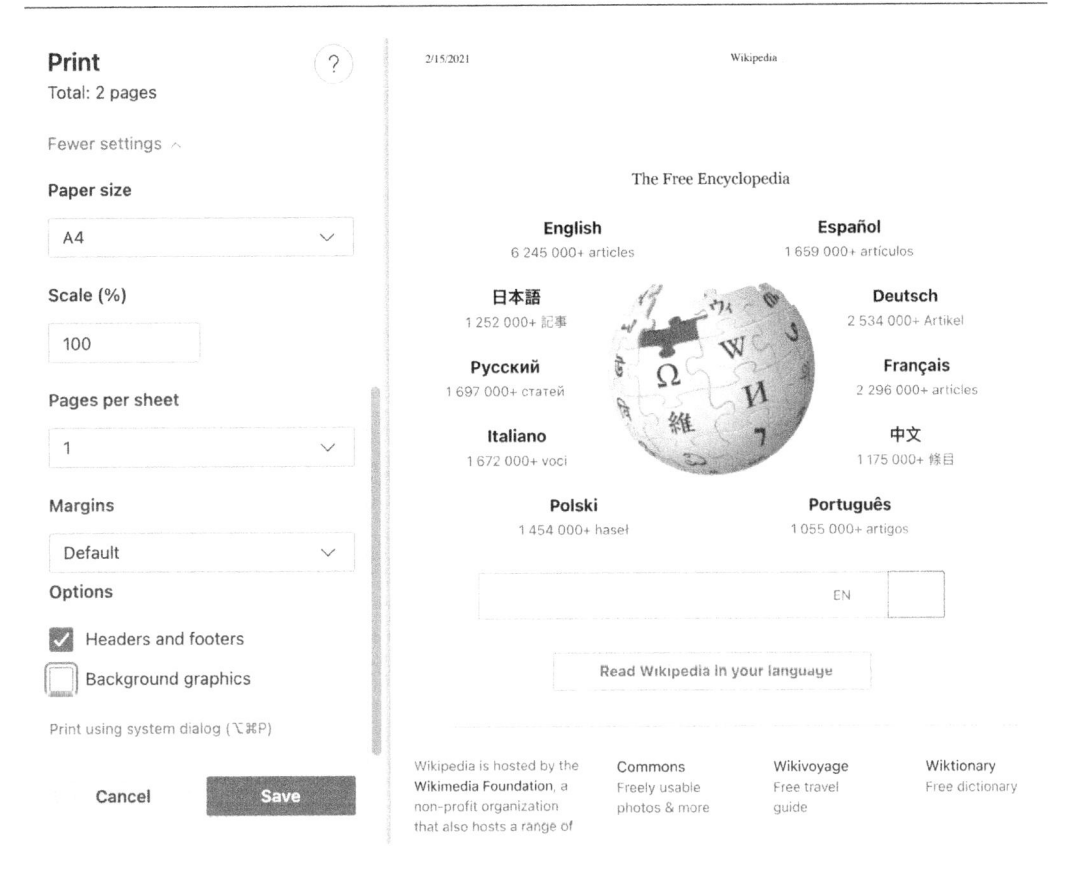

Wikipedia without the background graphics checked

As you can see, the Wikipedia title is missing if you don't check the **Background graphics** checkbox because it's the background image of a SPAN element. If you don't know about this flag, you might be scratching your head for several minutes, trying to see what's wrong with your code. Now you know that you have to consider printBackground.

There is one option that you won't see in the print dialog, and it's preferCSSPageSize. This property, whose default is false, will tell the browser to honor the @page size declared on the page over width/height or page format. Developers can use @page size (https://www.hardkoded.com/ui-testing-with-puppeteer/pagesize) to set the preferred page size when the page is printed.

The last option is the most important. The function's output works in the same way as in the screenshot function. If you set the path property, a file will be generated in that path. Either way, the function's return value will be a Buffer (https://nodejs.org/api/buffer.html) with the binary representation of the PDF file.

Time to take a look at some code. In the following code, which you can see in the `pdfdemo.js` file, we are going to print www.wikipedia.org using the options we have learned:

```
const browser = await puppeteer.launch({
    headless: true,
    defaultViewport: null});
const page = await browser.newPage();
await page.goto('https://www.wikipedia.org/');
await page.pdf({
    path: './headers.pdf',
    printBackground : true,
    displayHeaderFooter : true,
    headerTemplate: `
        <span style="font-size: 12px;">
            This is a custom PDF for
            <span class="title"></span> (<span class="url"></span>)
        </span>`,
    footerTemplate: `
        <span style="font-size: 12px;">
            Generated on: <span class="date"></span><br/>
            Pages <span class="pageNumber"></span> of <span class="totalPages"></span>
        </span>`,
    margin:{
        top:'100px',
        bottom: '100px'
    }
});
await browser.close();
```

The first thing to notice in this piece of code is that the `pdf` function only works in headless mode. If you call `pdf` while in headful, you will get an **Error: Protocol error (Page.printToPDF): PrintToPDF is not implemented**.

The second thing to notice is that you need to set up a margin if you want to use footer and header templates. In my personal experience, I wouldn't use very complex templates here. Things can get nasty and hard to debug.

The last thing to mention in the code is the CSS classes used in the template. As you can see, I'm leaving empty SPANs like `<span class="title"></span>` so the browser can replace them with real data.

This code will generate the following `headers.pdf` file:

PDF output

As you can see, we now have a custom header with a title and URL, a custom footer with the date and the pages, and, as we set `printBackground`, we are getting the Wikipedia logo.

You might think that's it, but it's not. We have one more way to generate content. We will build our own pages on the fly.

Creating HTML content

In this section, we will see a few simple features but pretty useful ones. You will be able to follow the code from this section in the `demohtml.js` file. Most of the time, you navigate pages using the HTTP protocol as we did with Wikipedia. If you open the `mediaprint.html` file, you navigated to that page using the pseudo protocol "file." Although it's not a real protocol, you should know that with Puppeteer, you can also navigate local files using a URL such as `file:///some/folder/of/my/computer/mediaprint.html`.

So, if you want to generate a social image, like the HolyJS conference one we saw in the first section, you could create a page on your website, navigate to that page using Puppeteer, take a screenshot, and use that image in your social post.

You could also have that file stored locally and navigate that file using the `file://` protocol.

What I want to show you in this section is that you don't necessarily need to have a file in your file system to generate that social image. You could have the HTML that you need in some external source, for instance, a content database, load that HTML in an empty page, and then take a screenshot.

We can do that using the `setContent` function. The signature is quite simple: `page.setContent(html[, options])`, where `html` is the HTML to load, and the `options` object, which supports two options you might already know: `timeout` and `waitUntil`. We need a `timeout` and a `waitUntil` property because the HTML we are loading might involve network requests, and we would need to wait for them.

Let's say we are assigned the task of creating that social media post. The content team tells us that we need to use the content `socialPostTemplate` from the `contentdb` component. We could do something like this:

```
const puppeteer = require('puppeteer');
const content = require('./contentdb');

(async () => {
    const browser = await puppeteer.launch({
    headless: true,
    defaultViewport: null});
    const page = await browser.newPage();
    await page.setContent(content.socialPostTemplate);
```

```
    await page.screenshot({path:'fromhtml.png'});
    await browser.close();
})();
```

We load `contentdb` using the `require` function. Then we call `newPage`, which will give us an empty canvas, the `about:blank` page. Once we have the empty canvas, we load the HTML using `setContent`, take the screenshot, and close the page.

Once you call `setContent`, the page will be fully functional. That means that you could even call the `evaluate` function to customize and populate that template's values.

One thing to consider is that the `setContent` function will override all the page content. You won't be able to append content using `setContent`.

Two more functions will come in handy while creating new content. The first one is `page.addScriptTag(options)`, which will allow you to inject script tags into any page. These are the options available:

- You can pass `url`, to inject a JavaScript file from a URL.
- You can also use `path` to inject a JavaScript file from a local file.
- If you have the script in a memory variable, you can use `content` and set the entire script there.
- Finally, you can pass `type`, which is the script type you can set to a script element (https://www.hardkoded.com/ui-testing-with-puppeteer/scriptelement).

You can use these two functions when you want to inject new functionality that wouldn't be solved with just an `evaluate` function call.

We also have `page.addStyleTag(options)`. It's just like `addScriptTag`, but instead of injecting a script, you can inject a CSS file or content. The `addStyleTag` function has the same options as `addScriptTag`, except for the `type` option, which is not a valid option of the link element used to add CSS files. If we go back to PDF generation, you can use the following code to inject CSS content before generating a PDF file:

```
await page.addStyleTag({
    content : `
    .search-input {
        display: none !important;
    }`
```

```
});
await page.pdf({…});
```

With this piece of code, we are hiding the search input before generating the PDF. This is a relatively simple change, but imagine all the things you would be able to set up in real-life scenarios.

Summary

In this chapter, we covered many of my favorite features. Creating content is an unexpected use for a browser automation tool.

We learned how to generate screenshots, use them for UI regression testing, and generate content for our websites. We also learned how to generate PDF files and all the options available. By the end of the chapter, we learned how to generate pages on the fly.

During this chapter, we also saw many features available in Chrome. I hope you learned some new tricks there.

In the next chapter, we will take our tests to the next level. We will learn how to test our websites by emulating different mobile devices and network conditions.

8
Environments emulation

I had the good luck of using the internet before it became popular. I was a teenager when *Windows 95 Plus* was launched to the market. Most people might remember *Windows 95 Plus* because it came with some cool themes and even the *Space Cadet Pinball* game. But this version of Windows brought a new software application whose name is still around these days, with haters and lovers. *Windows 95 Plus* came with *Internet Explorer 1.0 (IE 1.0)*.

My first internet connection was a free phone number that a local newspaper shared with its readers. I was able to convince my dad to get me a modem. The speed was 36.6 kbps. Today my speed test goes to 150 Mbps download and 30 Mbps upload, over 4,000 times faster than the speed I got as a teen.

I don't remember very well the specs of my computer. But I do remember using a 15" 800x600 monitor, and then upgrading to a 17" 1,024x768. LED? No way! What's that? There were some bulky, eye-burning CRT monitors.

SEO? Google? Nobody knew those words back then. I remember that my favorite search engine was *AltaVista*.

Why am I telling you all this? Because back then, the internet experience was consistent. It was slow, very slow, ugly, very ugly, and limited, very limited. But it was the same for everybody. If you were a developer back then, you knew that you had to develop a website for IE 1.0 to be displayed on an 800x600 screen and that your page would take over a minute to download. But you wouldn't have thought about all that. You would be happy creating your page with *Microsoft FrontPage*, pushing that to some server, and letting the world know about your site.

But now things are different. The ecosystem is more diverse than ever, and we need to be prepared to test all the different scenarios that we could come across. At the end of the day, it is our job to honor all our customers and try to understand their environments.

We will cover the following topics in this chapter:

- Understanding the browser's market share
- Emulating mobile devices
- Emulating network conditions
- Emulating localization
- Other emulations

By the end of this chapter, you will be able to get into your users' shoes and emulate how they experience your sites.

Let's get started.

Technical requirements

You will find all the code of this chapter on the GitHub repository (`https://github.com/PacktPublishing/UI-Testing-with-Puppeteer`) under the `Chapter8` directory. Remember to run `npm install` on that directory, and then go to the `Chapter0/vuejs-firebase-shopping-cart` directory and run `npm install` again.

Understanding the browser's market share

Before getting into all the emulation features Puppeteer provides, I would like to discuss how the browser's market share looks these days. I believe that will give you a clear picture of the importance of testing and emulating different scenarios.

The browser's popularity over the years

We have lived through lots of changes over the past 25 years. Browsers have been dramatically adopted and discarded. Let's take a look at this table made by Nick Routley in his post *Internet Browser Market Share (1996–2019)* (`https://www.visualcapitalist.com/internet-browser-market-share/`):

Browser	Peak Market Share	Peak Year
Netscape Navigator	90%	1995
Internet Explorer	95%	2004
Opera	3%	2009
Mozilla Firefox	32%	2010
Safari	7%	2012

Although I used *Netscape Navigator*, I wasn't there at its peak back in 1995. But I remember the days when the only browser that mattered was *Internet Explorer*.

The community was living through browser fatigue back in 2008, when *Google Chrome* was launched, causing a massive number of users to move to *Google Chrome* and *Firefox*, which had a peak in 2010.

If you didn't play the video on Nick's post, don't miss that. I took a screenshot from the moment that the video gets to 2013 Q1:

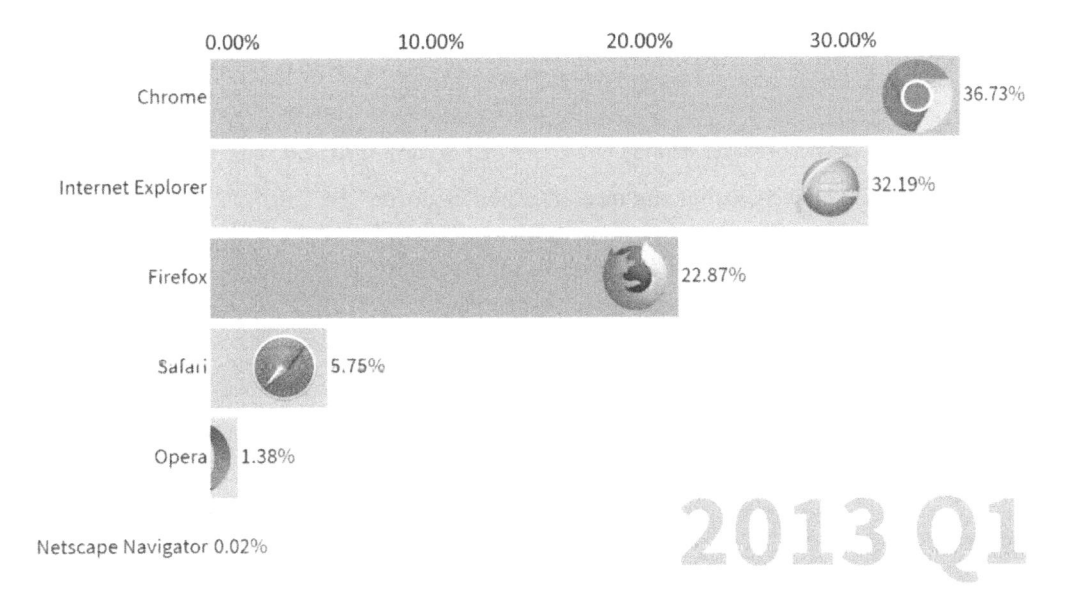

Chrome	36.73%
Internet Explorer	32.19%
Firefox	22.87%
Safari	5.75%
Opera	1.38%
Netscape Navigator	0.02%

2013 Q1

Market share in 2013

That was a challenging year for developers. You had four different browser engines behaving differently, processing CSS styles differently, having different JavaScript features. It was a mess. But I think that was a healthy web, with no clear market owner.

Browsers' popularity in 2020

According to *StatCounter* (https://gs.statcounter.com/), the picture is very different these days:

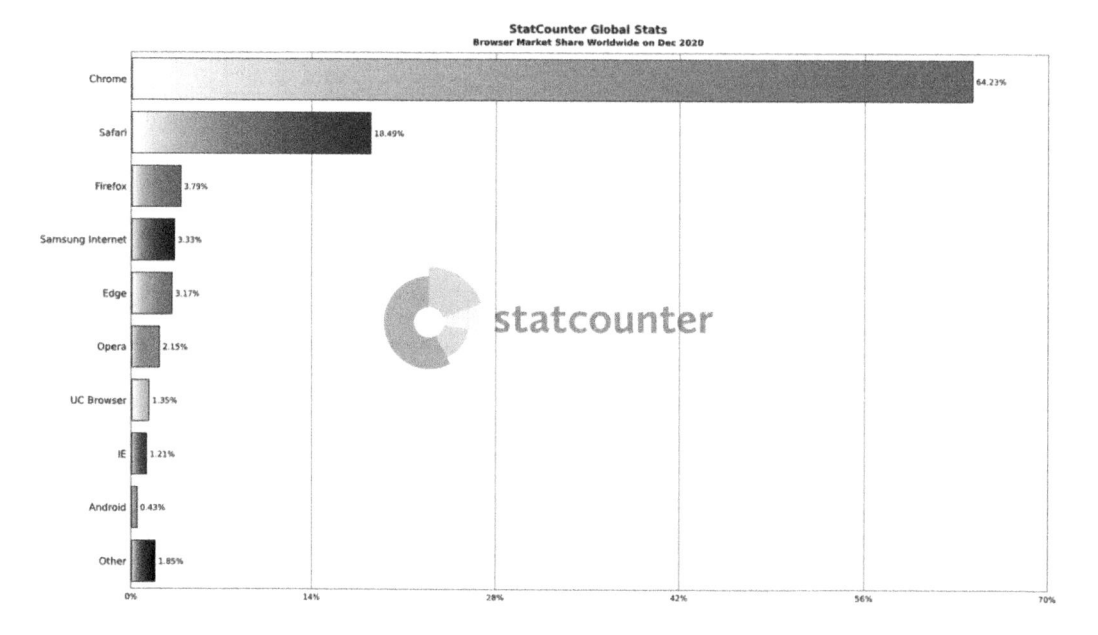

Browser market share in December 2020 according to StatCounter

Many people call *Google Chrome* the **new** Internet Explorer. The Chrome predominance gets even more important when you consider that *Edge* and *Opera* use the Chromium engine. When a browser gets to these levels of market share, it is good for developers, but it's not good for the web.

What if we take a look at operative systems?

Operative Systems market share

Operative systems play an essential part in how browsers work. They are responsible for providing the fonts and interacting with the hardware, among other things. Most browsers are cross-platform, but although they try to give the same experience across operative systems, they don't always work in the same way. That's why it's so important to know how the operative system market share looks:

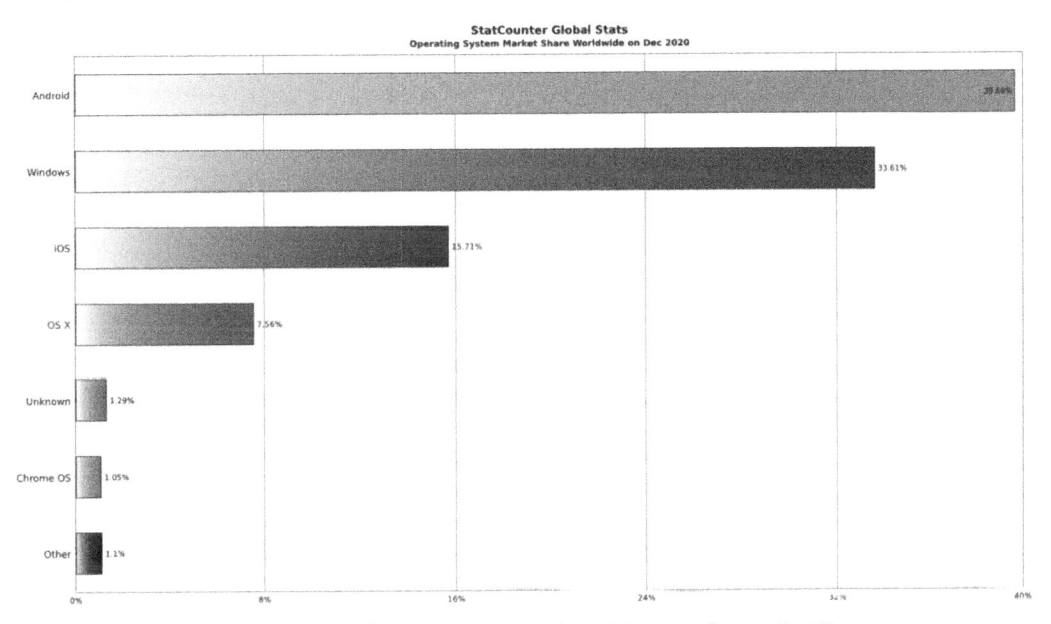

StatCounter Global Stats
Operating System Market Share Worldwide on Dec 2020

- Android: 39.66%
- Windows: 33.61%
- iOS: 15.71%
- OS X: 7.56%
- Unknown: 1.29%
- Chrome OS: 1.05%
- Other: 1.1%

Operative system market share in December 2020 according to StatCounter

I honestly found this surprising. Almost 55% of internet consumption is on mobile, and over 39% is on Android. These values should make us re-think how we develop and test our sites.

The last thing we can take a look at is screen resolutions.

Screen resolution distribution

Screen resolution is another important piece when we try to understand the whole web ecosystem. In *Chapter 3, Navigating through a website*, we talked about how developers can change a page layout based on the screen resolution. Let's see how the screen resolution is distributed according to **StatCounter**:

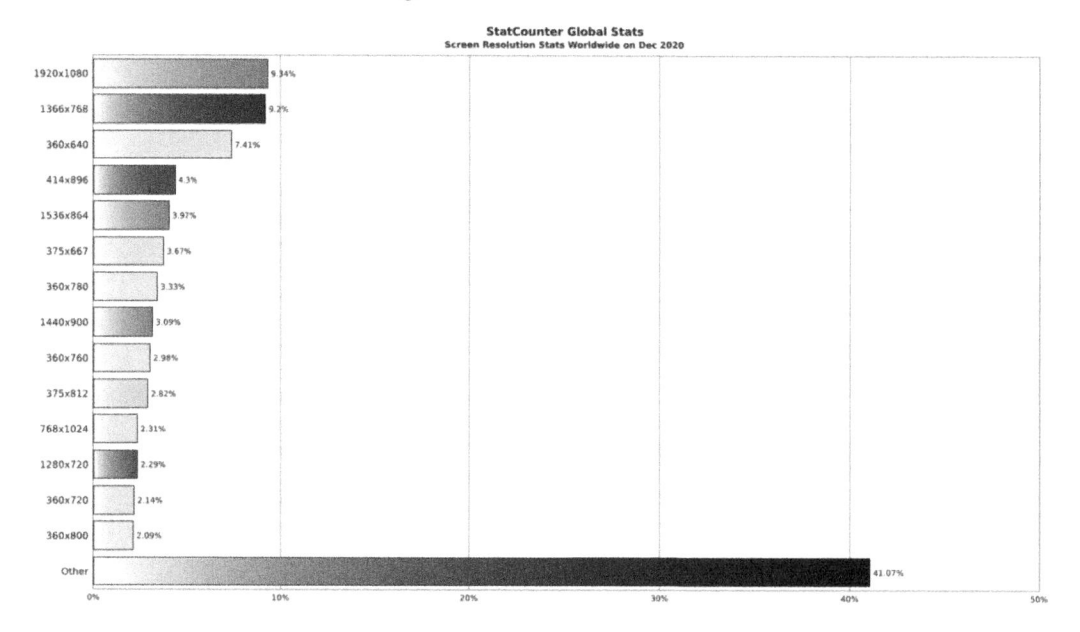

StatCounter Global Stats
Screen Resolution Stats Worldwide on Dec 2020

Resolution	Percentage
1920x1080	9.34%
1366x768	9.2%
360x640	7.41%
414x896	4.3%
1536x864	3.97%
375x667	3.67%
360x780	3.33%
1440x900	3.09%
360x760	2.98%
375x812	2.82%
768x1024	2.31%
1280x720	2.29%
360x720	2.14%
360x800	2.09%
Other	41.07%

Screen resolution market share in December 2020 according to StatCounter

The distribution of screen resolutions is crazy. There is not only a wide variety of resolutions, but we also have "**Other**" with 41%. We are far from that 800x600 standard.

The message I want to leave you with is that the internet ecosystem is more diverse than ever. The world where everything was just IE, 800x600, over a dial-up connection is long gone. Although there is one predominant browser, we have many possible scenarios, mobile devices, and screen resolutions, and we haven't talked about network speeds. We have Wi-Fi, 4G, 3G, or GPRS.

We sometimes make the error of thinking that all users have a crazy-fast internet and 27" 4K displays, and we are unable to understand why they feel frustrated with our site.

Do you know your users? Do you know whether they use your site on the street on their phones? Do you want your site to be used worldwide? Do you know that there are countries where they write right to left or where they don't have 4G coverage?

It's time to get into mobile users' shoes. Let's see how we can emulate mobile devices.

Emulating mobile devices

The first type of emulation I want to cover is mobile emulation. In this section, we will cover the three elements that Puppeteer can emulate: The viewport, the touchscreen, and the user agent. We have to keep in mind that it is a browser trying to **emulate** a mobile device. Puppeteer and Chromium won't be able to emulate any hardware limitations or any other specific features that certain mobile phones offer. There is no real device behind the curtains; it's just a browser trying to show you how a website would look on that device's screen.

As I mentioned previously, **55% of the internet traffic comes from mobile devices**. Most of the diversity we saw in the previous section is in the mobile world.

Let's take a look at some of the browser distribution in the mobile world:

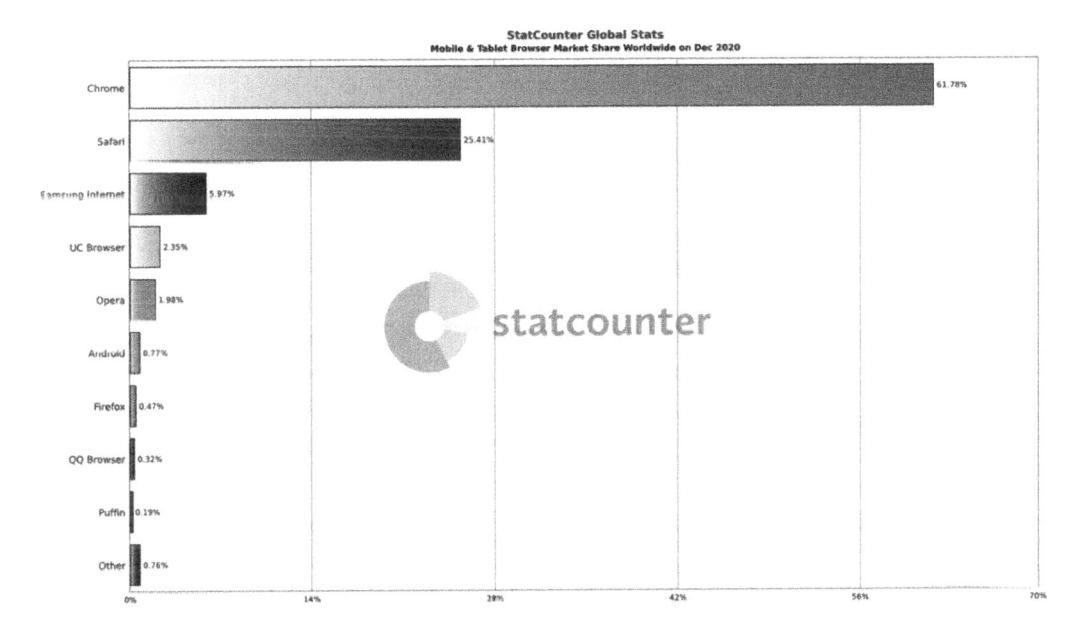

Browser market share in mobile devices according to StatCounter

The mobile market is mostly divided between *Chrome* and *Safari*. One thing you should know is that in *iOS*, the only available browser engine is *WebKit/Safari*. You have browsers such as *Chrome*, *Edge*, or *Firefox* available in *iOS*, but they cannot ship their own browser engine. They have to use *WebKit*. The only thing they can provide are features over that engine. The main feature you will see in those browsers is the synchronization between the desktop and the mobile browser.

Let's take a look at screen resolutions on mobile devices:

Screen resolutions on mobile devices according to StatCounter

You need 10 screen resolutions to reach 50% of the market share, compared with only three resolutions on desktop, 1,920x1,080, 1,366x768, and 1,536x864. The screen resolutions in the mobile world are highly diverse. Another thing that should call your attention in that chart is the resolutions that are pretty low. Who buys a phone with a 360x640 resolution? No one. We will find out in the next section who those 360x480 users really are.

So, it's time to talk about the elements that Puppeteer considers to emulate a mobile device.

The Viewport

We've talked a lot about the viewport in this book. It's time to give a clear definition of the viewport.

I like to explain the viewport by explaining what it's not. The viewport is not the screen resolution. It's not the size of the browser's window. And lastly, it's not the size of the page. The viewport is the rectangular portion of the screen the browser uses to render a page. From the user's point of view, the viewport is the part of the page you can see:

Emulating mobile devices   201

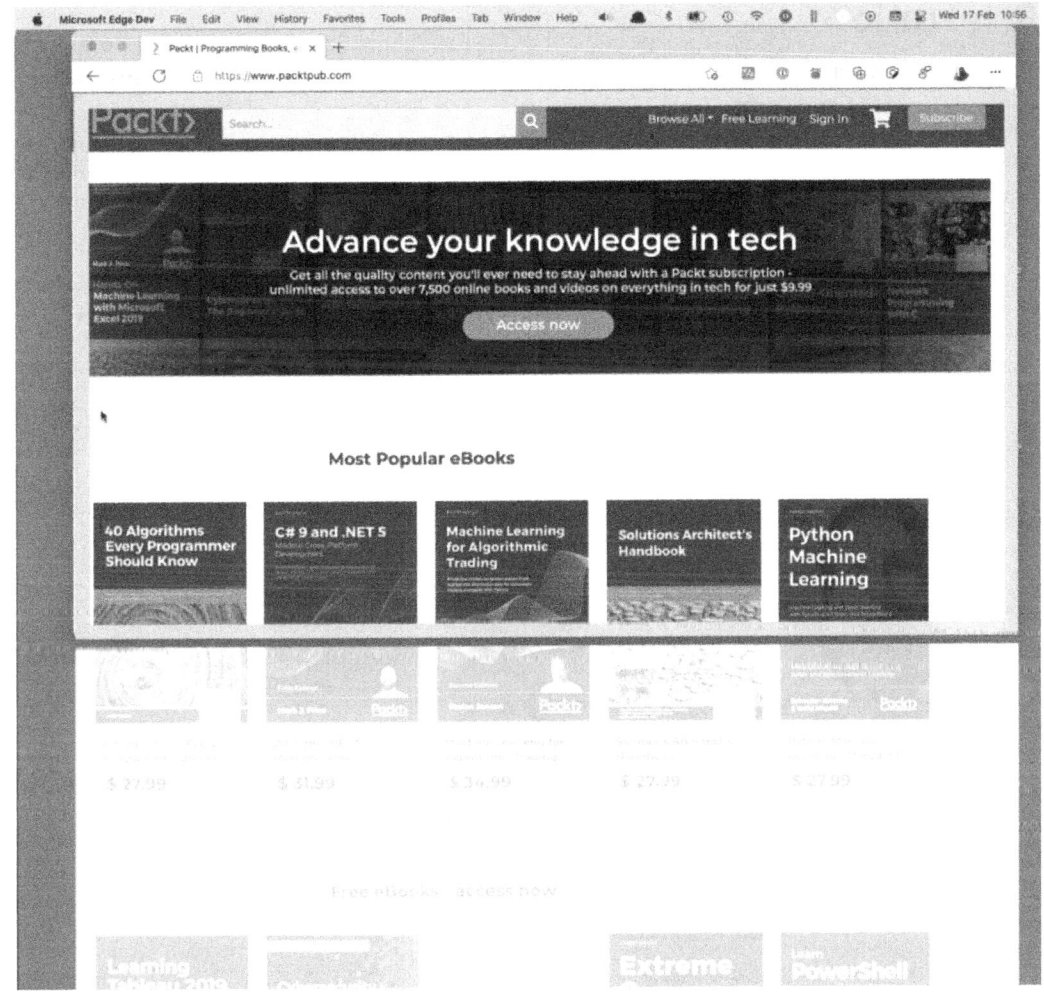

The viewport

I love the preceding visualization, not because I made it, but because it clearly shows the difference between the viewport and the screen size. The page can be huge. It can be way longer than what you can see. Even more, if you are a social media user, you would also know that pages can have an "infinite" height because sites such as *Facebook* and *Twitter* load new content when you are close to reaching the end of the page. Although it's not as common, a page could also be wider than the viewport. There was a wave of horizontal-scrolling pages when *Windows 8* was launched. The Microsoft *Azure* portal still shows its content using a horizontal layout.

The second element to take into consideration when you try to emulate a device screen is the pixel ratio.

Pixel ratio

What if I told you that the Samsung Galaxy S20, with a screen resolution of 1,440x3,200, has a viewport of 360x800?

No, that's not a typo, nor an error. That's the browser's viewport on that beautiful mobile phone. How's that possible? Let's see how a web page would be displayed on a Samsung S20 without a pixel ratio set:

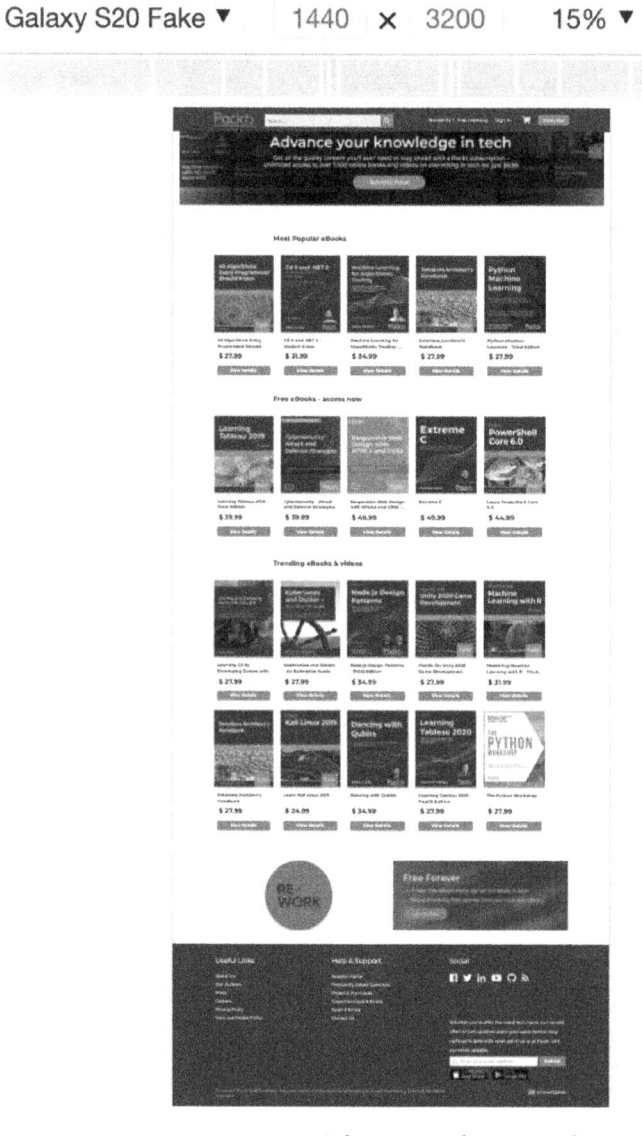

Galaxy S20 without a pixel ratio

Imagine if the browser honored the real resolution of the screen. That would be impossible to read, so you need to scale the resolution. You need to tell the browser to use a ratio to zoom the page and make it more usable. In the case of the Samsung Galaxy S20, the pixel ratio is 4, taking the viewport to 360x800, which is simple math (1,440/4) x (3,200/4). If we navigate the page using a pixel ratio of 4, we will see something like this:

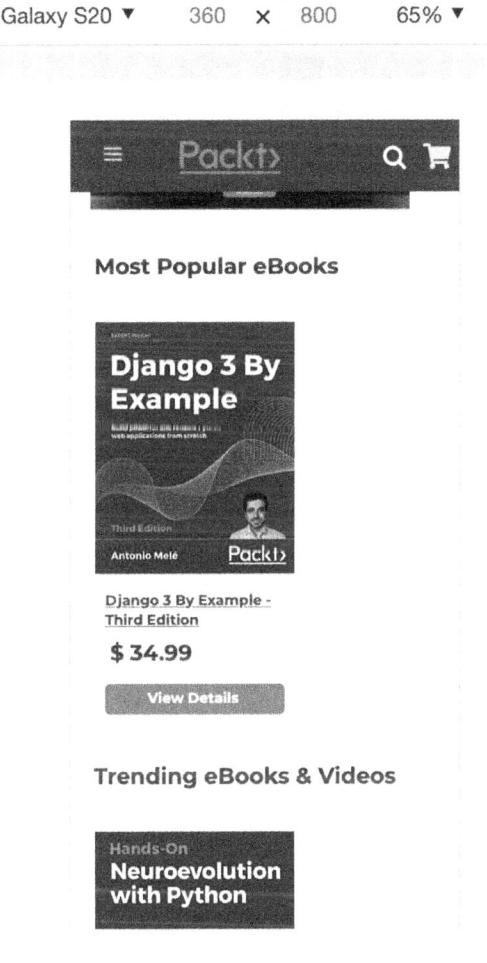

Galaxy S20 with the right pixel ratio

Now we have an S20 with a huge resolution, but pages are rendered in a way that we can read them.

If you're wondering how I've been emulating different devices, it's tool time!

If you open the developer tools (I hope that by now I don't have to tell you how to do that), you will find that there is a button called **Toggle device emulation**:

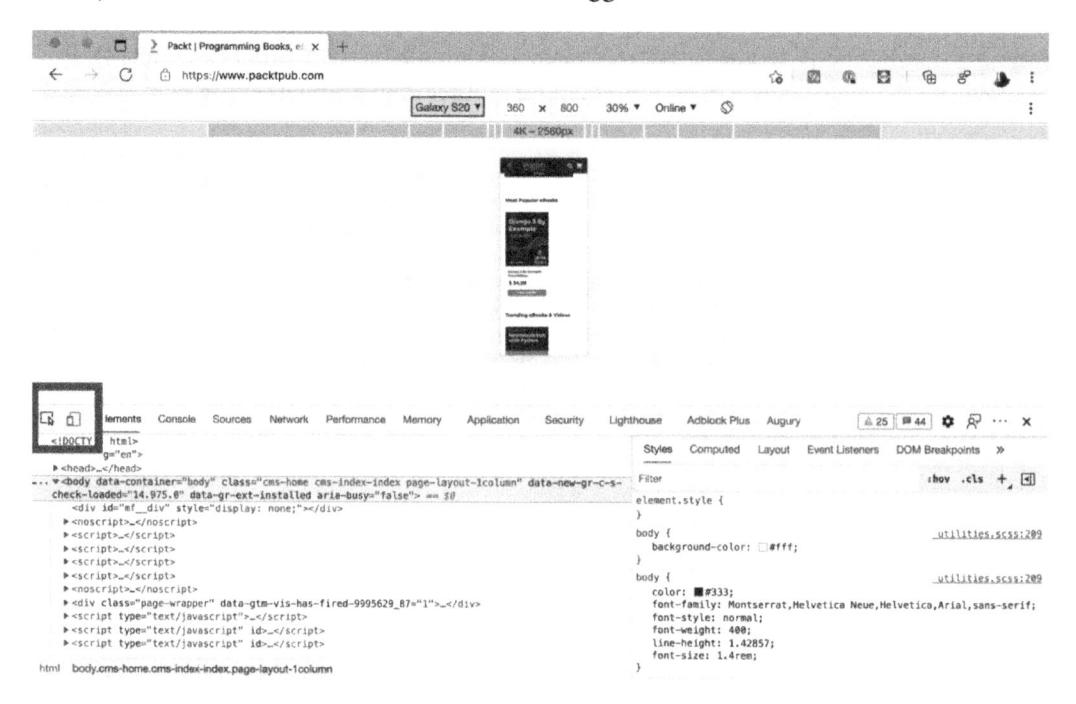

Toggle device emulation option

If you click on that button, you will activate the device emulation mode. From there, you will be able to pick any device to emulate, or create new ones. You will also be able to change the zoom. Notice that this zoom won't affect the viewport; it's just to zoom the emulator. Finally, you will have the option to emulate different network speeds. We will talk about that in the *Emulating network conditions* section.

The next element that Puppeteer takes into consideration is the touchscreen.

The touchscreen

If the device has a touchscreen, the browser will give developers an extra set of tools, **touch events** (`https://www.hardkoded.com/ui-testing-with-puppeteer/touchevents`). Single taps will be processed as click events. But the browser offers the chance of processing multi-touch interactions. Let's see how Chromium shows the touchscreen emulation:

Touch emulation

If you use the device emulation, you will see that Chromium will emulate taps with a black circle.

That takes us to the last thing that Puppeteer uses to emulate devices: the user agent.

The user agent

The user agent is one of those terrible decisions made on the web that are hard to eradicate. The user agent is a string (text) sent to the server on every request that identifies the browser/application, the operative system, the vendor, and its version.

According to MDN (https://www.hardkoded.com/ui-testing-with-puppeteer/userAgent), the format should be something like this:

```
User-Agent: <product> / <product-version> <comment>
```

If you open DevTools in Chrome and type `navigator.userAgent`, you will get something like this:

```
"Mozilla/5.0 (Macintosh; Intel Mac OS X 11_0_1)
AppleWebKit/537.36 (KHTML, like Gecko) Chrome/87.0.4280.88
Safari/537.36"
```

The only clear thing here is that I'm on a Mac, using an Intel processor, and the operating system version is `11_0_1`. It's also true that I'm on `Chrome/87.0.4280.88`. The rest are patches after patches, so the user doesn't get a "Your browser is not compatible" message. So, if the server checks for Mozilla, the user agent will match, but it's not Mozilla. Could you tell me what *KHTML, like Gecko* is? As you can see, the user agent system is broken.

Many developers would use the user agent to determine which device is on the other side. Let's take, for instance, the user agent on an iPad:

```
Mozilla/5.0 (iPad; CPU OS 11_0 like Mac OS X)
AppleWebKit/604.1.34 (KHTML, like Gecko) Version/11.0
Mobile/15A5341f Safari/604.1
```

If a developer wants to check whether the user is on an iPad, they can check whether the user agent contains the word **iPad**. But what if they want to check whether the user is using Safari? If they look for the word **Safari**, it will work on iPad, but, if you look at Chrome's user agent, it also has the word Safari, so we would think that Chromium is Safari. User agents are a mess.

If Puppeteer wants to emulate devices correctly, it needs to change the User-Agent in two places. First, it needs to change the User-Agent request header (https://www.hardkoded.com/ui-testing-with-puppeteer/userAgent) sent to the server. And second, as developers can also access the User-Agent from their JavaScript code using the `navigator.userAgent` property, the browser needs to change the value of that property as well. With these changes, both the server and the client will get a User-Agent that a real device would send.

Now it's time to see how we apply all this in our Puppeteer code.

Emulating mobile devices with Puppeteer

You toggle the emulation mode by calling page.emulate(options). I honestly think that the name options is wrong there. Compared with the other options we have seen in this book, this options argument is mandatory. The object will contain all the required data Puppeteer needs to emulate a device:

- viewport is the first property, and it includes the definition of the viewport and a little bit more:

  a) width, representing the viewport width.

  b) height, representing the viewport height.

  c) deviceScaleFactor, which is the pixel ratio we talked about before.

  d) isMobile is a Boolean property that will make the browser consider the meta viewport tag. You can read more about this on the MDN site (https://www.hardkoded.com/ui-testing-with-puppeteer/viewportMetaTag).

  e) hasTouch is a Boolean that will enable touch support.

  f) isLandscape is a Boolean that will emulate a device in landscape mode.

- The userAgent property will allow us to change the user agent on the request header and JavaScript, as we saw in the previous section.

I have some good news and some bad news for you. Good news first. The puppeteer class has a property called devices. It's a dictionary containing over 70 devices. We could do something like this in our code:

```
const iPhone = puppeteer.devices['iPhone 6'];
await page.emulate(iPhone);
```

That's the good news. The bad news is that you have to go to the source code for you to know the available list of devices: https://www.hardkoded.com/ui-testing-with-puppeteer/DeviceDescriptors. That's not ideal. The other option would be grabbing any Puppeteer code you have and printing the keys of the devices object:

```
console.log(Object.keys(puppeteer.devices));
```

If you do that, you will get all the devices included in Puppeteer. The other bad news is that the list of devices is not as up to date as you might expect. But I think it makes sense. First, because we get new devices every month, and keeping that list updated would be a tough job. And second, the website you want to automate shouldn't need to be tested on every single device. I think you should be able to have good test coverage using the provided devices.

If you do need to test a specific device, you could browse the spec on the web and manually pass a device setting. *yesviz.com* (`https://yesviz.com/devices.php`) has a nice list of devices' viewports. You can find a list of user agents at *DeviceAtlas* (`https://deviceatlas.com/blog/list-of-user-agent-strings`).

If we want to emulate an iPhone 12 device, which is not on the devices list, we can do something like this:

```
await page.emulate({
    userAgent:
        'Mozilla/5.0 (iPhone; CPU iPhone OS 12_0 like Mac OS X) AppleWebKit/605.1.15 (KHTML, like Gecko) Version/12.0 Mobile/15E148 Safari/604.1',
    viewport: {
        width: 360,
        height: 780,
        deviceScaleFactor: 3,
        isMobile: true,
        hasTouch: true,
        isLandscape: false,
    },
});
```

At the time of writing this book, I wasn't able to find the user agent sent by an iPhone 12, so I'm using the one from the iPhone XR. But if you are using this as a test tool, it would be a matter of asking your development team which values they are checking so you can then test the different user agents used by the team.

That takes us on to the next questions. How do we apply all these new concepts? How should we test mobile emulation?

Testing mobile UX

First, you need to check for **behavior changes**. Good developers make a great effort to give the best experience based on the device they infer you are using. Let's see how the www.packtpub.com website looks on mobile:

The packtpub site on an iPhone X

As we can see, the experience changes completely. The top menu is changed to a hamburger menu, and now you need to click on the magnifying glass to search for a book.

If you care about UI regressions, you will need to identify the different **layout changes**. Grids could become lists, and sections might be removed entirely to simplify the UI, fit the content on the screen, and make the user experience much nicer.

You might be thinking, "OK, but how do I test all that? Which devices should I test, all of them?". In order to know which devices to test, we need to know a little bit about **breakpoints**. No, not debugging breakings, **media query breakpoints**. Media query breakpoints are points that a developer can use to apply a different set of CSS styles based on the viewport width or height.

Do you remember how when we talked about generating PDF files, we mentioned that developers could use @media print to determine the style used to print a page? Well, @media print is not the only option we have there. We can also do stuff such as this:

```
/* Extra small devices (phones, 600px and down) */
@media only screen and (max-width: 600px) {...}

/* Small devices (portrait tablets and large phones, 600px and up) */
@media only screen and (min-width: 600px) {...}

/* Medium devices (landscape tablets, 768px and up) */
@media only screen and (min-width: 768px) {...}

/* Large devices (laptops/desktops, 992px and up) */
@media only screen and (min-width: 992px) {...}

/* Extra large devices (large laptops and desktops, 1200px and up) */
@media only screen and (min-width: 1200px) {...}
```

This example is taken from the *w3schools* site (https://www.hardkoded.com/ui-testing-with-puppeteer/breakpoints). We can see that developers can set specific styles depending on the width of the viewport. Functionally speaking, these days, we talk about five types of device categories:

- Mobile phones in portrait (up to 600 px)
- Tablets in portrait (up to 900 px)
- Tablets in landscape (up to 1,200 px)
- Desktops (up to 1,800 px)
- Big desktops (bigger than 1,800 px)

These numbers are relative, and you should team up with the development team and see which breakpoints they are using, and you should try to test edge scenarios using those breakpoints.

Emulating mobile devices 211

So maybe once you have met with the development team, you find that, based on the breakpoints they use, you should test the following devices:

- iPhone 6
- iPad
- iPad Landscape
- A desktop with a viewport of 1,280x1,080

We could improve our UI regression tests and test those devices:

```
it('Should visually match', async() => {
  for(const device of ['iPhone 6', 'iPad', 'iPad landscape',
''])
  {
    const target = differencify.init({ chain: false, testName:
'Home ' + device });
    await target.launch();
    const page = await target.newPage();

    if(device) {
      await page.emulate(puppeteer.devices[device]);
    } else {
      await page.setViewport({ width: 1600, height: 1200 });
    }
    await page.goto(config.baseURL);
    const image = await page.screenshot();
    const result = await target.toMatchSnapshot(image)
    await page.close();
    await target.close();

    expect(result).to.be.true;
  }
});
```

Here, I grabbed the same code from the previous chapter, but I wrapped it in a `for` loop that will iterate through the four devices we picked. We will assume that an empty string will be the default. If we get a device in the loop, we call the `emulate` function. If not, we set the **viewport** we had before.

Lastly, if you want to emulate user taps, you can replace calls to the `click` function with a call to the `tap` function. The `tap` function works just like the `click` function, but instead of using mouse emulation, it will use touchscreen emulation.

Now we have UI regression tests for mobile devices.

> **Tip**
> Device emulation is not only for UI testing. Web developers can benefit from this feature to check how a page looks on different devices. In the same way that we coded this test, you can create a small script that can loop through many devices, navigate a page, and take screenshots. Then you can check whether something is broken or not.

If you want to test a page's behavior on mobile devices, it won't be much different from the different Puppeteer tests we've been writing. You could create a new test file for mobile and add your tests there. You could create a `homepage.iPhone.tests.js`, and do something like this in the `beforeEach` function:

```
beforeEach(async () => {
    page = await browser.newPage();
    await page.emulate(puppeteer.devices['iPhone 6']);
    page.setDefaultTimeout(config.timeout);
    pageModel = new LoginPageModel(page, config);
    await pageModel.go();
})
```

The only thing new there is the call to the `emulate` function. From there, it is up to you to evaluate which tests you want to write for iPhone and which tests you don't. For instance, you might want to test layout changes, but tests such as prices or stock checks should be the same no matter the device.

In this section, we learned how to emulate different viewports, user agents, and touch devices. But there is more. Let's move on to bandwidth emulation.

Emulating network conditions

Networking is a challenging topic in computer science. If you tell a network engineer that Chromium emulates a 4G network, they will ask you to show them how it can emulate radio tower and weather conditions. Chromium does not pretend to emulate a network but a network condition. Chromium limits the scope to three variables that affect web development: Download speed, Upload speed, and Latency. That's it.

Emulating network conditions is something that you can now do on Chromium. You can open the developer tools and go to the **Network** tab, and you will find a drop-down list called throttling with the **Online** option selected by default, as in the following screenshot:

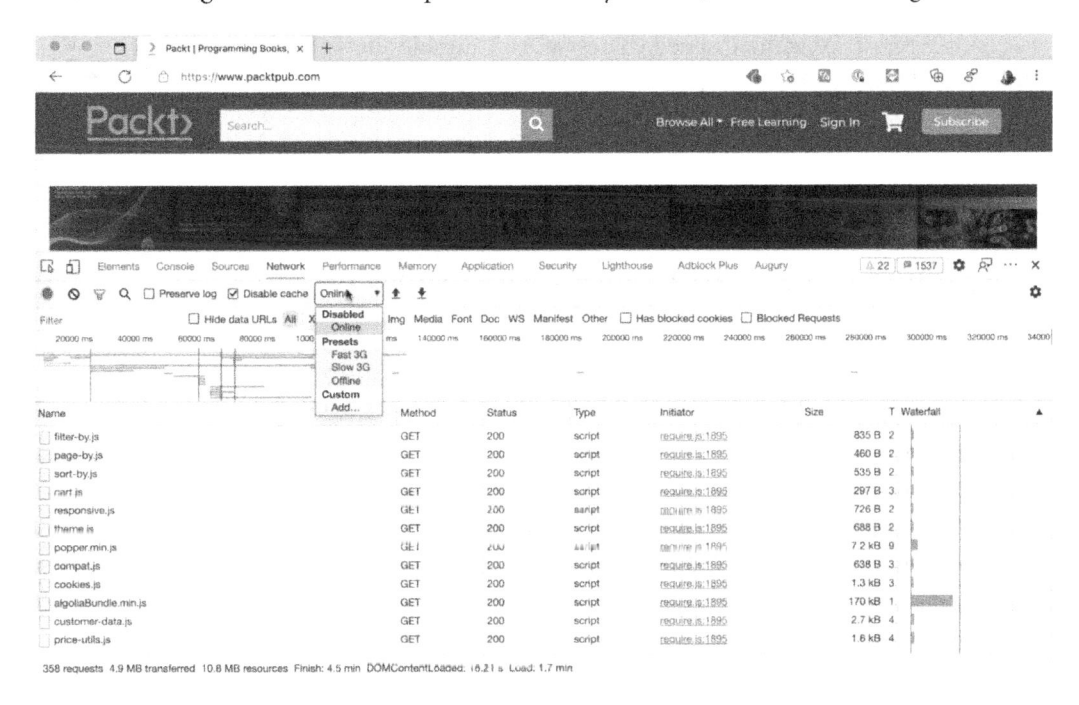

Emulating network conditions on Chromium

If you click on that drop-down list, you will find three other options: **Fast 3G**, **Slow 3G**, and **Offline**. Another cool feature is that you will be able to add custom profiles. There you will be asked about three variables we mentioned before, download, upload, and latency, and additionally, to provide a name so you can identify your new profile.

Emulating different network conditions is not something you want to add to every UI test. We want our tests to be as fast as possible. But it's a great tool to perform tests on demand. For instance, say one user of your e-commerce site reports that they're unable to finish the checkout process when they're using 4G. The company doesn't want to leave mobile users out, so they improve the site to work better on 4G. Now we have to write a test to ensure that the page will work on 4G.

You can emulate different network conditions by calling `page.networkConditions(networkConditions)`, where `networkConditions` is an object with the following properties:

- `download`: Download speed (bytes/sec). -1 disables download throttling.
- `upload`: Upload speed (bytes/sec). -1 disables upload throttling.
- `latency`: Minimum latency from the request sent to response headers received (ms).

The `puppeteer` object has a property called `networkConditions` that provides two network settings: `'Slow 3G'` and `'Fast 3G'`. This is how you can use them according to the official documentation:

```
const puppeteer = require('puppeteer');
const slow3G = puppeteer.networkConditions['Slow 3G'];
(async () => {
  const browser = await puppeteer.launch();
  const page = await browser.newPage();
  await page.emulateNetworkConditions(slow3G);
  // other actions...
  await browser.close();
})();
```

But we are not limited to the two options Puppeteer provides. We can create our own settings, or find examples on GitHub. For instance, The *porchmark* project (https://www.hardkoded.com/ui-testing-with-puppeteer/porchmark) has a great list. The project is under the MIT license so we can use it freely.

These are some values we can get from that project, and then use them in our own code to emulate different network conditions:

```
const NETWORK_PRESETS = {
    GPRS: {
        download: 50 * 1024 / 8,
        upload: 20 * 1024 / 8,
        latency: 500,
    },
    Good3G: {
        download: 1.5 * 1024 * 1024 / 8,
```

```
            upload: 750 * 1024 / 8,
            latency: 40,
    },
    Regular4G: {
            download: 4 * 1024 * 1024 / 8,
            upload: 3 * 1024 * 1024 / 8,
            latency: 20,
    }
};
export default NETWORK_PRESETS;
```

There are more in that repository. You can see the full list here: https://www.hardkoded.com/ui-testing-with-puppeteer/porchmark-presets. If you want to incorporate that file, you will need to rename the downloadThroughput property to download and uploadThroughput to upload, and remove the offline property. You will also find the networkPresets.js file in the project of this chapter with all the replacements already made.

We could test our login on a "Good 3G" network with all this information. We can go to our login.tests.js file and add this test:

```
it('Should login on 3G', async() => {
   await page.emulateNetworkConditions(NetworkPresets.Good3G);
   await pageModel.login(config.username, config.password);
   await page.waitForSelector('.thumbnail.card');
});
```

This is the same test as **Should login**, but adding a call to the emulateNetworkConditions function. If we don't want to use a NetworkPresets file, we could hardcode our network condition. Let's see how we can call page.emulateNetworkConditions using our own settings:

```
it('Should login on 3G with custom settings', async() => {
    await page.emulateNetworkConditions(
    {
       download: 750 * 1024 / 8,
       upload: 250 * 1024 / 8,
       latency: 100,
    });
```

```
    await pageModel.login(config.username, config.password);
    await page.waitForSelector('.thumbnail.card');
});
```

The end result will be the same. You can also have a fixed preset and add it to our existing `config.js` file.

We already covered a lot of ground in this chapter. In this section, we learned how to emulate different network conditions. We also learned how to execute methods from the DevTools protocol that are not exposed in the Puppeteer API. Now it's time to learn about localization.

Emulating localization

I love this topic. Maybe because English is not my mother tongue, so I have seen and felt the pain when a site fails to honor other cultures.

There are many debates about what localization is, what internationalization is, and the difference between them. While I bet there will be debate over whether I should treat both as a whole or not, we will treat both as a whole.

When we talk about localization, we're saying that a website should honor its audience:

- It should honor their language.
- It should honor their culture, such as how they read numbers, sort information, and read the content.
- It should honor their beliefs. For example, Green/Good Red/Bad might not apply in every culture.

Localization is a feature.

Ideally, every site on the web should consider localization. But localization can be quite a costly feature to implement. There is a high chance that your company is not Google or Amazon and you cannot afford to localize your site for every culture, so you need to know your audience.

You might be thinking: "I'm just a QA analyst. Should I care about that?". Let me tell you this: You should be the number-one person in the company defending and honoring your customers' culture.

Let me share a few real-life examples of having a clear scope of your audience.

I have found many times that buying local train tickets in Europe can be hard. They are only in the local language, or the English version of the site is extremely poor. The scope is evident. This site is for local people. If you are a tourist, go to *Rail Europe*.

One colleague from the United States wanted to buy a flight ticket on a Chilean website. He went to that site and found a flight at $186.992. He thought the flight price was 186 dollars and 992 cents. In fact, it was one hundred and eighty-six thousand, nine hundred and ninety-two Chilean pesos. The site didn't consider the way that my friend reads numbers. He wasn't part of the site's audience.

On the bright side, if you go to `www.google.com`, you will always get the site in your preferred language. The world is their audience.

If I go to `www.kayak.com`, I will get prices in my local currency, because I'm part of their audience. This is the full list of countries you will find on Kayak's website:

Argentina		India		România	
Australia		Indonesia	ID EN	Россия	
België	FR NL	Ireland		Schweiz	FR DE
Bolivia		Israël		Singapore	EN 简
Brasil		Italia		South Africa	
Canada	EN FR	日本		대한민국	
Chile		Malaysia	EN BM	Suomi	
中国		México		Sverige	
Colombia		Nederland		台灣	
Costa Rica		New Zealand		Türkiye	
Danmark		Nicaragua		United Arab Emirates	
Deutschland	DE EN	Norge		United Kingdom	
Ecuador		Panamá		United States	EN ES
El Salvador		Paraguay		Uruguay	
España	ES CA	Perú		Việt Nam	EN VI
France		Philippines		Österreich	
Ελλάδα		Polska		Česká republika	
Guatemala		Portugal		Україна	
Honduras		Puerto Rico		Saudi Arabia	
香港	EN 繁	República Dominicana		ประเทศไทย	TH EN

Kayak's audience

This might look like just a list of countries in Kayak. But that's, in fact, the definition of their audience.

If you don't know your site's audience, ask for it, and defend it in your tests.

Before getting into the code, there is one more thing you need to know regarding localization. There is no one way to implement it, and Puppeteer won't cover every scenario. But, let's take a look at the things we will be able to do with Puppeteer.

Emulating geolocation

With Puppeteer, we will be able to change the geolocation used by pages using the Geolocation API (https://www.hardkoded.com/ui-testing-with-puppeteer/geolocalization). I chose those words carefully. You won't be able to emulate geolocation completely. Most sites use IP-based geolocation. That means that when a site gets a request from your device, it will grab the IP, and it will infer your country based on an IP-to-country table they have on their server. In other words, you won't be able to change the country on *Netflix.com*.

So, what can we emulate? You will be able to emulate client-side geolocation, such as maps.google.com or even the google.com search itself.

Let's say we want to make Google tell us where to eat, but in Paris. We can do something like this:

```
const browser = await puppeteer.launch({ headless: false, defaultViewport: null});
const page = await browser.newPage();
const context = browser.defaultBrowserContext();
await context.overridePermissions('https://www.google.com/', ['geolocation']);
await page.setGeolocation({latitude: 48.8578349, longitude. 2.3249841});
await page.goto('https://www.google.com/');
await page.type('[name="q"]', 'where to eat');
await page.keyboard.press('Enter');
await browser.close();
```

Let's go through this code. You can find this script in the `wheretoeat.js` file. We already know what `puppeteer.launch` and `browser.newPage` do. The third line has something new: `browser.defaultBrowserContext`. OK, that's new for us, but that's not a big deal. It will give us the context of the new page we got in the previous line.

The next line does have something interesting: `context.overridePermissions`. This function allows us to bypass many permission checks that Chromium performs. If you open Google for the first time and you search for "where to eat," you will get something like this:

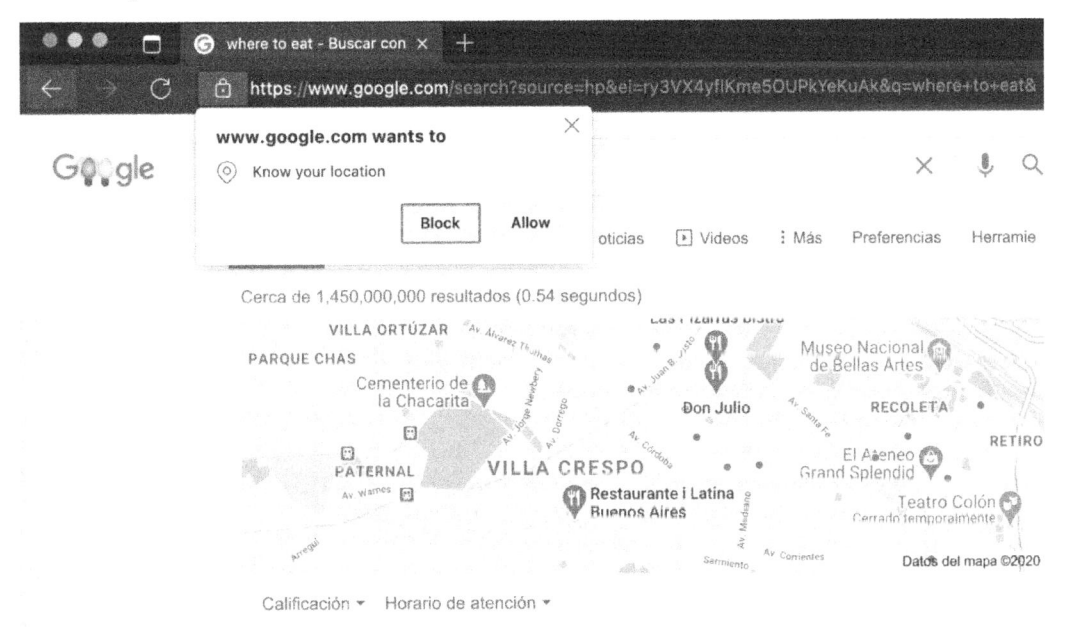

Geolocation permission request

That window is not something you can click on with Puppeteer. As we can't click on that, Puppeteer provides `context.overridePermissions` to tell the browser which permissions we want to grant automatically. The signature is quite simple: `browserContext.overridePermissions(origin, permissions)`, where `origin` is the page (the URL) we want to grant permission, and `permissions` is an array of strings accepting one of the following values:

- geolocation
- midi
- midi-sysex
- notifications

- push
- camera
- microphone
- background-sync
- ambient-light-sensor
- accelerometer
- gyroscope
- magnetometer
- accessibility-events
- clipboard-read
- clipboard-write
- payment-handler

You don't need to remember all these values; just come to this list when you get a permission request, and you need to know which value to use.

The next line is a fun one: `await page.setGeolocation({latitude: 48.8578349, longitude: 2.3249841})`. This function is also fairly straightforward. It only expects an object with three properties: `latitude`, which is a number between -90 and 90; `longitude`, which is a number between -180 and 180; and `accuracy`.

> **Pro tip**
> If you want to know the coordinates of a place, you can go to Google Maps (`https://www.google.com/maps`) and search for a place. The resulting URL will give you the coordinates. For instance, if you search for Paris, the URL should be `https://www.google.com/maps/search/Paris/@48.8590448,2.3257917,14.49z`; `48.8590448` will be the latitude, and `2.3257917` the longitude.

After setting the geolocation, we can navigate to Google, type **where to eat**, and the result will be where to eat in Paris:

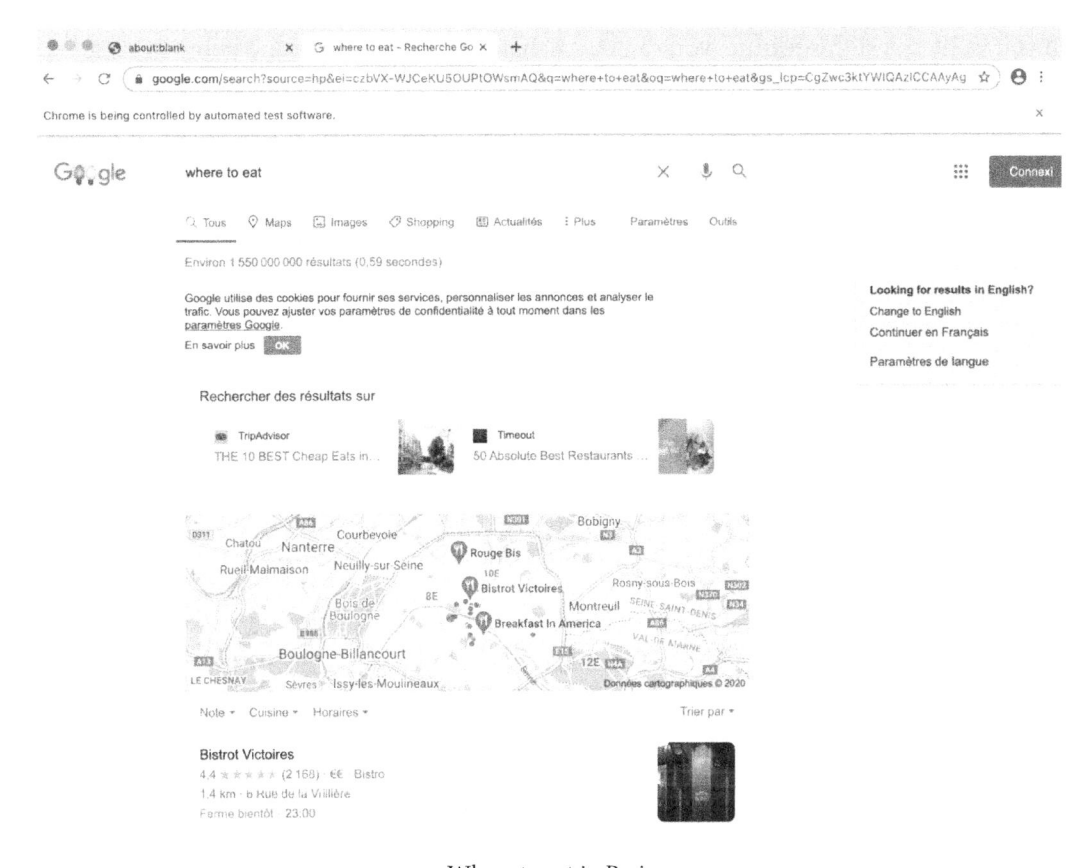

Where to eat in Paris

Puppeteer allows us to emulate not only a location but also a time zone. Let's see how we can travel around the globe with Puppeteer.

Emulating time zones

Finding a use case for time zone emulation is not easy, but there are a few. You can emulate time zones to test an application in some specific time zone, even if you are not there. This will be helpful when we talk about scraping in the next chapter.

One check that can be interesting is testing that your application saves data correctly, no matter the time zone.

The function to emulate time zones is pretty straightforward: `page.emulateTimezone(timezoneId)`, where `timezoneId` is an ICU's time zone. Chromium also has a list of ICU time zones in its source code. You can find it using the following link: `https://www.hardkoded.com/ui-testing-with-puppeteer/metazones`.

If you want to test this feature, you can try changing your time zone and going to a site that shows your current date. You can follow this script in the `timezones.js` file:

```
const browser = await puppeteer.launch({ headless: false, defaultViewport: null});
const page = await browser.newPage();
await page.emulateTimezone('Europe/London')
await page.goto('https://www.unixtimestamp.com/');
await browser.close();
```

There we set the time zone to "Europe/London," and go to `https://www.unixtimestamp.com/`, which shows dates and times in different formats. Not a fancy feature, but it might be useful someday.

The last thing we want to cover on this localization topic is language.

Emulating languages

Delivering the website in the user's language is the first thing developers cover when implementing localization. But there's one problem in our ecosystem. Let's cover the four common ways developers implement localization.

You will see sites that will show you the content **based on your IP**. If it detects your IP is from Spain, it'll show you content in Spanish. If it detects you're in France, it'll show you the site in French. What if you live in a country with five official languages? It just picks one. As we mentioned when we talked about geolocation, we won't be able to emulate IP-based language change.

Developers could also deliver **domain-based** solutions. If you go to `www.amazon.es`, you will see the content in Spanish. If you go to `www.amazon.fr`, you will see content in French. This will be easy to test. You just need to create a language domain map and use it in your tests.

Third, developers might offer a **preference-based** solution. If you go to `www.amazon.com`, you'll get the content in English, but it will show you a drop-down list somewhere to change your language. This one will also be easy to test. You could have one user per language in your test database, and then use them to test the website in different languages.

The last option I will cover here, although maybe there are more, is the one I believe is the proper way of inferring the user language: by reading the **Accept-Language header** value. According to MDN (`https://www.hardkoded.com/ui-testing-with-puppeteer/Accept-Language`), "*the Accept-Language request HTTP header advertises which languages the client is able to understand, and which locale variant is preferred. (By languages, we mean natural languages, such as English, and not programming languages.) Using content negotiation, the server then selects one of the proposals, uses it and informs the client of its choice with the Content-Language response header.*"

The browser tells the server which languages you prefer. When you navigate to a page, and on every subsequent request after that, the browser adds the **Accept-Language** header so that the server can act accordingly.

When you install a Browser, it will have a default list of languages, based on the download option you chose or the language of your Operative System. But you can then go to the preferences page and change that list of languages. If you go to your browser's preferences, you should be able to find a **Languages** section. You should be able to see something like this:

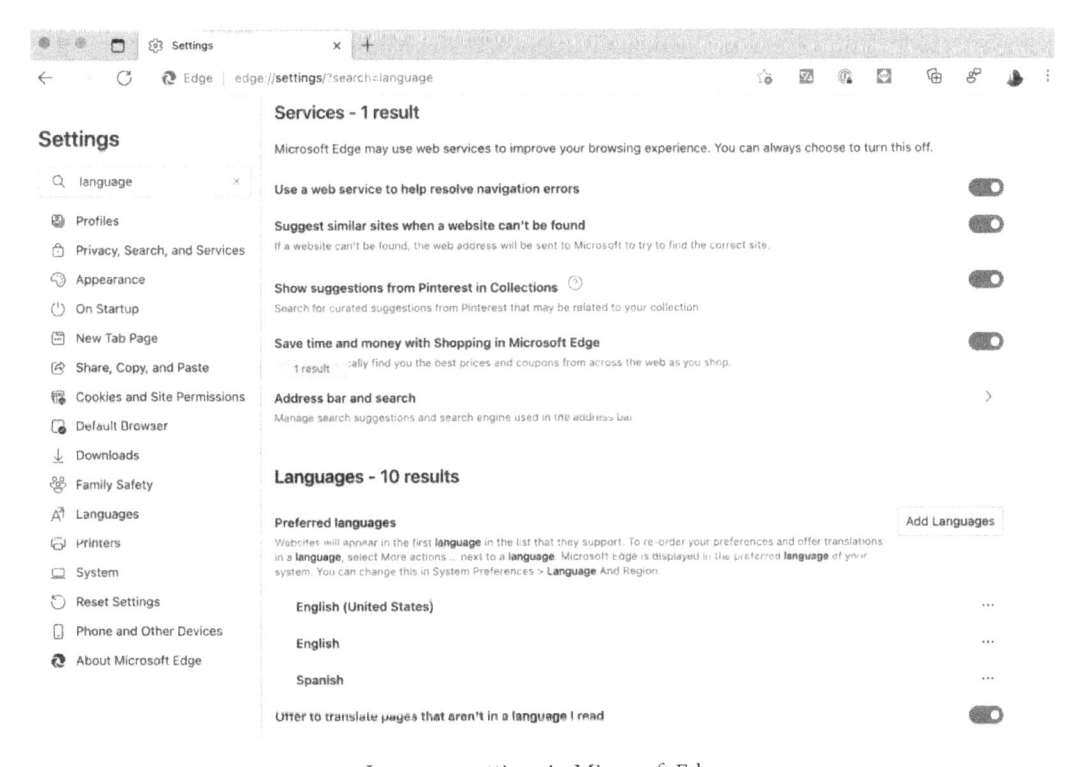

Language settings in Microsoft Edge

There, I have three languages: English (United States), English, and Spanish. All those three are set in the Accept-Language header. Sadly for us, according to Paul Reinheimer (`https://twitter.com/preinheimer`), only 7.2% of the top 10,000 sites supported Accept-Language in 2017 (`https://wonderproxy.com/blog/accept-language/`). That means that despite having the tools to infer the language based on the user's preference, most sites won't use it. I hope that changes over time. How can we test languages using the Accept-Language header? It's not that hard:

```
const browser = await puppeteer.launch({headless: false, defaultViewport: null});
const page = await browser.newPage();
await page.setExtraHTTPHeaders({
    'Accept-Language': 'fr'
});
await page.goto('https://www.google.com/');
await browser.close();
```

This is a way you can get Google's website in French. We will talk more about `page.setExtraHTTPHeaders` in the next chapter. But what you need to know is that you will be able to change the Accept-Language header the server gets.

I think we have now seen the most relevant emulation features that Puppeteer offers. But I don't want you to miss anything. Let me briefly show you a few more emulation tools.

Other emulations

To wrap up this chapter, I want to share three extra emulation functions with you.

The first one is related to **accessibility**. Localization and accessibility are two human topics. They talk about integration, about not leaving anyone out, not even from the web. I believe that your website could leave certain cultures out (read these words in context, please). You could say, "I don't plan to sell my products to this country, so I don't need to translate my site to X." As we said, localization could be expensive. But we do have to design sites to be inclusive. I think that in the same way we enforce shopping malls to have ramps for wheelchairs, we should enforce websites to be accessible. I could write lots of pages about this, but that's not the purpose of this book. But I encourage you to read about inclusive design on Microsoft's site: `https://www.microsoft.com/design/inclusive/`. I will leave you with this quote from that site:

> *Exclusion happens when we solve problems using our own biases.*

I'm taking the time to write these paragraphs in a UI testing book because I believe that Quality Assurance is the last line of defense for defending and including all users of the web.

Puppeteer won't cover every accessibility check you should do, but it will help you emulate different vision deficiencies. You can call the page.emulateVisionDeficiency(type) function to emulate the following vision deficiencies: **achromatopsia** (total color blindness), **deuteranopia** (green color blindness), **protanopia** (red color blindness), **tritanopia** (blue-yellow color blindness), and **blurredVision**, to check blurred vision. Let's see how we can use this new function:

```
const browser = await puppeteer.launch();
const page = await browser.newPage();
await page.goto('https://www.packtpub.com/');

await page.emulateVisionDeficiency('achromatopsia');
await page.screenshot({ path: 'achromatopsia.png' });

await page.emulateVisionDeficiency('blurredVision');
await page.screenshot({ path: 'blurred-vision.png' });

await browser.close();
```

If you run this check, you will get this result:

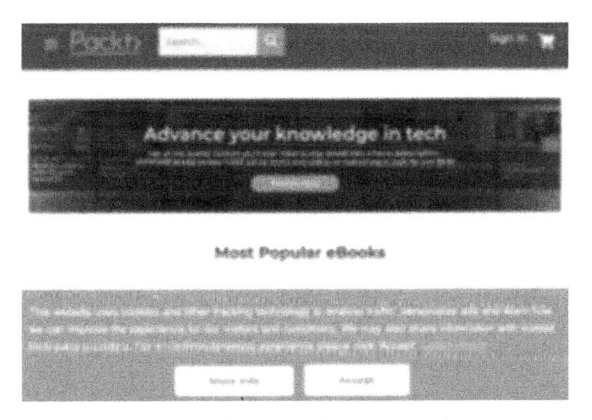

Packtpub under blurred vision emulation

You could write checks such as this and share them in a dashboard, so both the design and the development team can see how accessible the site is for people with visual impairments.

The next emulation I want to share with you is about emulating media features. The function is `page.emulateMediaFeatures(features)`. It accepts an array of **name/value** features you want to change. These are the two features that Puppeteer supports:

- `prefers-colors-scheme`, which will help you toggle between `dark` and `light` mode
- `prefers-reduced-motion`, which will reduce CSS animations with the `reduce` option or `no-preference`

This might not have been a popular feature a few years ago. But now, many sites are jumping onto the dark mode hype. This is how you can test dark mode:

```
const browser = await puppeteer.launch();
const page = await browser.newPage();
await page.goto('https://duckduckgo.com/');
await page.emulateMediaFeatures([{ name: 'prefers-color-scheme', value: 'dark' }]);
await page.screenshot({ path: 'dark.png' });
await browser.close();
```

As you can see, we can simply navigate to a page and emulate `prefers-color-scheme` with the value `dark`.

The last emulation I want to share in this chapter is media type emulation. We talked about media types when we talked about PDF generation. We have two media types: **screen** and **print**. This is an excellent feature if you need to test how a page would be printed. You could use it to test the receipt page, which might be printed by the user.

The function is `page.emulateMediaType(type)`, and the type is a string that can be `screen` or `print`:

```
const browser = await puppeteer.launch();
const page = await browser.newPage();
await page.goto('https://github.com/puppeteer/puppeteer');
await page.emulateMediaType('print');
await page.screenshot({ path: 'print.png' });
await browser.close();
```

Here we go to the Puppeteer repo and check how it would look if we were about to print the page.

Summary

This was another chapter full of content. I hope you enjoyed it as much as I enjoyed writing it.

We started the chapter by talking about the internet ecosystem. We talked about how the world is moving toward mobile experiences. This is an excellent time to reach out to the person in charge of analytics in your company and see whether the charts we saw in this chapter represent your website's users.

Then we moved on to mobile emulation. There, we learn about the viewport, the pixel ratio, a fundamental concept in mobile resolution, touchscreen emulation, and the user agent.

We also learned how to emulate different network conditions. We will see in *Chapter 10, Evaluating and Improving the Performance of a Website*, how critical speed is in the mobile experience.

At the end of this chapter, we covered localization emulation. We learned how to emulate geolocation, time zones, and languages.

I didn't want to leave any emulation out of this chapter. That's why we also learned about other available emulations. We covered accessibility, dark mode, and media type emulation. Testing dark mode will become more important with all the dark mode hype we live in these days.

The next chapter will be about Scraping. We will demystify the concept of scraping and learn some new techniques so that you can use Puppeteer not only for testing but also for other fun stuff.

9
Scraping tools

Back in *Chapter 1, Getting started with Puppeteer,* we talked about the different uses for web automation. Of all those use cases, web scraping is the one that excites developers the most. When I give talks about automation, I know that I will get the crowd's full attention when I start talking about task automation, but even more when I get into the topic of **web scraping**.

Don't get me wrong, I think that UI testing is important. As we saw in the previous chapters, it's not just about running automation tests but also about taking care of your customers. But web scraping has that fun spark, a hacker feeling, and I didn't want to leave this topic out of the book.

A few months ago, I read a book about web scraping that included a chapter about UI testing at the end of the book. We are going to do the same, but the other way around. This is a UI testing book with a scraping chapter at the end.

We will begin this chapter by defining and demystifying web scraping. Is it just for hackers? Is it even legal? We will also talk about scraping ethics, such as when it is OK to scrape and when it is not.

The second part of the chapter will discuss the different tools available to scrape with Puppeteer.

We will cover the following topics in this chapter:

- Introduction to web scraping
- Creating scrapers
- Running scrapers in parallel
- How to avoid being detected as a bot
- Dealing with authentication and authorization

By the end of this chapter, you will be able to apply all the concepts you have learned during the course of this book in a brand-new field of web automation.

Let's get started.

Technical requirements

You will find all the code of this chapter on the GitHub repository (`https://github.com/PacktPublishing/UI-Testing-with-Puppeteer`) under the `Chapter9` directory. Remember to run `npm install` on that directory.

Introduction to web scraping

The best way to introduce a new concept is by giving a few concrete and straightforward definitions. Let's begin by defining **data scraping**. According to Wikipedia (`https://www.hardkoded.com/ui-testing-with-puppeteer/data-scraping`), "*Data scraping is a technique in which a computer program extracts data from human-readable output coming from another program.*" Any information coming out from a computer can be extracted and processed. The first scrapers were called "screen scrapers." A screen scraper is something as simple as an application that can capture the screen. Then, by running **Optical Character Recognition** (**OCR**), it extracts the text from that image for further processing.

Web scraping takes this idea to the next level. *Web scraping is a technique used to extract data from one or multiple websites using a piece of software.*

You might be wondering: Is that even legal? Amazon is a public site. I can freely navigate through the site; why wouldn't I be able to run a script to extract data that is already public? Well, it depends. Let me share with you some scenarios from the real world that have similar ethical dilemmas to web scraping.

First scenario

A small grocery store owner goes to a big mall to compare their products and prices. She can't go and get a box of milk and leave without paying, but she can walk around and take notes of the product prices, take that list to her shop, and compare their prices. The price is not a product. She's not stealing anything. Also, the mall is too big, and they can't control every person walking around taking notes. But what if the same person goes to a small grocery store on the next block and starts taking notes? I bet the owner already knows her, and it's too evident that she's taking notes, and that will probably threaten their business. Is it illegal? No. But she might get into a fight.

Second scenario

Some exclusive furniture stores won't let you take photos inside the store.

Last scenario

You can't count cards in the casino! They will kick you out and ban you for life.

These are real-life "scrapers." People are trying to extract information in the real world. Scraping the web is quite similar. You will be able to scrape a site as long as a) the site welcomes (implicitly or explicitly) scrapers, b) your attitude is considerate while scraping, and c) what you are scraping is allowed. Let's unpack these concepts.

Does the site allow scrapers?

The first reaction to this question would be: "No! why would the owner of a website allow scrapers?" But that's not necessarily true. What if you own a hotel? If an aggregator website scrapes your booking page, then it shows those results on their website with a link back to your site, they will make some profit from that, and you will get more customers: win-win. Or, if you own a non-profit site such as Wikipedia or a government website, scraping might not be an issue. As it's a non-profit website, you shouldn't care much about bots coming to your site to extract data unless they affect your website's performance. But if your site is about song lyrics, you won't want anybody to come to your site and extract the lyrics. Lyrics are your product, your assets.

In this chapter, we will see many techniques to bypass some validations, but my personal rule is: If the site doesn't want to be scraped, I won't scrape it. No means no.

So, how do we know whether we can scrape a website? The owner of a website can express that in at least four different ways.

Terms and conditions

The first thing you should check before scraping a website is the terms and conditions. The website owners can make it very clear that they don't want it to be scraped.

The terms and conditions is that huge block of text we often ignore when installing an app. I bet you've also had emails telling you that a website has changed its terms and conditions, and you said "yeah, whatever" and archived the email.

But we shouldn't do that. According to iubenda (`https://www.hardkoded.com/ui-testing-with-puppeteer/iubenda-terms`), *"'Terms and Conditions' is the document governing the contractual relationship between the provider of a service and its user. The Terms and Conditions are nothing other than a contract in which the owner clarifies the conditions of use of its service."* Sometimes we might think that when we buy digital content (software, music, e-books) on a website, we then own that product, when, in fact, if you read the terms and conditions, you have bought the right to use the product, but you don't own it.

The terms and conditions also states what they allow you to do on a website. Many sites make that very clear. Let's take the example of the terms and conditions of www.ebay.com:

3. Using eBay

In connection with using or accessing the Services you will not:

use any robot, spider, scraper or other automated means to access our Services for any purpose;

bypass our robot exclusion headers, interfere with the working of our Services, or impose an unreasonable or disproportionately large load on our infrastructure.

As we can see, eBay makes it very clear. You can't scrape their site. eBay v. Bidder's Edge's (`https://www.hardkoded.com/ui-testing-with-puppeteer/ebay-vs-edge`) was a well known case back in the 2000s. eBay alleged that Bidder's Edge activities constituted a trespass of eBay's chattels (`https://www.hardkoded.com/ui-testing-with-puppeteer/Trespass-to-chattels`). In other words, Bidder's Edge's scraping affected the servers that are eBay's property. I bet you don't want to go to court against eBay.

Now, let's take a look at Ryanair's terms and conditions (`https://www.hardkoded.com/ui-testing-with-puppeteer/ryanair-terms`):

Use of any automated system or software, whether operated by a third party or otherwise, to extract any data from this website for commercial purposes ("screen scraping") is strictly prohibited.

Ryanair doesn't like scrapers either, but it says "for commercial purposes," which would mean that you could code your scraper to look for the best price for your next vacation.

If the terms and conditions is not clear regarding scrapers, the second way a site owner can express their relationship with scrapers is through the `robots.txt` file.

robots.txt file

Wikipedia, again, has a great definition of the robots file. According to Wikipedia (`https://www.hardkoded.com/ui-testing-with-puppeteer/Robots-exclusion-standard`), the robots exclusion protocol *"is a standard used by websites to communicate with web crawlers and other web robots. The standard specifies how to inform the web robot about which areas of the website should not be processed or scanned. Robots are often used by search engines to categorize websites."*

The keyword in that definition is "inform." The website owner can express in the robots file which parts of the site can be scraped. Most websites only use the `robots.txt` file to tell search engines where they can find the sitemap to scrape:

```
User-agent: *
Sitemap: https://www.yoursite.com/sitemap.xml
```

With these two simple lines of code, they tell search engines, such as Google, to get that Sitemap file and scrape those pages. But you can find more complex definitions in that file. For instance, the `robots.txt` file on Wikipedia has over 700 lines! That tells us that the site is being scraped quite a lot. Let's see some examples of what we can find in that file:

```
# Please note: There are a lot of pages on this site, and there are
# some misbehaved spiders out there that go _way_ too fast. If you're
# irresponsible, your access to the site may be blocked.
```

I love that the file begins with a message to us! They expect us to come to this page to read it. The next section is interesting:

```
# Crawlers that are kind enough to obey, but which we'd rather
not have
# unless they're feeding search engines.
User-agent: UbiCrawler
Disallow: /
User-agent: DOC
Disallow: /
User-agent: Zao
Disallow: /
# Some bots are known to be trouble, particularly those
designed to copy
# entire sites. Please obey robots.txt.
User-agent: sitecheck.internetseer.com
Disallow: /
```

Here, Wikipedia informs that they don't want scrapers identified with the user-agent **UbiCrawler, DOC, Zao,** and **sitecheck.internetseer.com** to scrape the site. And the file closes with general rules for all user-agents:

```
User-agent: *
Allow: /w/api.php?action=mobileview&
Allow: /w/load.php?
Allow: /api/rest_v1/?doc
Disallow: /w/
Disallow: /api/
Disallow: /trap/
Disallow: /wiki/Special:
...
```

They basically say that all the rest (`User-agent: *`) can scrape the whole site except some URLs such as `/w/`, `/api/`, and so on.

If we don't find anything useful in the terms and conditions or in the `robots.txt` file, we might find some hints in the page response.

Are you a human?

I bet no one in real life has asked you whether you are a human, but many websites ask us that question all the time:

Bot check by reCAPTCHA

What started as a simple "type the word you see" turned into more and more complicated challenges:

Complex CAPTCHAs

Should we check the third square of the first row? Who knows… But their goal is clear. In a friendly way, using the UI, they want to kick scrapers out.

When a site puts a CAPTCHA, like the one in the previous screenshot, it's not always because they don't want to be scraped. Maybe they want to protect their users. They don't want malicious bots to test users and passwords or stolen credit card numbers. But the intention is clear: that page is for humans.

I call these validations a "friendly" way to kick bots out. But you can also get some unfriendly responses from the server:

> **Forbidden**
>
> You don't have permission to access /wp-content/uploads/2018/06/ on this server.
>
> *Apache/2.4.10 (Debian) Server at blogsdna.com Port 80*

Page returning a 403 HTTP error

If a page you would typically be able to access now returns a 403 when you scrape it, it means that the server considered your actions as an attack on the server and banned your IP.

That's terrible news. It means that you won't be able to access that site using your current IP. The ban could be for a few hours or forever. That would also mean that if you share your public IP with other computers, for instance, inside an organization, no one will be able to access that site. There are two ways to fix this issue. One is by reaching out to the site owner, apologizing, and asking them to remove your IP from the forbidden list. Or you could keep playing badly, trying to change your public IP or using proxies. But if you got caught once, you will get caught twice.

The last way a site can tell you not to scrape is by giving you an API.

Using the Website API

In this context, an API is a set of URLs that the website exposes that instead of returning a page, return some data, generally in JSON format:

Wikipedia API

The question here is, why would you waste time parsing HTML elements, wait for network calls, and so on, if you can hit a URL to get all the information you need?

I think this is an excellent way for a site to tell you: **hey, don't scrape me, here is the data you might need. You are welcome to come here and fetch the information you need**.

APIs also give the website's owner the chance to set the rules, such as the rate limit (how many requests you can make per second or minute), the data the API exposes, and what will remain hidden for consumers.

These are some ways the site can communicate what we can and can't do. But our attitude toward the site being scraped is also important.

Our attitude

This part is quite simple, and it can be reduced to two words: be nice. You have to think that on the other side of the page you are trying to scrape, there are people like you whose goal is to keep the site up and running. They have to pay for a server and network bandwidth. Remember, they are not your enemy. They are your friends. They have the data you need, so be nice.

You should look at available APIs first. If a website exposes an API with the data you want, there is no need to scrape the site.

Next, you should consider your scraping rate/speed. Although you might want to scrape a site as fast as possible, I would try to make the scrape process close to real user interaction. Later in this chapter, we will see tools to scrape pages in parallel, but I would use those tools very carefully.

There is one thing that many scrapers using Puppeteer forget. You should always identify yourself as a bot. In the next section, we will see that the idea is telling the server that you are a bot and not a real user.

The last thing we need to consider is to evaluate what data we are extracting.

What's the data we are scraping?

I think this is common sense. Are we extracting copyrighted data? Are we extracting the assets of the site? For instance, if we go to a lyrics website and extract the lyrics, we are taking the very purpose of the website. But if we go to an airline's website and check for flight prices, the price is not the company's asset. They sell flights, not prices.

The other thing to consider is what the data we extracted will be used for. We should consider whether our actions will empower the scraped site, for instance, in the case of the hotel booking website, they might get more customers, or threaten it, for instance, if we scrape lyrics to create our own lyrics site.

Truth be told, lots of the sites we know today used scraping techniques to seed their websites. You might see that on real-estate websites. Who would want to go to an empty real-estate website? No one. So, these websites would be seeded with postings from other websites to make them more appealing to new customers.

Enough theory. Let's create some scrapers.

Creating scrapers

Let's try to scrape book prices from the Packt site. The terms and conditions said nothing about scrapers (`https://www.hardkoded.com/ui-testing-with-puppeteer/packtpub-terms`). But the `robots.txt` file has some clear rules:

```
User-agent: *
Disallow: /index.php/
Disallow: /*?
Disallow: /checkout/
```

```
Disallow: /app/
Disallow: /lib/
Disallow: /*.php$
Disallow: /pkginfo/
Disallow: /report/
Disallow: /var/
Disallow: /catalog/
Disallow: /customer/
Disallow: /sendfriend/
Disallow: /review/
Disallow: /*SID=
```

They don't want us to go to those pages. But the site has a pretty massive `sitemap.xml`, with over 9,000 lines. If `robots.txt` is the "don't go here" sign for scrapers, `sitemap.xml` is the "please, check this out" sign. These are the first items on the `sitemap.xml` file:

```
<?xml version="1.0" encoding="UTF-8"?>
<urlset xmlns="http://www.sitemaps.org/schemas/sitemap/0.9"
    xmlns:image="http://www.google.com/schemas/sitemap-image/1.1">
    <url>
        <loc>https://www.packtpub.com/web-development</loc>
        <lastmod>2020-12-15T12:22:50+00:00</lastmod>
        <changefreq>daily</changefreq>
        <priority>0.5</priority>
    </url>
    <url>
        <loc>https://www.packtpub.com/web-development/ecommerce</loc>
        <lastmod>2019-09-13T07:29:53+00:00</lastmod>
        <changefreq>daily</changefreq>
        <priority>0.5</priority>
    </url>
    ...
</urlset>
```

240   Scraping tools

Based on this XML, we are going to build a **crawler**. A crawler is a program that will navigate through the website scraping all the pages. This will be our plan:

- We are going to build an array of book category URLs. To make the run shorter, we will scrape only category pages, such as `https://www.packtpub.com/web-development`. We will also limit the list to 10 categories, so we are nice with the server.

- Once we get that list, we will navigate each page, getting book links. We don't want to get duplicates in there, so we need to be careful.

- Once we get the list of books, we navigate each book page and get the price for the print book plus the e-book and the print book alone:

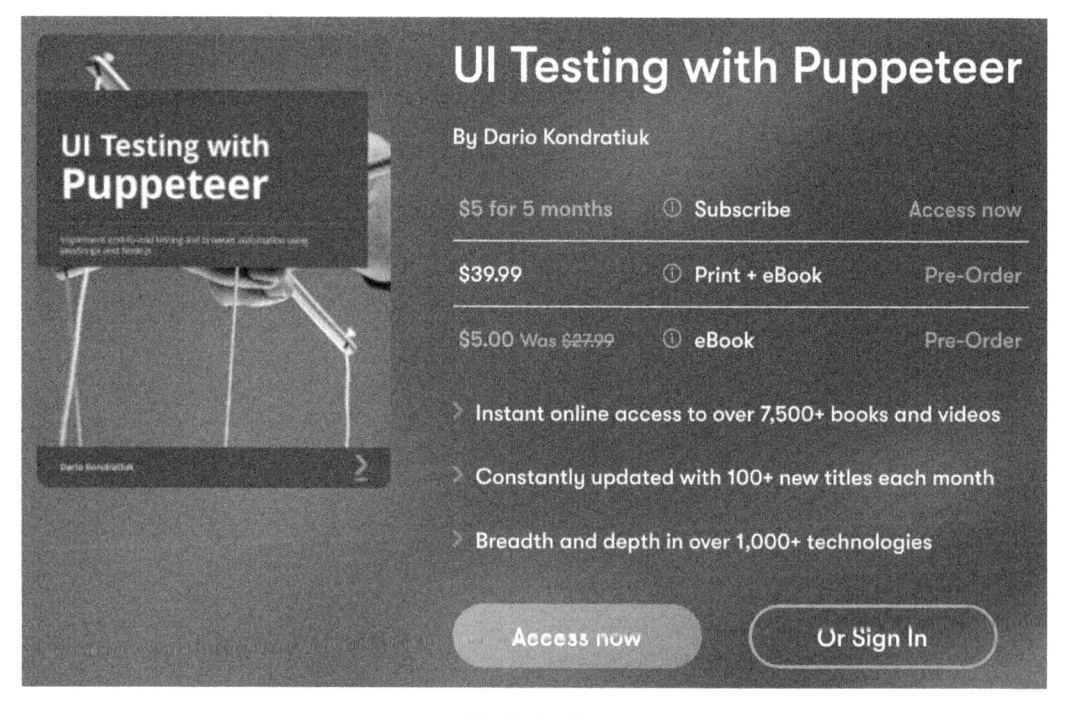

Book details

- Those prices will be collected in a JSON array and sent to disk at the end of the process.

Let's get started! You can get the code of this section in the `crawler.js` file. We will get the `sitemap.xml` file and get the first 10 categories:

```
const https = require('https');
(async function() {
    const sitemapxml = await getSitemap();
})();
function getSitemap() {
    let resolve;
    const promise = new Promise(r => resolve = r);
    https.get('https://www.packtpub.com/sitemap.xml',
function(res) {
        let body = '';
        res.on('data', (chunk) => body += chunk);
        res.on('end', () => resolve(body));
    });
    return promise;
};
```

There we are using the native `https` package to download the `sitemap.xml` file. We create a Promise that will be resolved when we call the `resolve` function. Then we call the `get` function to fetch the file. We collect the information being downloaded in the `data` event, and when we receive an `end` event, we resolve the Promise by returning the body string we were collecting. It might take a while to get the code's flow, but it's very straightforward once you get used to it.

That `sitemapxml` variable is a string. We need first to parse the XML and then get a JavaScript model from there. `xml2js` will do most of the job for us. Let's install that module using `npm install` in our terminal:

npm install xml2js

Once we have that module, we can start using it in our code:

```
const xmlParser = require('xml2js').parseString;
```

We will be able to parse the sitemap by calling the `xmlParser` function:

```
(async function() {
    const sitemapxml = await getSitemap();
    const categories = await getCategories(sitemapxml);
```

```
})();
function getCategories(sitemapxml) {
    let resolve;
    const promise = new Promise(r => resolve = r);
    xmlParser(sitemapxml, function (err, result) {
        const output = result.urlset.url
            .filter(url => url.loc[0].match(/\//g).length === 3)
            .slice(0, 10)
            .map(url => url.loc[0]);
        resolve(output);
    });
    return promise;
};
```

As you can see, we are using the same `Promise` pattern we used before. When we call `xmlParser`, we will get the parsed `result` in the result argument of the callback we just passed in. Once we get the result, we prepare the output. It might be helpful to read the code while looking at the `sitemap.xml` file to get more context. We get URL elements from the `result.urlset.url` array. Then we `filter` URL elements with a `loc` with three slashes (such as https://www.packtpub.com/web-development). Then, we grab only the first 10 elements using the `slice` function. Lastly, we use the `map` function to return only the resulting URL, returning an array of strings containing category URLs.

Now it's time to use Puppeteer. We will navigate each of the categories we grabbed from the `sitemap.xml` and return book URLs. We are not going to scrape only the first page of the category page. I'll leave that feature to you as homework.

Let's begin by creating a browser that we are going to use across the program:

```
(async function() {
    /*Previous code*/
    const books = [];
    const page = await getPuppeteerPage();
})();
async function getPuppeteerPage() {
    const browser = await puppeteer.launch({
        headless: false,
        slowMo: 500
    });
```

```
        const userAgent = await browser.userAgent();
        const page = await browser.newPage();
        await page.setUserAgent(userAgent + '
UITestingWithPuppeteerDemoBot');
        return page;
}
```

I bet you are pretty familiar with this piece of code. The first new thing we can see here is that we are passing the `slowMo` option. That means that we are going to wait 500 milliseconds after each action that Puppeteer will perform. We will also use the `userAgent` function to get the user-agent from the browser. Then, we grab that string, and we append ' UITestingWithPuppeteerDemoBot', so the server admins in the publisher will know that's us.

Let the scraping begin!

```
(async function() {
    /*Previous code*/
    for(const categoryURL of categories) {
        const newBooks = await getBooks(categoryURL, page);
        if(newBooks) {
            books.push(...newBooks);
        }
    }
    page.browser().close();
})();
async function getBooks(categoryURL, page) {
    try {
        await page.goto(categoryURL);
        await page.waitForSelector('a.card-body');
        return await page.evaluate(() => {
            const links = document.querySelectorAll('a.card-body');
            return Array.from(links).map(l =>
l.getAttribute('href')).slice(0, 10);
        });
    }
    catch {
        console.log(`Unable to get books from ${categoryURL}`);
```

```
        }
    }
```

We will iterate through the `categories` list in the main function, and we will call `getBooks`, passing `categoryURL` and a Puppeteer page. That function will return a list of book URLs that we will append to our `books` array using the `push` function. We are using `slice(0, 10)`, so we return only the first 10 items.

We wrapped all the code into a `try/catch` block because we don't want the code to fail if one category has failed.

Let's now take a look at the `getBooks` function. It looks pretty straightforward. We go to `categoryURL` and wait for an element using the `a.card-body` CSS selector. That selector will give us book URLs. Once the books are loaded, we will call `evaluate` so we can get all the links with `a.card-body`, and then, using the `map` function, we will return the `href` attribute of the link, which will give us the URL.

Scraping books won't be that different:

```
(async function() {
    /*Previous code*/
    const prices = [];
    for(const bookURL of books) {
        const price = await getPrice(bookURL, page);
        if(price) {
            prices.push(price);
        }
    }
    fs.writeFile('./prices.json', prices);
    page.browser().close();
})();
async function getPrice(bookURL, page) {
    try
    {
        await page.goto(bookURL);
        await page.waitForSelector('.price-list__item .price-list__price');
        return await page.evaluate(() => {
            const prices = document.querySelectorAll('.price-list__item .price-list__price');
```

```
                if(document.querySelectorAll('.price-list__name')
[1].innerText.trim() == 'Print + eBook') {
                    return {
                        book: document.querySelector('.product-
info__title').innerText,
                        print: prices[1].innerText,
                        ebook: prices[2].innerText,
                    }
                }
            });
        }
        catch {
            console.log(`Unable to get price from ${bookURL}`);
        }
}
```

Here we are applying everything we have already learned in this book. We go to a page, wait for a selector, and then we will call the `evaluate` function, which will return an object. We haven't used the `evaluate` function in this way yet.

Inside `evaluate` we get the prices using the `.price-list__item .price-list__price` CSS selector, and we get the book title using the `.product-info__title` CSS selector. Then, if the product name is "Print + eBook", because the site also offers videos, we return an object with three properties: `book`, `print`, and `ebook`.

The last thing to highlight is that we are wrapping the code in a `try/catch` block. If we fail in fetching one book, we don't want the entire program to fail.

The main function will collect those results and then save them to the file using `fs.writeFile`. In order to use that function, you will need to import `fs` by adding `const fs = require('fs');` in the first line of the program.

If everything goes as expected, we will get a `prices.json` file with something like this:

```
[
    {
        "book": "Kubernetes and Docker - An Enterprise Guide",
        "print": "$39.99",
        "ebook": "$5.00 Was $27.99"
    },
    {
```

```
    "book": "The Docker Workshop",
    "print": "$39.99",
    "ebook": "$5.00 Was $27.99"
  },
]
```

And we have our first scraper. From there, you have the data in the filesystem ready to be analyzed by other tools.

Can this be made better? Yes, it can. We could try to see whether we can do some parallel scraping.

Running scrapers in parallel

I'm not saying this just because I coded it, but our scraper has a pretty good structure. Every piece is separated into different functions, making it easy to identify which parts can run in parallel.

I don't want to sound repetitive, but remember, the site being scraped, in this case, Packt, is our friend and even my publisher. We don't affect the site; we want to look like normal users. We don't want to run 1,000 calls in parallel. We don't need to do that. So, we will try to run our scraper in parallel but with caution.

The good news is that we don't have to code a parallel architecture to solve this. We will use a package called **puppeteer-cluster** (https://www.npmjs.com/package/puppeteer-cluster). This is what this library does according to the description at npmjs:

- Handles crawling errors
- Auto restarts the browser in case of a crash
- Can automatically retry if a job fails
- Offers different concurrency models to choose from (pages, contexts, browsers)
- Is simple to use, small boilerplate
- Offers progress view and monitoring statistics (see the following code snippet)

Sounds pretty promising. Let's see how we can implement it. First, we need to install the package:

```
npm install puppeteer-cluster
```

That will get us the package ready to be used. You can get the code of this section in the `crawler-with-cluster.js` file. Let's import the cluster in our scraper by calling `require` in the first line of our code:

```
const { Cluster } = require("puppeteer-cluster");
```

Now that we have imported the `Cluster` class, we can create a new **cluster** in the main function:

```
const cluster = await Cluster.launch({
    concurrency: Cluster.CONCURRENCY_PAGE,
    maxConcurrency: 2,
    retryLimit: 1,
    monitor: true,
    puppeteerOptions: {
        headless : false,
        slowMo: 500
    }
});
```

The `Cluster.launch` function has many options, but I think that, for now, we only need to know about these options:

- `concurrency` will tell the cluster the level of isolation we want to use. The default is `Cluster.CONCURRENCY_CONTEXT`. These are all the options available:

  a) Using `Cluster.CONCURRENCY_CONTEXT`, each job will have its own context.

  b) Using `Cluster.CONCURRENCY_PAGE`, each job will have its own page, but the same context will be shared across all jobs.

  c) Using `Cluster.CONCURRENCY_BROWSER`, each job will have its own browser.

- `maxConcurrency` will help us set how many tasks we want to run simultaneously.
- With `retryLimit`, we can set how many times the cluster will run a task if it fails. The default is 0, but we will give it one more chance to do the task, setting this to 1.
- If we set the `monitor` option to `true`, we will get a nice console output, showing the current process.
- The last option we will cover here is `puppeteerOptions`. The cluster will pass this object to the `puppeteer.launch` function.

One thing that the package description mentions is that it supports error handling. Let's add the error handling they have in the example:

```
cluster.on('taskerror', (err, data, willRetry) => {
    if (willRetry) {
        console.warn(`Encountered an error while crawling ${data}. ${err.message}\nThis job will be retried`);
    } else {
        console.error(`Failed to crawl ${data}: ${err.message}`);
    }
});
```

That looks pretty solid. When a task fails, the cluster will fire a `taskerror` event. There we can see the error, the data, and whether the action will be retried.

We don't need to change how we download and process `sitemap.xml`. There is nothing to change there. But once we have the category, instead of calling the `getBooks` function, we will use `queue` for that task:

```
for(const categoryURL of categories) {
    cluster.queue(categoryURL, getBooks);
}
```

We are telling the cluster that we need to run `getBooks` by passing that `categoryURL`.

I have more good news. Our scraping functions are almost ready to be used in a cluster – **almost ready**. We need to change four things:

```
async function getBooks({page, data}) {
    const userAgent = await page.browser().userAgent();
    await page.setUserAgent(userAgent + ' UITestingWithPuppeteerDemoBot');
    await page.goto(data);
    await page.waitForSelector('a.card-body');

    const newBooks = await page.evaluate(() => {
        const links = document.querySelectorAll('a.card-body');
        return Array.from(links).map(l => l.getAttribute('href')).slice(0, 10);
    });
```

```
        for(const book of newBooks) {
            cluster.queue(book, getPrice);
        }
    }
}
```

First, we changed the signature a little bit. Instead of expecting (page, categoryURL), it will expect an object with a page property and a data property, where page will be the page created and managed by the cluster, and the data property will be the categoryURL instance we passed in when we queued the task.

> **Tip**
> The first argument to pass to the queue function doesn't need to be a URL. It doesn't even need to be a string. You can pass in any object, and the function will get that object in the data property.

The second thing we had to do was to add the call to setUserAgent as the page is created by the cluster itself.

Then, instead of returning the list of books, we added more tasks to the queue, but in this case, we enqueued the getPrice function, passing the book URL.

The last thing we had to do is remove the try/catch block because the cluster will handle that for us.

Now it's time to update the getPrice function:

```
async function getPrice({ page, data}) {
    const userAgent = await page.browser().userAgent();
    await page.setUserAgent(userAgent + ' UITestingWithPuppeteerDemoBot');
    await page.goto(data);
    await page.waitForSelector('.price-list__item .price-list__price');
    prices.push(await page.evaluate(() => {
        const prices = document.querySelectorAll('.price-list__item .price-list__price');
        if(document.querySelectorAll('.price-list__name')[1].innerText.trim() == 'Print + eBook') {
            return {
                book: document.querySelector('.product-info__title').innerText,
```

```
                    print: prices[1].innerText,
                    ebook: prices[2].innerText,
            }
        }
    }));
}
```

We did pretty much the same. We changed the signature, added the call to `setUserAgent`, removed `try/catch`, and instead of returning the price, we are pushing to the `prices` array inside the function.

Finally, we need to wait for the cluster to finish its work:

```
await cluster.idle();
await cluster.close();
```

The call to `idle` will wait for all the tasks to complete, and then the `close` function will close the browser and the cluster. Let's see if all this works!

```
> node crawler-with-cluster.js
== Start:      2020-12-29 08:50:14.475
== Now:        2020-12-29 08:51:28.078 (running for 1.2 minutes)
== Progress:   6 / 70 (8.57%), errors: 0 (0.00%)
== Remaining:  13.1 minutes (@ 0.08 pages/second)
== Sys. load:  6.1% CPU / 95.3% memory
== Workers:    2
   #0 WORK https://www.packtpub.com/security
   #1 WORK https://www.packtpub.com/all-products
```

The output of `puppeteer-cluster` is amazing. We can see the elapsed time, the progress, and what the workers are processing.

Until now, we played by the rules. But what if we want to avoid being detected as scrapers? Let's find that out.

How to avoid being detected as a bot

I hesitated about adding this section after everything I mentioned about scraping ethics. I think I made my point clear when I said that when the owner says no, it means no. But if I'm writing a chapter about scraping, I think I need to show you these tools. It's then up to you what to do with the information you have learned so far.

Websites that don't want to be scraped, and are being actively scraped, will invest a good amount of time and money in trying not to be scraped. The effort would become even more important if the scrapers damage not only the site's performance but also the business.

Developers in charge of dealing with bots won't rely only on the user agent because, as we saw, that could be easily manipulated. They should rely only on evaluating the number of requests from an IP because, as we also saw, scrapers can slow down their scripts, simulating an interested user.

If the site can't stop scrapers by checking the user agent and monitoring traffic spikes, they would try to catch scrapers using different techniques.

They would begin by introducing CAPTCHAs. But, as we will see in this section, scrapers can solve some of them.

Then, they would try to evaluate the time between requests. Did you click a link after 500 milliseconds? Did you fill a form in less than 1 second? You might be a bot.

They could also add JavaScript code to check your browser capabilities. Don't you have plugins? Not even the ones that come with Chrome by default? Don't you have a language set? You might be a bot.

Finally, they will try to set traps to catch you. For instance, Packt knows that you might be scraping links using the a.card-body CSS selector. They could add a hidden link with that selector, but in that case, the link's URL could be https://www.packtpub.com/bot-detected. If you got to the bot-detected URL, you would get caught. In the case of forms, they could add hidden inputs that a typical user wouldn't complete because it is hidden. If the server gets a value in that hidden input, sorry—you were caught again.

This is a cat-and-mouse game. The mouse will always try to find new ways to sneak in, and the cat will work hard to cover the holes in the wall.

That being said, let's see what tools we have if we are the mouse in this game.

Antoine Vastel has a great bot detection demo page (https://arh.antoinevastel.com/bots/areyouheadless). You can get the code of this section in the bot.js file. Let's try to take a screenshot of that page using Puppeteer:

```
const puppeteer = require('puppeteer');

(async function() {
    const browser = await puppeteer.launch({});
    const page = await browser.newPage();
```

```
    await page.goto('https://arh.antoinevastel.com/bots/
areyouheadless');
    await page.screenshot({ path : './bot.png'});
    browser.close()
})();
```

Simple Puppeteer code. We open the browser in headless mode, navigate to the page, and take a screenshot. Let's see what the screenshot looks like:

Are you chrome headless?

You are Chrome headless

This page runs a simple test to determine whether or not you are Chrome headless. For research purpose, I also collect a more complex browser fingerprint. It does not use detection any of techniques presented in these blog posts (post 1, post 2) or in the Fp-Scanner library. Known spoofing/escape techniques such as the ones presented in this repository are totally useless. Since I use a simple test and don't try to correlate its value with other known tests, false positives/negatives may occur on less popular browsers. Under the hood, I only verify if browsers pretending to be Chromium-based are who they pretend to be. Thus, if your Chrome headless pretends to be Safari, I won't catch it with my technique, but because of the differences, it could be easily caught using many other techniques.

Antoine Vastel's bot detection

Antoine got us. We were detected as a bot, but that's not the end of the game. There are a few things we can do. Let's start by incorporating `puppeteer-extra` (https://github.com/berstend/puppeteer-extra). The `puppeteer-extra` package allows us to add plugins to Puppeteer. This package will allow us to use the `puppeteer-extra-plugin-stealth` plugin (https://www.npmjs.com/package/puppeteer-extra-plugin-stealth). This package is like a mouse master in this game. It will add all the tricks (or many tricks), so our code is not detected as a bot.

The first thing we need to do is install those two packages from the terminal:

```
npm install puppeteer-extra
npm install puppeteer-extra-plugin-stealth
```

Now we can replace this line:

```
const puppeteer = require('puppeteer');
```

We replace it with these three lines:

```
const puppeteer = require('puppeteer-extra');
const StealthPlugin = require('puppeteer-extra-plugin-stealth');
puppeteer.use(StealthPlugin());
```

There, we import `puppeteer`, but from `puppeteer-extra`. Then, we import the stealth plugin and install it using the `use` function. And that's it!

Antoine Vastel's bot detection bypassed

The `puppeteer-extra-plugin-stealth` package is not bulletproof. As I mentioned before, it's a cat-and-mouse game. There are many other extras you can use. You can see the full list in the package's repository (https://www.hardkoded.com/ui-testing-with-puppeteer/puppeteer-extra-packages). There, you can find `puppeteer-extra-plugin-anonymize-ua`, which will change the user agent in all the pages, or `puppeteer-extra-plugin-recaptcha`, which will try to solve reCAPTCHA (https://www.google.com/recaptcha/about/) challenges.

A scraping chapter wouldn't be complete if we didn't talk, at least a little, about how to deal with authorization.

Dealing with authorization

Authentication and authorization is a vast topic in web development. Authentication is how a website can identify you. To make it simple, it's the login. On the other hand, authorization is what you can do on the site once you are authenticated, for instance, checking whether you have access to a specific page.

There are many types of authentication modes. We covered the simplest one in this book: a user and password login page. But things can get more complicated. Testing integration with Facebook or single sign-on logins could be quite challenging, but they would be about automating user interaction.

There is one authentication method that you won't be able to perform by automating the DOM—**HTTP basic authentication**:

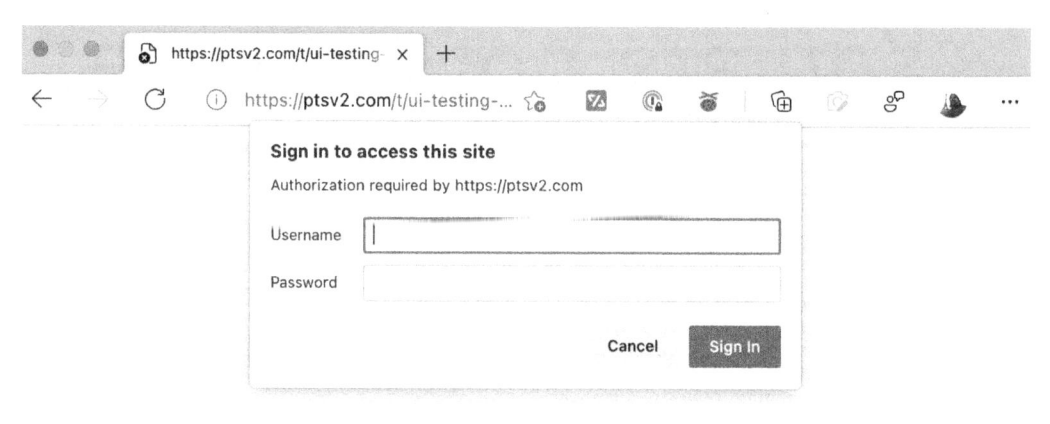

HTTP basic authentication

That login popup is not popular these days. In fact, I don't think they ever were popular. But you might have seen them if you have set up a router. That modal is like the dialogs we saw in *Chapter 5, Waiting for elements and network calls*. Puppeteer won't help us out with this authentication because there is no HTML to automate there. Luckily for us, automating this is easy. You can get the code of this section in the `authentication.js` file:

```
(async function() {
    const browser = await puppeteer.launch();
    const page = await browser.newPage();
    await page.authenticate({username: 'user', password:
'password'});
    await page.goto('https://ptsv2.com/t/ui-testing-puppeteer/
post');
    await page.screenshot({ path : './authentication.png'});
    browser.close()
})();
```

The only thing we need to do to authenticate into `https://ptsv2.com/t/ui-testing-puppeteer/post` is to call the `authenticate` function before calling `goto`. The `authenticate` function expects an object with two properties: `username` and `password`.

Once we are authenticated, we need to tell the server who we are on every request, so they can authorize us (or not) to perform certain tasks. The web server is, in theory, stateless. It doesn't have a way to know who we are unless 1) they inject some information in their responses, using cookies, or 2) we tell them. The most common way is with HTTP Headers. But that can be solved by passing a key as a Query String argument or as part of the HTTP post data.

When you want to alter the authentication data, you need to get that information elsewhere. You might need to open your browser, log in to the site you want to scrape, and extract the authentication data from there, so you can then use that data in your scraper.

Let's say that you want to scrape the Packt website, but this time you want to scrape it being logged in. So, you open your browser, log in and then you can use a tool such as the *Export cookie JSON file for Puppeteer* extension (you can find it with that name in the Chrome web store) to export all the cookies generated by the site. Once we have the JSON file named `account.packtpub.com.cookies.json` with all the cookies, you can copy that file into your workspace and do something like this:

```
const puppeteer = require('puppeteer');
const cookies = require('./account.packtpub.com.cookies.json');
(async function() {
    const browser = await puppeteer.launch({defaultViewport : { width: 1024, height: 1024}});
    const page = await browser.newPage();
    await page.setCookie(...cookies);
    await page.goto('https://account.packtpub.com/account/details');
    await page.waitForSelector('[autocomplete="given-name"]');
    await page.screenshot({ path : './cookies.png'});
    browser.close()
})();
```

The new element in this code is a call to the `setCookie` function. That function expects a list of cookies. As we have all the cookies in a JSON file, we load that JSON file and pass the content to the `setCookie` function. Let's take a look at what a cookie looks like inside that file:

```
{
  "name": "packt_privacy",
  "value": "true",
  "domain": ".packtpub.com",
  "path": "/",
  "expires": 1611427077,
  "httpOnly": false,
  "secure": false
}
```

The structure is quite simple and straightforward. You don't need to use an extension and load a cookie from a JSON file. You can call the `setCookie` function passing an object with the `name`, `value`, `domain`, `path`, and `expires` properties (the latter is a Unix time in seconds), whether it's `httpOnly`, and whether it should be marked as `secure`.

Now it's time to see how we can handle authorizations implemented using HTTP headers. You might find sites using the `authorization` HTTP header to pass some kind of user identifier. The `authorization` header would look something like this:

```
Authorization: <type> <credentials>
```

According to MDN (https://www.hardkoded.com/ui-testing-with-puppeteer/authentication-schemes), you can find the following types: `Basic`, `Bearer`, `Digest`, `HOBA`, `Mutual`, and `AWS4-HMAC-SHA256`. If those names sound scary, don't worry about that. There is a high chance that you will only see the `Bearer` type. What would be the credentials? Well, that's what you will need to find out while coding your scraper. You would need to see what information is being sent when you use a website for real and try to mimic that.

For our example, we will use `Basic` because that's the same HTTP basic authentication we saw before. When you log in using the authentication popup, the browser will send the authorization header passing `basic` and `username:password` in Base64. In our example, the username was `user`, and the password was `password`. So, we can use any Base64 encoder available, for instance, https://www.base64encode.net/, and get `user:password` in base64: `dXNlcjpwYXNzd29yZA==`.

We can inject this header in two ways. The first one is using the `setExtraHTTPHeaders` function. You can see this code in the `header-inject.js` file:

```
(async function() {
    const browser = await puppeteer.launch();
    const page = await browser.newPage();
    await page.setExtraHTTPHeaders({
        authorization: 'basic dXNlcjpwYXNzd29yZA=='
    });
    await page.goto('https://ptsv2.com/t/ui-testing-puppeteer/post');
    await page.screenshot({ path : './authentication-header.png'});
    browser.close()
})();
```

`setExtraHTTPHeaders` expects an object where the property name is the header name, and the value is the header value. Here we are adding the `authorization` header with the value `'basic dXNlcjpwYXNzd29yZA=='`. And that's it. Puppeteer will add that header to every request that the page will make.

But what if the site we are trying to scrape needs an authorization header not in every request, but only in some of them? Well, it will be quite tricky, but not that hard. You can follow this code in the `header-inject2.js` file:

```js
const puppeteer = require('puppeteer');

(async function() {
    const browser = await puppeteer.launch();
    const page = await browser.newPage();
    await page.setRequestInterception(true);
    page.on('request', r => {
        const overrides = {
            headers: r.headers()
        };

        if(r.url() == 'https://ptsv2.com/t/ui-testing-puppeteer/post')
            overrides.headers.authorization = 'basic dXNlcjpwYXNzd29yZA==';

        r.continue(overrides);
    });
    await page.goto('https://ptsv2.com/t/ui-testing-puppeteer/post');
    await page.screenshot({ path : './authentication-header.png'});
    browser.close()
})();
```

We are first telling Puppeteer we want to intercept every request the page will make. We do that by calling the `setRequestInterception` function with the first argument as `true`. Then we start listening to the `request` event. If the request meets the condition we need, in this case, if it matches our URL, we create an `overrides` object with a `headers` property and then call the `continue` function of the request object. We cannot override the headers. The `overrides` object can also have the `url`, `method` (the HTTP method), and `postData` properties.

The request object also has a function called `abort`. With this function, you can cancel that request. For instance, you could check whether the request is an image and `abort` it. The result will be a website with no images.

> **Important Note**
> If you call `setRequestInterception`, you need to implement a `request` event listener. And you need to `continue` or `abort` every request you listen to.

As I mentioned when I opened this section, this doesn't cover all the different authentication and authorization schemes, but it will have you covered in more than 90% of cases. Now it's time for a wrap-up.

Summary

Although this is not a scraping book, we covered a lot of ground here. I hope the first section gave you a good idea of what scraping is, as well as covering what you can do and what you shouldn't do. We also learned how to create our own scrapers. We created a crawler in less than 100 lines. We added two new tools to our toolbox: `puppeteer-cluster` and `puppeteer-extra`. We closed this chapter learning a little bit about authentication and authorization, giving you almost everything you need to get started in the scraping world.

If you weren't that excited about scraping before this chapter, I hope it is the spark that will make you start creating your own scrapers. If you knew about scraping, I hope this chapter gave you more tools to scrape as a professional.

Our next and final chapter will be about performance and how we can measure it using Puppeteer.

10
Evaluating and Improving the Performance of a Website

Many things can make a website a success or a complete failure. In *Chapter 9, Scraping tools*, we talked about a real estate website that can't be launched without content. On many websites, content is the number-one feature. `Amazon.com` could be the best website in the world, but if it doesn't have the book you are looking for, you will go somewhere else.

For other websites, functionality is the number-one feature. A website such as `Trello.com` is a success because you can move cards from one list to another easily and intuitively. But functionality is not only about rich web pages. If we go back to the Amazon website, the website is pretty straightforward. It doesn't use any cool UI framework, but it has a great search and well-planned navigation.

The website design can also be considered a feature. While some websites such as `www.google.com` might look simple and focused on delivering content, you can see that other websites, such as `www.apple.com`, invest a lot in design. You can see that design is the number-one feature on `www.apple.com`.

But most websites will share the same feature: **speed**. **Speed is a feature**. When planning a website, the stakeholders might argue whether they want to invest in a rich client or not. They can discuss whether they should hire a designer or not. But if you ask about the speed, there is only one answer: "We need the website to be fast."

In this chapter, we will learn how to use performance metrics to solve several issues that can arise with websites. We will look at functionality, speed, and how we can measure these key performance points with Google Lighthouse.

We will cover the following topics in this chapter:

- The issue of performance
- Getting started with Google Lighthouse
- Tracing pages
- Analyzing code coverage

By the end of this chapter, you will be able to implement performance metrics on your website and help the development team improve the website's performance.

Let's get started.

Technical requirements

You will find all the code of this chapter on the GitHub repository (`https://github.com/PacktPublishing/UI-Testing-with-Puppeteer`) under the `Chapter10` directory. Remember to run `npm install` on that directory, and then go to the `Chapter10/vuejs-firebase-shopping-cart` directory and run `npm install` again.

The Issue of Performance

As I mentioned in the introduction, speed is a feature. You might be asked to make a simple website, but no one, ever, will tell you to make a slow website. Websites need to be fast. **Performance is the key to success**. Performance increases user satisfaction; it results in high conversion rates and higher revenue. Let me share some facts with you:

- Rebuilding Pinterest pages for performance increased conversion rates by 15% (`https://www.hardkoded.com/ui-testing-with-puppeteer/pinterest-case`).

- By reducing the response size of the JSON needed for displaying comments, Instagram saw increased impressions (`https://www.hardkoded.com/ui-testing-with-puppeteer/instagram-case`).

- Walmart saw a 1% increase in revenue for every 100 ms improvement in page load (`https://www.hardkoded.com/ui-testing-with-puppeteer/walmart-case`).

As you can see, performance puts money in your pocket.

There is one more thing on which I'm sure you will agree with me: No matter the website, no matter what they sell or offer, performance is the number-one feature in the mobile experience. When you are on the street, you don't care about the style; you don't care about functionality. The first thing you need is the website to load, and load fast. You need to measure the performance on mobile.

The problem with this feature is that, in general, people don't know how to measure speed. If we go back to the other features, they are easy to measure. It's easy to discuss content. Content is easy to measure:

- I want to ship the website with content.
- How many items?
- Over 1,000.

Functionality is, in general, something you can write down on a spec:

- I want an e-commerce site with an outstanding search experience.
- What does that mean?
- It should support typos, and I should be able to search for part of a word.

Design is about whether you want to put effort into the look and feel or not:

- We need a website with a great design
- OK, we need three designers.
- Perfect.

But speed is hard to discuss:

- The website needs to be fast.
- How fast?
- I don't know… fast?
- But how fast do you think it should be?
- I don't know… faster?

The second problem is that we tend to react to performance issues. We don't realize something needs to be fast until we realize it's slow.

Third, speed is a matter of expectation and comparison. The user would say that the website is slow. They would also say that they use Google Drive and that it's way faster. The developer would reply that the website seems fast in their opinion, and, of course, that they don't have Google's budget.

And the last problem is that we don't know how to test the website's performance. We would get a bug report from a user, saying that the website is slow, and the QA analyst would grab that bug report to validate it, but what's the tool that the analyst has to validate that issue? Going to the website and checking whether it "feels" slow to them.

That is the perfect cocktail for a disaster: No way to measure, no plan—it's all about feelings and different expectations.

We won't be able to solve all these problems in just one chapter in a web automation book. But, we will see some strategies and tools to help you and your team to measure and improve your website's performance. Let me share some tips with you to get started.

First, **choose what you need to measure**. If it's the entire website, that's OK. But I would start with the most popular pages first. Begin with the home page. Then, continue with the main workflow of the website. For instance, for an e-commerce website, you would want to test the product details and the checkout page. Ask the people in charge of analytics what pages bring more conversions, and focus on those pages.

Second, **define the maximum amount of time a page can take to load**. You could say that the home page should never take more than 30 seconds to load, under any circumstances. This is an excellent use for *Checkly*, the platform we saw in *Chapter 6, Executing and Injecting JavaScript*. You could code a test to check that the page doesn't take more than 30 seconds to load in production and keep that check running on *Checkly*. We will see how to implement this later in this chapter. Once you have set up that check, you and your team can set more strict goals. For instance, the search page should never take more than a second to load.

Third, **measure performance degradation**. Many times, setting a limit is hard, and it can become a guessing game. You can start by measuring how the performance evolves over time. Is the website becoming faster or slower? Are we getting better or worse? This is a great approach, but it requires a little bit more work. You need to start storing data over time and build something to visualize that information.

And lastly, use the tools you learned in this book. We talked about Checkly, but remember all the emulation techniques we learned back in *Chapter 8, Environments emulation*? You can set different goals for different network speeds.

This is all you can do to measure a website's performance. In this chapter, I want to show you which tools you have to implement these ideas. Let's start with Google Lighthouse, a tool we can use to measure several important metrics.

Getting started with Google Lighthouse

As we saw in the previous section, it's not easy to determine how fast "fast" is. Google came up with an idea. They built Lighthouse, "*an open-source, automated tool for improving the quality of web pages. You can run it against any web page, public or requiring authentication. It has audits for performance, accessibility, progressive web apps, SEO and more*" (https://www.hardkoded.com/ui-testing-with-puppeteer/lighthouse).

Lighthouse will grab the website you choose, apply a list of metrics and recommendations it finds important, and give you a score from 0 to 100. It will analyze the website under five categories:

- **Performance**: The most popular category. Lighthouse will measure how optimized the website is, that is, how fast it gets ready for user interaction.
- **Accessibility**: I would love to see developers paying more attention to this category. Here, Lighthouse will evaluate how accessible the website is.
- **Best practices**: This is another popular category. Lighthouse will evaluate a few good practices to incorporate into the website.
- **SEO**: This category is used a lot by people in charge of marketing. Some companies even have SEO experts looking at this. This category is about how optimized the website is for search engines. You might agree or not on how the other categories are measured, but here Google is telling you: "This is how we measure your website." You will want a score of 100 if you want to secure your spot on the first page of Google.

- **Progressive Web App**: If the website is a progressive web app, this category will evaluate aspects of that progressive web app.

> **Important Note**
> **Progressive web apps (PWAs)** are websites prepared to be installed as native applications. Many PWAs have offline capabilities and try to get close to a native app experience.

In this chapter, we will focus only on the Performance category. But before getting into the details of the performance category, let's see how we can run this tool. Lighthouse comes in four flavors, which we will cover in the following sections.

As part of Chrome DevTools

If you open DevTools, you will find a **Lighthouse** tab. If you can't find it, you can add it by clicking on the three dots in the tool's right corner, then going to **More tools**, and then finding the **Lighthouse** options. You should see something like this:

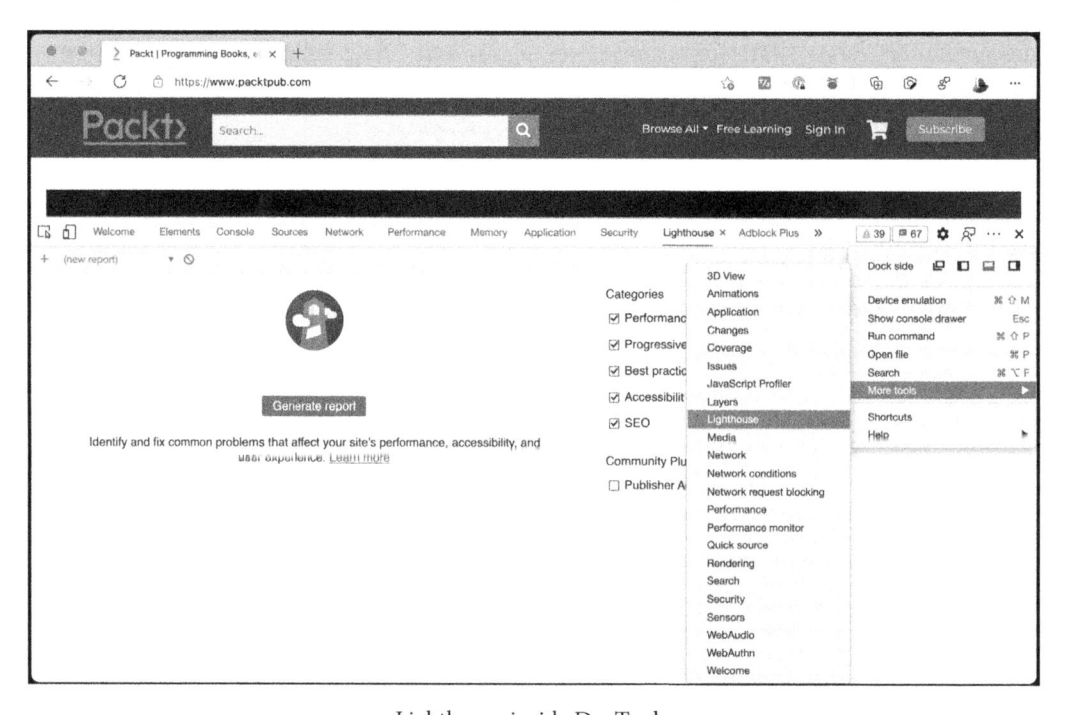

Lighthouse inside DevTools

You should now have the tab there with all the options to generate the report. The process will run Lighthouse locally, which is good, but that would mean that the Lighthouse results will be based on your hardware, CPU, available RAM, network speed, and so on.

Using PageSpeed Insights

Google saw that results might fluctuate based on your hardware, so they made a PageSpeed Insights (https://www.hardkoded.com/ui-testing-with-puppeteer/pagespeed) where you can run Lighthouse using Google's hardware. That would make it more stable, but you could get different results even using Google's hardware.

Using the command line

You can also use Lighthouse from the command line. I wasn't that excited about having Lighthouse in the command line first. But then I realized that it's way more productive to use it from the command line than opening a browser, going to DevTools, and so on.

You can install the Lighthouse **CLI (command-line interface)** by installing the Lighthouse module globally. This is the first time we do this in this book, but it's no different from how we installed the Puppeteer module. We just need to add the -g flag like this:

```
npm install -g lighthouse
```

> **NPM global modules**
>
> When you run `npm install` with the -g flag, the module will be installed in a shared directory rather than in the node_modules folder, and it will be accessible by any app. Additionally, if the module provides an executable command, it will be accessible from the command line like this Lighthouse module.

Once installed, you will be able to launch `lighthouse` from the command line, passing the URL and, additionally, extra command-line arguments such as --view, which will launch the report after evaluating the website.

With this line of code, you will be able to see the Lighthouse result for www.packtpub.com:

```
lighthouse https://www.packtpub.com/ --view
```

Wondering what the result is? We'll get there.

The last option available is one that we will use a lot, and it's using the node module as part of our code.

Using the node module

We will be able to use Lighthouse in our unit tests using the node module. Let's take a look at the example from the Lighthouse repository (https://www.hardkoded.com/ui-testing-with-puppeteer/lighthouse-programmatically):

```
const fs = require('fs');
const lighthouse = require('lighthouse');
const chromeLauncher = require('chrome-launcher');
(async () => {
  const chrome = await chromeLauncher.launch({chromeFlags: ['--headless']});
  const options = {logLevel: 'info', output: 'html', onlyCategories: ['performance'], port: chrome.port};
  const runnerResult = await lighthouse('https://example.com', options);
  const reportHtml = runnerResult.report;
  fs.writeFileSync('lhreport.html', reportHtml);
  console.log('Report is done for', runnerResult.lhr.finalUrl);
  console.log('Performance score was', runnerResult.lhr.categories.performance.score * 100);
  await chrome.kill();
})();
```

The code is not very complicated. We launch a Chrome browser using the chrome-launcher module. Then we launch lighthouse, passing a URL and a set of options. The lighthouse function will return an object, I called it runnerResult, which contains a report property with the report as HTML and also a property called lhr (Lighthouse result) with all the results as an object. We will use that property to assert the minimum values we want to get.

Now that we know how to launch Lighthouse, let's see how the report looks. In order to avoid hurting feelings, we will run Lighthouse against the very same Lighthouse website: `https://www.hardkoded.com/ui-testing-with-puppeteer/lighthouse`. Let's see whether it is as fast as they say. As I mentioned before, I felt really comfortable with the command-line tool, so I will run this command:

```
lighthouse https://developers.google.com/web/tools/lighthouse
--view
```

After running that, I got a new tab in my browser with the following result:

Lighthouse result

To be honest, I picked a Google website on purpose. As you can see in the screenshot, the results can be rough. A score of 55 doesn't mean that your site is terrible. It just means that the website can be improved a lot.

You also have to keep in mind that a single company made this scoring system and, although many companies use it as a marketing number to show off how good the score is, this is not the final word. It's just one way to measure the performance of your website.

Another thing to keep in mind is that although it measures many things, its focus is on the time taken to load the page, and you should know that performance is more than that.

Let's dive into the performance category details.

The performance category

Each category in Lighthouse consists of three sections: metrics, opportunities, and diagnostics. Although only the metrics are used for the category score, it is by implementing the opportunities and looking at the diagnostics that you will improve the metrics.

Each category has its own set of metrics, opportunities, and diagnostics. In particular, the performance category has 6 metrics, 17 opportunities, and 13 diagnostics.

Let's take a look at the performance metrics.

Performance metrics

The first metric is **First Contentful Paint**. It has a weight of 15% on the overall performance score. According to Google, this metric "*measures how long it takes the browser to render the first piece of DOM content after a user navigates to your page. Images, non-white <canvas> elements, and SVGs on your page are considered DOM content; anything inside an iframe isn't included.*" You will get a green score if this metric is under 2 seconds. You can read more about this metric and how to improve the score at `https://web.dev/first-contentful-paint/`.

The second metric is **Speed Index**. It has a weight of 15% on the overall performance score. According to Google, this metric "*measures how quickly content is visually displayed during page load. Lighthouse first captures a video of the page loading in the browser and computes the visual progression between frames. Lighthouse then uses the* `Speedline Node.js module` *to generate the Speed Index score.*" You will get a green score if this metric is under 4.3 seconds. You can read more about this metric and how to improve the score at `https://web.dev/speed-index/`.

With a weight of 25%, the third metric is **Largest Contentful Paint** and is one of the most important metrics. According to Google, this metric "*measures the render time of the largest image or text block visible within the viewport.*" You will get a green score if this metric is under 2.5 seconds. If you are interested in how they get to know what the "largest contentful element" is, check out their article at `https://web.dev/lcp/`.

The fourth metric is **Time to Interactive**. It has a weight of 15% on the overall performance score. According to Google, this metric "*measures how long it takes a page to become fully interactive.*" You will get a green score if this metric is under 3.8 seconds. You can read more about this metric and how to improve the score at `https://web.dev/interactive/`.

The fifth metric is **Total Blocking Time**, which is the second metric with a weight of 25% on the overall performance score. According to Google, this metric "*measures the total amount of time that a page is blocked from responding to user input, such as mouse clicks, screen taps, or keyboard presses.*" You will get a green score if this metric is under 300 milliseconds. You can read more about this metric and how to improve the score at `https://web.dev/lighthouse-total-blocking-time/`.

With a weight of just 5%, the last metric is **Cumulative Layout Shift**. According to Google, this metric "*measures the sum total of all individual layout shift scores for every unexpected layout shift that occurs during the entire lifespan of the page.*" You will get a green mark if the score is under 0.1. You can read more about this metric and how to improve the score at `https://web.dev/cls`.

I came to a few conclusions after digging into all these metrics. First, it's clear that they were made by web performance professionals. It would have been impossible for me to build all these metrics in my daily job. The research behind these metrics is impressive.

On the other side, when you look at the weights and thresholds, while they look well thought out, they might sound quite arbitrary. Why is total blocking time more important than time to interactive? Or why do I get a green mark on a speed index under 4.3 seconds? Why not 4.2? Why not 4.4? But this is better than nothing.

You might also have had the feeling of this being too complicated or hard to understand. Some concepts, such as **Largest Contentful Paint**, sound like rocket science, at least to me. That's why you might find it easier to understand and follow the opportunities section of the report.

Performance opportunities

Opportunities are calls to action. These are not just simple recommendations. Here, Lighthouse will get to the point: "If you do this, you might get this bump in performance."

As I mentioned before, there are 17 opportunities under the performance category. We won't cover all of them. But I would like to go through a few of them so you get an idea of what this section is about.

Let's cover only the opportunities shown when we process the Lighthouse website. These are the opportunities I got in my report:

Opportunity	Estimated Savings
▲ Properly size images	28.2 s
▲ Serve images in next-gen formats	27.31 s
▲ Eliminate render-blocking resources	1.7 s
▲ Remove unused JavaScript	1.65 s
▒ Remove unused CSS	0.75 s

Opportunities — These suggestions can help your page load faster. They don't directly affect the Performance score.

Performance opportunities for the Lighthouse website

Here, we have five opportunities. Let's unpack them:

- **Properly size images**: Lighthouse found images that are bigger than the size shown on the page.

- **Serve images in next-gen formats**: Here, Lighthouse checks whether you are using JPEG or PNG files instead of "next-gen" formats such as WebP. I'm not particularly a fan of this opportunity. Although WebP is supported in most popular browsers these days, it is not a popular format in general yet.

- **Eliminate render-blocking resources**: I think this is a critical opportunity. Here, Lighthouse found that many resources are blocking the first paint of the page. Paying attention to this opportunity would improve your metrics considerably.

- **Remove unused JavaScript**: Lighthouse found JavaScript code that is not being used. Although this would be easy to detect by Lighthouse, this issue is not that easy to solve by developers. Developers these days use bundlers to pack all their JavaScript code, and shrinking the final code to only the code that the page needs can be challenging.

- **Remove unused CSS**: This opportunity is similar to the previous one, but it's related to CSS styles.

I love this section because Lighthouse doesn't just tell you what the opportunities are; it also gives details showing you where the opportunity is and what would be the performance bump. Let's see, for instance, what we get when we click on the **Properly size images** row:

Opportunity			Estimated Savings
▲ Properly size images			28.2 s ⌃

Serve images that are appropriately-sized to save cellular data and improve load time. Learn more.

Show 3rd-party resources (0)

URL	Resource Size	Potential Savings
…images/extension.png (developers.google.com)	1,945.8 KiB	1,696.9 KiB
…images/audits.png (developers.google.com)	1,824.1 KiB	1,590.8 KiB
…images/cdt-report.png (developers.google.com)	1,823.1 KiB	1,589.9 KiB
…images/report.png (developers.google.com)	701.8 KiB	612.0 KiB
…images/lighthouse-psi.png (developers.google.com)	168.0 KiB	133.5 KiB
…images/viewer.png (developers.google.com)	123.4 KiB	24.1 KiB

Properly size images section

As you can see there, Lighthouse is showing us which images we can improve and what the potential savings we could get are. You will get the same kind of details on every opportunity.

The last section within a Lighthouse category is the diagnostics.

Performance Diagnostics

I see the diagnostics section as a list of things you should consider to improve your website. As I mentioned before, the performance category has 13 diagnostics, but you will see this number change over time.

This is how the diagnostics section looks:

Diagnostics — More information about the performance of your application. These numbers don't directly affect the Performance score.

- ▲ Ensure text remains visible during webfont load

    Warnings: Lighthouse was unable to automatically check the `font-display` value for the origin https://fonts.gstatic.com.

- ▲ Reduce the impact of third-party code — Third-party code blocked the main thread for 270 ms
- ▲ Some third-party resources can be lazy loaded with a facade — 1 facade alternative available
- ▲ Image elements do not have explicit `width` and `height`
- ▲ Avoid enormous network payloads — Total size was 8,044 KiB
- ▲ Minimize main-thread work — 4.1 s
- ■ Serve static assets with an efficient cache policy — 9 resources found
- ● Avoid chaining critical requests — 8 chains found
- ● Keep request counts low and transfer sizes small — 91 requests • 8,044 KiB
- ● Largest Contentful Paint element — 1 element found
- ● Avoid large layout shifts — 5 elements found
- ● Avoid long main-thread tasks — 12 long tasks found
- ● Avoid non-composited animations — 11 animated elements found

Performance diagnostics for the Lighthouse website

As you can see, you will have the same level of detail as in the opportunities section, but these diagnostics sound more like recommendations to improve over time on your website. For instance, let's take a look at the **Minimize main-thread work** section:

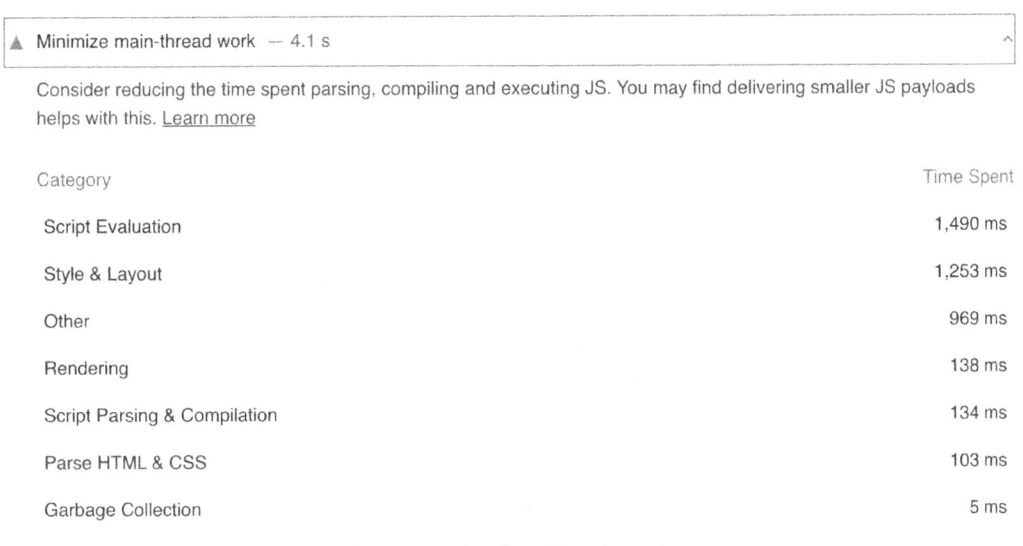

Category	Time Spent
Script Evaluation	1,490 ms
Style & Layout	1,253 ms
Other	969 ms
Rendering	138 ms
Script Parsing & Compilation	134 ms
Parse HTML & CSS	103 ms
Garbage Collection	5 ms

Minimize main-thread work section

As you can see, it seems to make sense what the diagnostics section reports. There is some script evaluation that is taking 1,490 ms. But that doesn't sound like a call to action. It's more something to consider if you need to improve the website's performance.

Now that we have learned about what Lighthouse is, let's see how we can test our website's performance by adding Lighthouse to our tests.

Using Lighthouse for testing

Let's be clear, Lighthouse is not a testing tool. It's a tool used more for developers to check their websites' performance. But, as we mentioned many times in this book, the role of QA is to honor the customer. It's to ensure that the customer gets the best product the team can deliver. We will use Lighthouse to ensure that the customer will get the fastest website we can deliver.

I can think of three ways we can test a Lighthouse report:

- Ensure that a page has a minimum performance score.
- Ensure that a metric is below a threshold.
- Ensure that an opportunity is not found.

Let's begin by checking the performance score.

Ensure that a page has a minimum performance score

The first test we can make using Lighthouse is making sure that our page performance won't degrade over time. We will check that our page never falls below a specific score. How can we pick the minimum score? As we want to be sure that our website won't degrade over time, let's see the current performance score and enforce that. Let's go to the `vuejs-firebase-shopping-cart` directory, under `Chapter10` of the repository, and we will run `npm run serve` and launch the web application:

```
npm run serve
```

That command should start the website. Once started, let's open another terminal and run Lighthouse on the home page:

```
lighthouse http://localhost:8080/ --view
```

The result of that process was a score of 30 for performance. We can set our target score at 25. Time to write our test.

> **Important Note**
> As Lighthouse runs locally, you might get different results on different machines. You should consider that when picking your score goal.

We are going to add our test in the `homepage.tests.js` file. But before creating the test, we need to install the `lighthouse` module by running the following command:

```
npm install lighthouse
```

That will get us Lighthouse in our tests. The next step is importing the lighthouse module using the `require` function. Let's add this line at the top of the file:

```
const lighthouse = require('lighthouse');
```

This will make Lighthouse available in our tests. Now, let's see how our test would look:

```
it('Should have a good performance score', async() => {
  const result = await lighthouse(config.baseURL, {
    port: (new URL(browser.wsEndpoint())).port,
    onlyCategories: ['performance']
  });

  expect(result.lhr.categories.performance.score >= 0.25).
```

```
to.be.true;
});
```

We solved the test using only two statements. We first call `lighthouse`, passing the URL we want to process, in this case, `config.baseURL`, and then we pass an `options` object. There we are passing the `port` it has to use to connect to the browser that Puppeteer is using. We get it by doing `new URL(browser.wsEndpoint())).port`, and then we tell Lighthouse we only want to process the `performance` category. We won't cover all the available options here. You can take a look at the full list of options at https://www.hardkoded.com/ui-testing-with-puppeteer/lighthouse-configuration.

In the next line, we just assert that the score of the performance category is greater or equal to 0.25. When you see the report, scores are in the range of 0 to 100. But in the JSON object, the range is from 0 to 1. That's why we need to use 0.25 instead of 25.

The next test is checking for specific metrics.

Ensure that a metric is below a threshold

We can also be more specific. We could say that, for instance, regardless of the performance score we want to check, **First Contentful Paint** should never take longer than 30 seconds. Our code will be similar to our previous test:

```
it('Should have a good first contentful paint metric', async() 
=> {
  const result = await lighthouse(config.baseURL, {
    port: (new URL(browser.wsEndpoint())).port,
    onlyCategories: ['performance']
  });

  expect(result.lhr.audits['first-contentful-paint'].
numericValue).lessThan(30000);
});
```

Here, we can see that the `lhr` object also contains an `audits` dictionary with all the metrics. We can grab the `first-contentful-paint` entry call and check that `numericValue` (in milliseconds) is under 30,000 (30 seconds expressed in milliseconds).

How can we know what the available metrics are? The easiest way is to add a breakpoint in your test and add a watch to see the value of `result.lhr`. You will see something like this:

```
∨ WATCH                                                                    + 🗗 🗗 ⊙
  ∨ result.lhr: {userAgent: 'Mozilla/5.0 (Macintosh; Intel Mac OS X 10_1…ike Gecko) Chrome/85.0.4182.0 Safari/53…
    ∨ audits: {first-contentful-paint: {…}, largest-contentful-paint: {…}, first-meaningful-paint: {…}, speed-ind…
      > bootup-time: {id: 'bootup-time', title: 'JavaScript execution time', description: 'Consider reducing the …
      > critical-request-chains: {id: 'critical-request-chains', title: 'Avoid chaining critical requests', descr…
      > cumulative-layout-shift: {id: 'cumulative-layout-shift', title: 'Cumulative Layout Shift', description: '…
      > diagnostics: {id: 'diagnostics', title: 'Diagnostics', description: 'Collection of useful page vitals.', …
      > dom-size: {id: 'dom-size', title: 'Avoids an excessive DOM size', description: 'A large DOM will increase…
      > duplicated-javascript: {id: 'duplicated-javascript', title: 'Remove duplicate modules in JavaScript bundl…
      > efficient-animated-content: {id: 'efficient-animated-content', title: 'Use video formats for animated con…
      > estimated-input-latency: {id: 'estimated-input-latency', title: 'Estimated Input Latency', description: '…
      > final-screenshot: {id: 'final-screenshot', title: 'Final Screenshot', description: 'The last screenshot c…
      ∨ first-contentful-paint: {id: 'first-contentful-paint', title: 'First Contentful Paint', description: 'Fir…
          description: 'First Contentful Paint marks the time at which the first text or image is painted. [Learn …
          details: undefined
          displayValue: '18.3 s'
          errorMessage: undefined
          explanation: undefined
          id: 'first-contentful-paint'
          numericUnit: 'millisecond'
          numericValue: 18341.727199999994
          score: 0
          scoreDisplayMode: 'numeric'
        > should (get): f shouldGetter() {\n        if (this instanceof String\n           || this instanceof Number\…
        > should (set): f shouldSetter(value) {\n      // See https://github.com/chaijs/chai/issues/86: this makes…
          title: 'First Contentful Paint'
          warnings: undefined
```

Result.lhr content

There you will be able to see not only the available entries but also `numericUnit`, among many other properties.

Based on this example, making sure that an opportunity is not found will be easy.

Ensure that an opportunity is not found

I think this is the most solid way to use Lighthouse. We introduced some arbitrary numbers in our previous examples, 30 for the score and 30 seconds for the metric. Now, let's say we don't want to get a certain opportunity; for instance, we don't want any images of the wrong size. We can look at the audits and try to find an entry with the name user-responsive-images. With that entry, we can write the following test:

```
it('Should have properly sized images', async() => {
  const result = await lighthouse(config.baseURL, {
    port: (new URL(browser.wsEndpoint())).port,
    onlyCategories: ['performance']
  });

  result.lhr.audits['uses-responsive-images'].numericValue.should.equal(0);
});
```

The code is the same as the previous example, but here, we assert that the metric value should be 0. That will mean that all the images are properly sized.

It's impressive all we can do with Lighthouse, but to be honest, you won't see many teams applying these ideas to their project. If you get to test your website's performance using Lighthouse, you will add a lot of value to your team.

Lighthouse is kind of a black box that you call, get values, and act in response. But what if you want to build your own metric? What if you want to analyze the performance of a page in a more granular way? Let's now explore all the **tracing** features Puppeteer offers.

Tracing Pages

In this section, we will cover how to get performance information using the tracing object you can find on the **page.tracing** property. I saw this question more than once on Stack Overflow: How can I get the Performance tab's information using Puppeteer? The answer is: You can get all that information from the tracing result. There is a high chance that you will get a reply like: "Yes, I say that, but the result is too complex." And yes, the tracing result is quite complicated. But we will try to see what we can get from that object in this section.

280 Evaluating and Improving the Performance of a Website

If you open DevTools, you should see a **Performance** tab like this one:

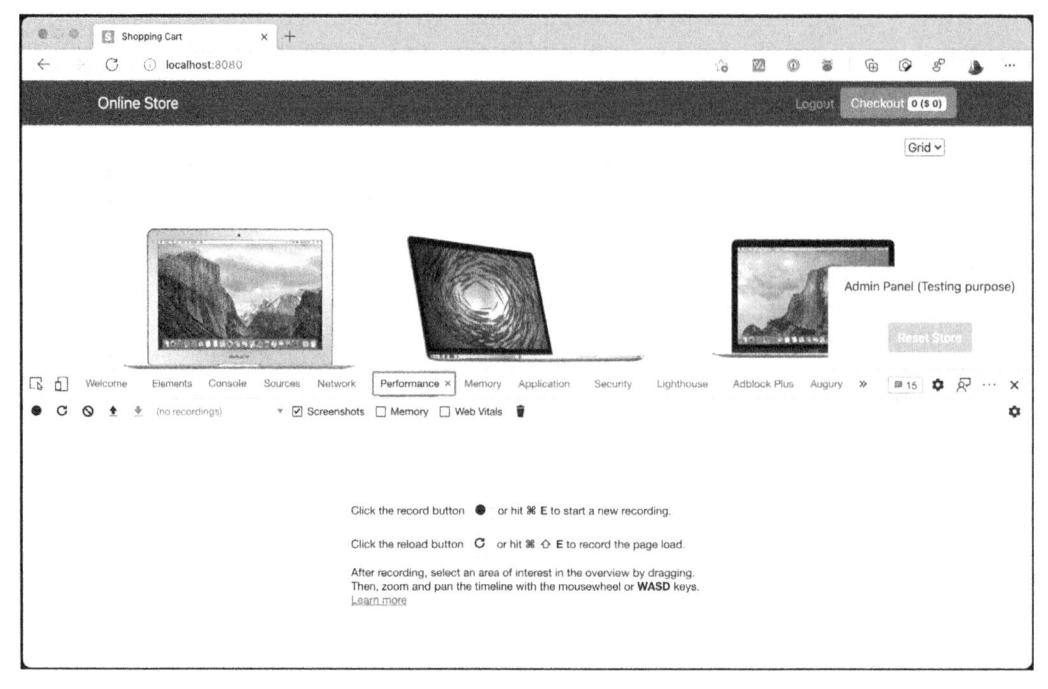

Performance tab

As you can see, the **Performance** tab is not processing information all the time because it's a costly process. You need to start "recording" the tracing, Chrome will begin collecting lots of data from the browser, and then you have to stop the tracing process.

If you click on the second button, which looks like a reload, it will automatically reload the page and start the tracing. If you click on that button and then stop the tracing when the page loads, you will get something like this:

Tracing Pages   281

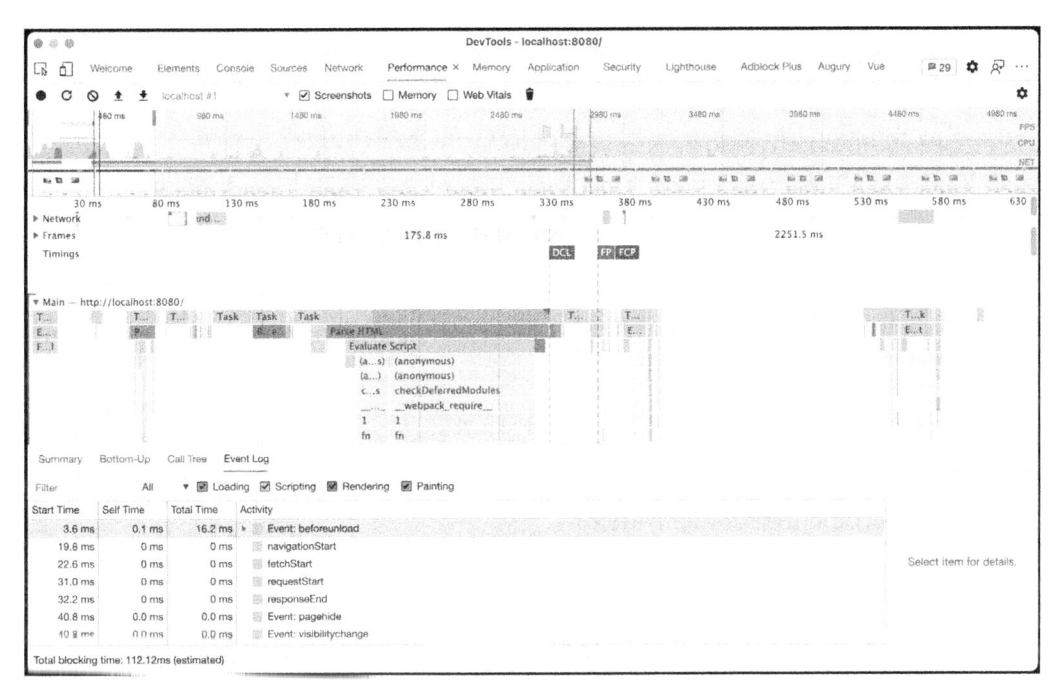

Performance result

The level of detail of that panel is impressive. You get to see every paint action, every HTML parsing, every JavaScript execution, everything the browser did to render the page there.

We can get the same using the `tracing` object. Let's create a test called `Should have a good first contentful paint metric using tracing` in our `homepage.tests.js` file, but we will add only the tracing calls for now:

```
it('Should have a good first contentful paint metric using
tracing', async() => {
    await page.tracing.start({ screenshots: true, path: './
homepagetracing.json' });
    await page.goto(config.baseURL);
    await page.tracing.stop();
});
```

The code is straightforward. We start the tracing, we go to the page, and we stop the tracing.

The `start` function expects an `options` object, which has three properties:

- The `screenshots` property will determine whether we want Chromium to take screenshots during the tracing.
- If you set the `path` property, the tracing result will be written in that JSON file.
- Finally, you'll find a `categories` property, where you will be able to pass an array of properties you want to trace.

There is no fixed list of categories, but these are the categories I find more relevant to us:

- Under the **rail** category, we will find many useful traces such as **domInteractive**, **firstPaint**, and **firstContentfulPaint**.
- If you set `screenshots` to `true`, you will find all the screenshots under the **disabled-by-default-devtools.screenshot** category.
- You will find that lots of entries will come under the **devtools.timeline** category. This category represents one of those items you see in the performance timeline.

When you call the `stop` function, you will get the result in the file you passed to the `start` function, and, whether you passed a path or not, the `stop` function will return the result as a `Buffer`.

The resulting JSON will be an object with two properties: A `metadata` object with information about the trace and the browser, and a `traceEvents` array, with all the trace information.

In my simple test example, `traceEvents` gave me `16,693`. That was just for navigating to the page. I think now you get why this can be scary for some users.

The shape of each trace event might vary based on the category. But you will find these properties:

- `cat` will tell you the categories for the event, separated by commas.
- `name` will give you the name of the event, as you would see it in the **Performance** tab.
- `ts` will give you the tracking clock, expressed in microseconds (1 microsecond is 0.000001 seconds). Most events are relative to the beginning of the trace.
- `pid` is the process ID. I don't think you will care about that.

- `tid` is the thread ID. You won't care about that either.
- `args` will give you an object with specific information for that event type. For instance, you will get the URL and the HTTP method of a request. For a screenshot, you will get the image in Base64 format.

With all this information, let's code our first contentful paint test using tracing values. We are going to write a test that will start the tracing, navigate to a page, and then evaluate the results. It would be something like this:

```
it('Should have a good first contentful paint metric using tracing', async() => {
  await page.tracing.start({ screenshots: true, path: './homepagetracing.json' });
  await page.goto(config.baseURL);
  const trace = await page.tracing.stop();
  const result = JSON.parse(trace);
  const baseEvent = result.traceEvents.filter(i=> i.name == 'TracingStartedInBrowser')[0].ts;
  const firstContentfulPaint =result.traceEvents.filter(1=> i.name == 'firstContentfulPaint')[0].ts;
  expect((firstContentfulPaint - baseEvent) / 1000).lessThan(500);
});
```

We have some tricks to explain here. After stopping the trace, we get the result and parse it. That will give us the `result` with a `traceEvents` property. As `ts` is based on the beginning of the trace, we need to find the `baseEvent`, looking for an event with the name `TracingStartedInBrowser`. Then we look for the event with the name `firstContentfulPaint`, and finally, we calculate the difference. As it's in microseconds, we need to divide it by 1,000, so we can compare it with our target goal of 500 ms.

Notice that in this example, our goal is 500 ms versus the 30 seconds we used in the Lighthouse example. This is because, by default, Lighthouse performs several runs emulating different conditions.

Another thing we could do here is export the screenshots generated by the tracing tool for later analysis. We can add something like this at the end of the test:

```
const traceScreenshots = result.traceEvents.filter(x => (
    x.cat === 'disabled-by-default-devtools.screenshot' &&
    x.name === 'Screenshot' &&
    x.args &&
    x.args.snapshot
));

traceScreenshots.forEach(function(snap) {
  fs.writeFile(`./hometrace-${snap.ts - baseEvent}.png`, snap.args.snapshot, 'base64', function(err) {});
});
```

There, we are filtering screenshots events with a valid screenshot, and then we just write all those Base64 snapshots to the filesystem. With that, you will see how the page was being rendered during the loading process. You would even code your own first contentful paint algorithm with those images.

Now you might be wondering whether you should use Lighthouse or Puppeteer's tracing. I think there are some pros and cons to every approach. Lighthouse is easy to use, and as we saw, it gives us metrics that would take us lots of effort to build by ourselves. With Lighthouse, you just call the `lighthouse` function and evaluate the results. But it can be slow, even if you select only one category.

On the other hand, Puppeteer's tracing can be hard to read and process, but if you know how to take the metric you need from the tracing result, it will be way faster than Lighthouse. Another important difference is that Lighthouse only evaluates the page load, whereas with Puppeteer's tracing, you could start the tracing at any moment. For instance, you could go to a page, start the tracing, click on a button, and then evaluate what the browser did to process that click. At the end of the day, it's about picking the right tool for your job.

Lighthouse also gives us two interesting metrics: **Remove unused JavaScript** and **Remove unused CSS**. Let's see how we can solve those metrics using Puppeteer.

Analyzing code coverage

In this last section, we will see how we can get code coverage using the `Coverage` class from Puppeteer. Code coverage is a metric that can be applied to any piece of code. To get the code coverage of a piece of code, you need some kind of tool to trace which lines of code are being executed, execute that code, and get the tracing result. It's like the performance tracing, but instead of measuring time, it measures executed lines of code.

You can see the code coverage on a page on Chrome using the **Coverage** tab. I didn't have that tab by default, so I needed to add it using the **More tools** option, as in the following screenshot:

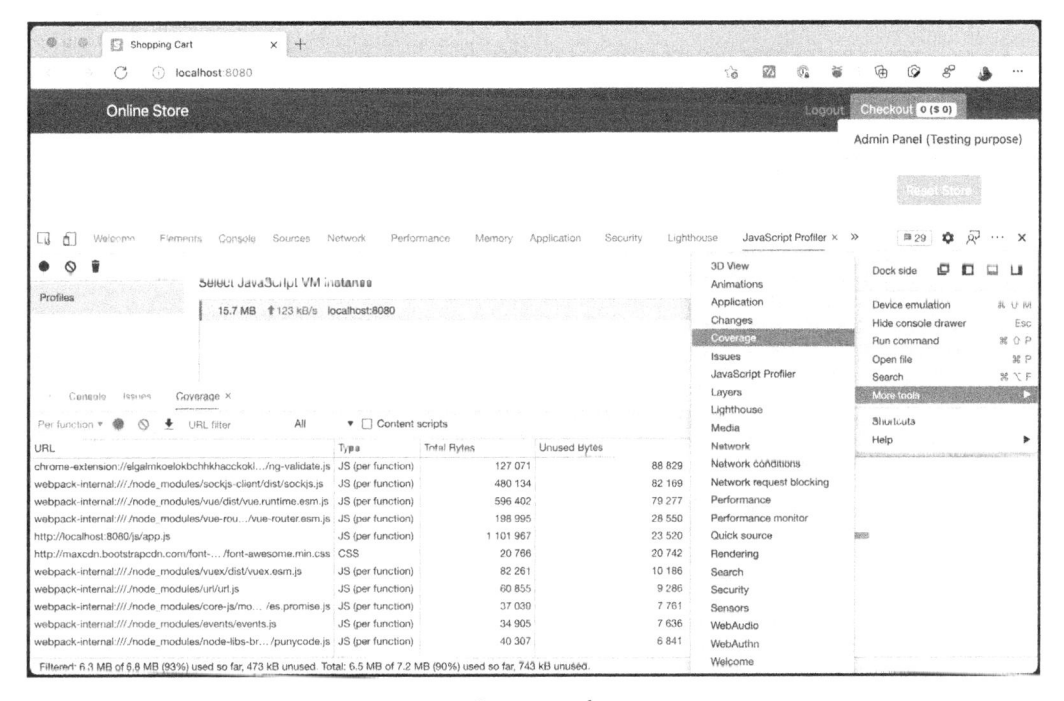

Coverage tab

The **Coverage** tab works like the **Performance** tab. You need to start the tracing, run the page, or perform an action, then stop the tracing to get the results.

The result will be something like what we see in the preceding screenshot: A list of resources with the total bytes of that resources and the unused bytes. At the bottom of the window, we can see that over 90% of the code was used (executed) during the tracing. That's pretty good. We could write a test to ensure that we will always have a code coverage of over 90%.

The JavaScript and the CSS code coverage have two sets of functions in Puppeteer. If you want to get the JavaScript code coverage, you need to run `startJSCoverage` to start the coverage and `stopJSCoverage` to stop it. `startJSCoverage` supports an `options` argument with two properties:

- `resetOnNavigation` is a Boolean property we can use to tell Puppeteer to start over with the tracing if navigation was detected.
- `reportAnonymousScripts` is a Boolean property we can use to tell Puppeteer to ignore, or not, dynamically generated JavaScript code.

If we want to get CSS coverage, we need to use the `startCSSCoverage` and `stopCSSCoverage` functions. `startCSSCoverage` also expects an `options` argument, but, in this case, it only has the `resetOnNavigation` property.

Once we run the coverage, both `stopCSSCoverage` and `stopJSCoverage` will return the same type of value. Both will return an array of objects with these properties:

- `url` will give us the resource URL.
- `content` will be the CSS or the script content.
- `ranges`, which will contain an array of objects telling us which were the portion of code that has been executed. Each entry will contain two properties, `start` and `end`, telling us where that text range starts and ends.

Now we have all this information, we can write our code coverage test. Let's take a look at it:

```
it('It should have good coverage', async() => {
    await Promise.all([page.coverage.startJSCoverage(), page.coverage.startCSSCoverage()]);
    await page.goto(config.baseURL);
    const [jsCoverage, cssCoverage] = await Promise.all([
        page.coverage.stopJSCoverage(),
        page.coverage.stopCSSCoverage()
    ]);
    let totalBytes = 0;
```

```
    let usedBytes = 0;
    const coverageTotals = [...jsCoverage, ...cssCoverage];
    for (const entry of coverageTotals) {
        totalBytes += entry.text.length;
        for (const range of entry.ranges) usedBytes += range.end
 - range.start - 1;
    }
    const percentUnused = parseInt((usedBytes / totalBytes) *
 100, 10);
    expect(percentUnused).greaterThan(90);
});
```

We start our test by starting both code coverages. We put `startJSCoverage` and `startCSSCoverage` inside `Promise.all`, so we wait for both coverages to be confirmed. Then we go to the page, and after that, we stop both coverages. That will give us two arrays that we can join (because they share the same shape) using `[...jsCoverage, ...cssCoverage]`.

Once we have both coverages, we get the total size of the resource by using `entry.text.length`, and then we get the size of the coverage by adding the length of all the ranges.

The result will give us the total code coverage of our tracing, which we will check whether it's over 90%.

The pros and cons of this solution compared with Lighthouse are the same as we saw in the previous section. On one side we have Lighthouse, which gives us all the numbers already cooked. But here, we have more control over what we want to measure. This test was quite simple, but you could improve it by filtering out all the resources you don't want to measure. You can also download that result to a file and share it with your team if the test fails.

Now it's time to wrap up this chapter and this book.

Summary

If you get to apply performance tests in your team, you will be on a whole new level.

We started the chapter by talking about Lighthouse. We only covered the Performance category. But now that you know how it works, I encourage you to keep digging into the other categories and think about how to create tests for that. I would love to see more tests about accessibility.

We also learned how to use Lighthouse in our tests. That's not something you will see quite often. You will be able to test very complex metrics using two lines of code.

Most developers would run away from Puppeteer's tracing results. Although what you can get from there is way more than what we covered, we learned the foundations of such a powerful tool in this chapter.

The size of a page is critical for performance; that's why we learned about code coverage and how to measure it.

And this is also a wrap on this book. When I planned this book, my goal was to write a book that would cover the entire Puppeteer API, without being a reference book. And I think we accomplished that goal. We learned how to write high-quality end-to-end tests using Puppeteer and, at the same time, we covered most of the Puppeteer API.

With this goal in mind, we covered topics that were not strictly related to unit testing. We talked about PDF generation and Web Scraping. We also covered topics that many people would run away from, such as the tracing model.

If you read this book from cover to cover, I can assure you that you will know way more about Puppeteer than the average user of this library.

But I also hope you learned more than just a Node package. In this book, we also learned about the foundations of the web, and how to write good tests. We talked about the internet ecosystem, scraping ethics, and web performance. You have also empowered your role. QA is more than just about testing web pages. It's about honoring your users by delivering high-quality software they can enjoy using.

Packt>

Packt.com

Subscribe to our online digital library for full access to over 7,000 books and videos, as well as industry leading tools to help you plan your personal development and advance your career. For more information, please visit our website.

Why subscribe?

- Spend less time learning and more time coding with practical eBooks and Videos from over 4,000 industry professionals
- Improve your learning with Skill Plans built especially for you
- Get a free eBook or video every month
- Fully searchable for easy access to vital information
- Copy and paste, print, and bookmark content

Did you know that Packt offers eBook versions of every book published, with PDF and ePub files available? You can upgrade to the eBook version at packt.com and as a print book customer, you are entitled to a discount on the eBook copy. Get in touch with us at customercare@packtpub.com for more details.

At www.packt.com, you can also read a collection of free technical articles, sign up for a range of free newsletters, and receive exclusive discounts and offers on Packt books and eBooks.

Other Books You May Enjoy

If you enjoyed this book, you may be interested in these other books by Packt:

End-to-End Web Testing with Cypress

Waweru Mwaura

ISBN: 978-1-83921-385-4

- Get to grips with Cypress and understand its advantages over Selenium
- Explore common Cypress commands, tools, and techniques for writing complete tests for web apps
- Set up and configure Cypress for cross-browser testing
- Understand how to work with elements and animation to write non-flaky tests
- Discover techniques for implementing and handling navigation requests in tests

Modern Web Testing with TestCafe

Dmytro Shpakovskyi

ISBN: 978-1-80020-095-1

- Understand the basic concepts of TestCafe and how it differs from classic Selenium
- Find out how to set up a TestCafe test environment
- Run TestCafe with command-line settings
- Verify and execute TestCafe code in the browser
- Automate end-to-end testing with TestCafe using expert techniques
- Discover best practices in TestCafe development and learn about the future roadmap of TestCafe

Packt is searching for authors like you

If you're interested in becoming an author for Packt, please visit `authors.packtpub.com` and apply today. We have worked with thousands of developers and tech professionals, just like you, to help them share their insight with the global tech community. You can make a general application, apply for a specific hot topic that we are recruiting an author for, or submit your own idea.

Leave a review - let other readers know what you think

Please share your thoughts on this book with others by leaving a review on the site that you bought it from. If you purchased the book from Amazon, please leave us an honest review on this book's Amazon page. This is vital so that other potential readers can see and use your unbiased opinion to make purchasing decisions, we can understand what our customers think about our products, and our authors can see your feedback on the title that they have worked with Packt to create. It will only take a few minutes of your time, but is valuable to other potential customers, our authors, and Packt. Thank you!

Index

A

accessibility 224, 225
Accessible Rich Internet
  Applications (ARIA) 91
action elements 88, 89
AJAX call 67
application program interface (API) 2, 3
Arrange, Act, Await approach 131, 132
assertions 34
asynchronous programming
  in JavaScript 19, 20
authorization 254-259
automation 2
Automator 2

B

base64 encoder
  URL 257
Bidder's Edge
  reference link 232
bot detection
  avoiding 250-253
breakpoints 117
browser automation 3

Browserless.io 9
browsers
  market share 194
  popularity 195, 196
  popularity, in 2020 196

C

Checkly
  URL 141
  used, for running checks 167-169
Chrome DevTools 266, 267
Chromium 5
chromium-based browsers
  examples 5
Chromium DevTools Protocol (CDP) 6, 7
close event 138
closure 147
code
  organizing 44, 45
code coverage
  analyzing 285-287
command line
  using 267
command-line interface (CLI) 267

console event 139
container elements 89, 90
continuous integration (CI) 73-81
Cascading Style Sheets (CSS) 85
CSS Selectors 94

D

data dash attributes 91
data scraping 230
default viewport 60
dialog event
  about 140
  alert type 140
  beforeunload type 141
  confirm type 140
  prompt type 140
differencify
  reference link 179
DIVs 89
Document Object Model (DOM) 68, 91-93
document structure elements 87
drop-down lists
  options, selecting in 105-107

E

ebay
  URL 232
element handles
  about 103
  manipulating, with JavaScript code 150-152
elements
  about 127, 128
  finding 95-99
  finding, with JavaScript 156
  finding, with XPath 100
  information, obtaining from 152-154
  input elements 104
  interacting with 104
emulation, functions
  about 224
  accessibility 224, 225
  media features 226
  media type emulation 226
end-to-end tests 31, 32
environment
  setting up 12
executablePath option 59
expressions 148

F

fire and forget approach 41, 133, 134
functions 157-163

G

generic timeouts 66
geolocation
  emulating 218-221
GitHub.com 108
Google Lighthouse
  categories 265
  Chrome DevTools 266, 267
  command line, using 267
  node module, using 268-270
  PageSpeed Insights, using 267
  performance category 270
  using, for testing 275-279
  working with 265, 266

Google Lighthouse, performance category
  diagnostics 273, 275
  metrics 270, 271
  opportunities 271, 273
Google Maps
  URL 220

H

headful mode 57
headless browsers 4-6
headless option 57
headless recorder 141-143
hello world program
  in Puppeteer 18, 19
HTML5 90
HTML content
  creating 190, 191
HTTP basic authentication 254
HTTP status code
  reference link 70
HyperText Markup Language (HTML)
  about 85, 87
  action elements 88, 89
  container elements 89, 90
  document structure elements 87
  input elements 90, 91
  text elements 88

I

input elements 90, 91, 104
iubenda
  URL 232

J

JavaScript
  used, for finding elements 156
  variable scopes 146-148
JavaScript code
  element handles, manipulating 150-152
  executing 146
Jest
  about 35
  URL 35
jest-image-snapshot 36
jest-puppeteer 35
JSHandle 150

K

Kayak
  URL 217
keyboard emulation 108-111

L

languages
  emulating 222, 224
local functions 163-165
localization
  about 216
  emulating 217, 218
Long-Term Support (LTS) 12

M

media query breakpoints 209
mobile device emulation
  about 199, 200
  with Puppeteer 207, 208

mobile device emulation, elements
  about 200
  pixel ratio 202-204
  touchscreen 204
  user agent 205, 206
  viewport 200, 201
mobile UX
  testing 209-212
Mocha
  about 36
  URL 44
mocha-puppeteer 36
mocha-snapshots 36
mouse emulation 111-115

N

navigation timeouts 65
network calls 130, 131
network conditions
  emulating 213-216
networking 212
Node.js
  setting up 12, 13
  URL 12
node module
  using 268-270
NPM
  URL 15

O

Open Graph
  about 172
  URL 172
operative systems market share 197
Optical Character Recognition (OCR) 230

P

page
  loading 121-125
page events
  close event 138
  console event 139
  dialog event 140
  popup event 138
  targetcreated event 139
  waiting for 135-137
Page Object Model (POM) 45-48
PageSpeed Insights
  using 267
page.tracing 279-284
PDF files
  generating 182-189
Pixelmatch
  reference link 179
pixel ratio 202-204
popup event 138
porchmark project
  reference link 214, 215
progressive web apps (PWAs) 266
Promise.all 21, 134
Promise.race 21
promises
  fulfilling 22
  states 20
Puppeteer
  about 3, 8
  hello-puppeteer project 14, 15
  hello world program 18, 19
  installing 15-17
  versioning 17
  working 4
Puppeteer 7 17

Puppeteer browser, creation
  about 55
  arguments 62
  default viewport 60, 61
  executablePath option 59
  headless option 57, 58
  mobile options 63-65
  product 62
  Puppeteer.launch function, using 56, 57
  user data directory 58
puppeteer-cluster 246
puppeteer-extra-plugin-stealth
  reference link 252
Puppeteer object model
  about 9
  browser 9
  browser context 10
  execution context 10
  frame 10
  page 10
  worker 10
Puppeteer pyramid
  components 8
Puppeteer repository
  reference link 8
Puppeteer-Sharp
  reference link 8
Puppeteer, use cases
  about 10
  content generation 11
  end-to-end testing 11
  task automation 11
  web scraping 11

Q

Quality Assurance (QA) 24

R

race conditions 131
Raf 158
reCAPTCHA
  reference link 254
referrer 68, 69
regression tests
  screenshots, using for 178-182
response object
  using 69
response status code
  obtaining 70-73
response URL
  obtaining 69
Ryanair's terms and conditions
  reference link 233

S

scrapers
  creating 238-246
  running, in parallel 246-250
screen resolution
  about 198
  distribution 198
screen scrapers 230
screenshots
  about 172-177
  using, for regression tests 178-182
select options
  in drop-down lists 105-107
selectors
  combining 95
Selenium
  about 3
  working 3, 4

Semantic Elements 90
Semantic Versioning Specification
    (SemVer) 17
server rules
  enforcing 155
service tests
  about 28, 30
  users 29
site navigation 65
snapshot tool 35

T

targetcreated event 139
Test-Driven Development (TDD) 26
Testing Pyramid 25
test project
  creating 37-44
test runner
  about 35
  features 32-34
  Jest 35
  Mocha 36
tests
  debugging, with Visual Studio
      Code 115-117
tests sites 52-55
text elements 88
timeouts 66
time zone
  emulating 221, 222
Toggle device emulation 204
touch events
  reference link 204
touchscreen 204, 205
trespass to chattels
  reference link 232

U

UI regression test 178
unit tests
  about 26
  benefits 27
  users 26
user agent 205, 206
user data directory 58

V

variable scopes, JavaScript 146-148
viewport 200, 201
Visual Studio Code
  setting up 13, 14
  URL 14
  used, for debugging tests 115-117

W

wait function 128-130, 157
waitUntil option 66, 67
WebDriver
  reference link 3
web scraping
  about 230
  scenarios 231
website
  performance issue 262-265
website, scraping
  403 HTTP error 236
  Complex CAPTCHAs 235
  data, scraping 238
  permissions 231
  reCAPTCHA 235

robots.txt file 233, 234
terms and conditions 232
Website API, using 236, 237

X

XML content
  basic elements 86
XML parsers 86
XPath 100
XPath, used for finding elements
  about 100
  contains text 102, 103
  filter by attribute 101
  filter by text 102
  select all elements 101
  select from current node 101
  select from root 101

Made in the USA
Las Vegas, NV
12 March 2021